PRAISE FOR

Eye of My Heart

"So many different perspectives and vantage points are woven seamlessly that no matter what their personal relationship to the word 'grandmother' is, readers will find much to make them laugh out loud—and also to break their hearts."
— *Christian Science Monitor*

"Spry and unsentimental. . . . Truth-telling with dollops of love."
— *O, The Oprah Magazine*

"In illuminating, unsentimental essays, twenty-seven writers offer up insights on the tricky art of grandmothering."
— *People*

"These stories are so fresh and fundamental, wrenching and joyful, that one is left feeling that the subject has never been cracked open before."
—Harriet Lerner, Ph.D., author of *The Dance of Anger*

"Finally, a look at grandmothering that is decidedly unsentimental. These clear-eyed essays offer humor and insight as they take on the multigenerational lives many of us now lead."
— Cokie Roberts, author of *We Are Our Mothers' Daughters*

"Insightful and candid, sometimes painfully so. . . . Women who have achieved grandmotherly status will appreciate this engaging, honest volume of essays by twenty-seven writers who articulate shared emotions about their grandchildren."
— *Publishers Weekly*

Eye of My Heart

Eye of My Heart

27 Writers Reveal the Hidden Pleasures and
Perils of Being a Grandmother

EDITED BY
BARBARA GRAHAM

INTRODUCTION BY
MARY PIPHER, Ph.D.

HARPER

NEW YORK · LONDON · TORONTO · SYDNEY

HARPER

A hardcover edition of this book was published in 2009 by Harper, an imprint of HarperCollins Publishers.

An extension of this copyright page appears on pages 311–312.

HarperCollins books may be purchased for educational, business, or sales promotional use. For information please write: Special Markets Department, HarperCollins Publishers, 10 East 53rd Street, New York, NY 10022.

FIRST HARPER PAPERBACK PUBLISHED 2010.

Designed by Eric Butler

Library of Congress Cataloging-in-Publication Data is available upon request.

ISBN 978-0-06-147416-3

10 11 12 13 14   OV/RRD   10 9 8 7 6 5 4 3 2 1

To Isabelle Eva
and Azalia Luce

In memory of Bessie Kopelman Glick
and Esther Lewin Graham

"The Laws of Primogeniture"

My grandson has my father's mouth
with its salty sayings
and my grandfather's crooked ear
which heard the soldiers coming.

He has the pale eyes of the cossack
who saw my great-great-grandmother
in the woods, then wouldn't stop
looking.

And see him now, pushing
his bright red firetruck towards
a future he thinks he's inventing
all by himself.

—LINDA PASTAN

Contents

Contents

Contents

Preface

On the one hand, it seemed so simple. There was a new baby, Isabelle Eva, who looked as if she had just arrived fresh from heaven. There was nothing to do except love her, this pearl of a granddaughter, born on a full moon. That was the one hand. The other hand revealed itself in the days and months following Isabelle's birth—and that hand, belonging to her parents, held all the cards. I soon learned that I could love my granddaughter fiercely, with a passion that made me hunger for her when she was out of range, but I could have no say—in anything. She was mine but not mine. Most of all, I had to win over her parents. They loved me—I knew that—but did they trust me? In the early days I felt as though I were auditioning for the role of grandmother: Did I hold Isabelle properly? Was I capable of changing her diaper? Didn't I know that you *never* put a newborn down on her stomach? (Wait, wasn't that stomach-down position just what Dr. Spock advised?) And that was just the beginning.

Margaret Mead wrote: "The closest friends I have made all through life have been people who grew up close to a loved and loving grandmother or grandfather." In part, she attributed the strong bond between grandchildren and grandparents to the fact that they were united against a "common enemy"—the parents. Even before Isabelle was brought home from the hospital, it had begun to dawn on

me that this grandmother business was much more complicated than I'd imagined.

But since I was the first among my close friends—some
of whom still have children in high school and college—to
become a grandmother, I sought wisdom in the one place
I always turn to: books. Surely, novelists, memoirists, and
other chroniclers of the heart must have tackled one of life's
most profound passages—becoming a grandmother, a role
that is as primal as parenthood, as universal as childhood,
yet stirs unforeseen conflicts and expectations within families that can blindside you and set you spinning. I searched
and searched for literature on the subject and was astonished to find: nothing. Nothing literary, nothing narrative,
nothing that began to limn the power and complexity of
grandmotherhood itself. Oh, plenty of women had written about their own grandmothers, and there are enough
self-help books offering guidance to the new grandparent to line a bookshelf. There are also countless humor
books that reinforce the cultural cliché of grandmothers
as adorable and adoring creatures, as devoted and doting
as puppies. Where, I wondered, were the real stories? The
working women, the non-doters, the grandmothers who
were raising their grandchildren or kept from them by
angry adult children? Where were the stories of women
grappling with the role itself, trying to figure out just what
sort of grandmother to be in a world that differs in so many
ways from the world in which our role models—our own
grandmothers—lived?

The very word *grandmother* sounds archetypal, ancestral.
It evokes a sense of history, of a lineage going back generations
and going forward, too—far beyond us. For me, stepping

into the shoes of a grandmother was sobering and thrilling, scary yet comforting: Although the coming of Isabelle Eva secured the continuity of some fragment of the ancestral essence I carry from my own Russian-Polish-German-Jewish stew—sparking in me an unexpected but palpable sense of relief—I was also acutely aware that her arrival moved me up a notch in the life cycle. Often, in the weeks following her birth I would stand gazing at the mirror and wonder: Is *this* what a grandmother looks like? And this: Over time grandmothers, whether loving or absent, attain near-mythic status in the memories of their grandchildren. Yet for the most part a grandmother isn't around long enough to know the children of her children beyond their young adulthood. So I wondered too: how will I be remembered? Which of my quirks and character flaws will become family legend?

When I couldn't find books that revealed the cracks as well as the wonder and, occasionally, the absurdity of my new status, I decided there must be other women with nuanced feelings about being a grandmother, and so I started asking around. I tracked down writers whose work I love and put out feelers: Were they grandmothers? Did they have something to say on the subject? One contributor's response was typical: "This essay will force me to explore and articulate emotional areas I have avoided." Suddenly there were stories and more stories. Out of this rich tapestry, *Eye of My Heart* was born.

In this collection you will encounter tales that are heartbreaking, hilarious, touching, and transformative—and of course there are love stories, too. Lynne Sharon Schwartz probes the nature of the love that grandmothers feel toward their grandchildren and concludes, "There's something suspiciously viral about the condition: relentless, forceful, and all-consuming." But though some grandmothers, including Jill Nelson and Claire Roberts, may be stirred by love for their grandchildren, thorny relationships with their adult children keep them from fully expressing this very particular form of middle-aged ardor. Still others have found unexpected joy: Lynn Lauber, who as a teenager gave up for adoption the only child she ever had, gets in grandmotherhood a taste of the happiness that she missed out on as a mother. So do authors Sandra Benitez and Beverly Lowry, for very different reasons. And because of her strict Hindu upbringing, Bharati Mukherjee's pride in her multicultural, multinational family—including two adopted granddaughters born in China—would have once seemed unimaginable.

The glories and glitches are more subtle for others as they adjust to the role and learn to negotiate with the "common enemy." Anne Roiphe, for one, has learned to keep her mouth shut and stifle the wisdom and expertise she gained through years of motherhood, unless her daughters directly solicit her opinions. And in her witty account of a trip from Amsterdam to Paris with her daughter and her three-year-old granddaughter, Molly Giles manages, most of the time, to bite her tongue. Judith Guest, however, isn't quite so successful at maintaining her image as the perfect grandmother during a weeklong stay at a dude ranch with her three prepubescent granddaughters.

Other writers grapple with the role itself: Susan Shreve, whose longing for motherhood seemed hardwired, took years to accept the fact that she is now the *grand*mother. Beverly Donofrio and Rona Maynard—unconventional mothers, each in her own way—must redefine grandmotherhood for themselves, just as they once redefined motherhood. And Susan Griffin, reflecting on her experience as both grandmother and granddaughter, notes her growing awareness of the passage of time. "In the eyes of our grandchildren," she writes, "we are the past come to meet them, a living link ready to connect them to a larger lineage, their own history, ours, the history of the planet; we are the doorway to the vast continents of time that existed before they were born, and that will exist after they too pass."

Although these and the other stories in this book vary in the particulars, most have a common thread: a love for grandchildren that knows no bounds, despite very earthly— and, occasionally, impassable—boundaries and limitations. Mary Pipher, whose lovely introduction illuminates the role of grandmother, writes that the mutual affection she shares with her grandchildren continues to teach her about "pure and nearly perfect love." It is in the gap between this purest of loves and the realities of complex human entanglements that the stories in *Eye of My Heart* are located.

BARBARA GRAHAM

Eye of My Heart

Introduction

In the 1950s, I grew up in Beaver City, Nebraska, a sleepy town of 420 people along Beaver Creek. Today, my three grandkids are growing up in another small town in Nebraska, along the Platte River. They live on the edge of town in a big old-fashioned house much like the one I grew up in. Their days are spent doing what I used to do—reading, listening to stories, playing games, and frolicking outside. Their family owns a television, but they rarely watch it. They move in a world of relatives, neighbors, and animals. They visit the river and their friends on nearby farms.

My grandchildren are nurtured and protected. I was not. My parents were busy, preoccupied, often absent. When I was a baby, my mother started medical school in Colorado, and soon after that my father was sent to war in Korea. While they were away, my siblings and I were left with various sitters. We grew up as feral children. I spent much of my childhood alone or caring for my younger sister and brothers. I found comfort in books and animals.

My grandchildren have wonderful parents who read them endless stories, take them on outings, and notice when they need their hair combed. Jamie, my daughter-in-law, is with them every day, nurturing, teaching, and correcting them in the hundreds of ways that small children require if they are to grow up properly. My son Zeke is a fun-loving, affectionate dad. Watching Jamie and Zeke with their children,

I have begun to understand what I missed. But of course, at the same time, I take great pleasure in seeing my grandchildren thrive.

At six, Kate has long dark hair and wears wonky glasses. She is tall for her age and, as her dad says, when she sits on your lap it feels as if you are holding a baby giraffe. She watches people closely, is curious about everything, and forgets nothing. Like me, Kate is a big sister—responsible, kindhearted, and prone to worry. Once when a cousin had hurt her foot and could not swim, Kate volunteered to give up swimming to keep her company. When my husband's father was dying, Kate sat by his bed, rubbed his head, and told him she loved him. At bedtime, Kate prays for goodness.

Kate and I have much the same relationship I had with Grandma Page. My grandmother founded the library in her little town in eastern Colorado. When I visited, she would ask me what I was reading, and we'd discuss it. She admonished me to choose my books as carefully as I chose my friends. She appointed me her helper and we talked as we washed dishes, shelled peas, or picked peaches from her orchard.

When Kate was barely two, we lay on a couch and I read her twenty-six books in a row. When I was finished she asked me to do it again. I still read to her, but now she also reads to me. When we are together we never stop talking. My grandmother's nickname for me was Bright Eyes, and that is what I call my Kate.

Aidan Blair, whom I refer to as A.B., is four years old. With his curly brown hair and soulful blue eyes, he resembles his dad at that age. He is outgoing and energetic. Like his father, A.B. is easy to spot in a swimming pool. We look for the place with the most white water. He sometimes chokes because he can't quit smiling. Once my husband, Jim, put on goggles to watch A.B. after he jumped off the diving board. He grinned all the way to the bottom.

A.B. is the somersault king of Nebraska. He once somersaulted two blocks to show me he could. He has invented many new forms including one that does not require hands or feet.

He is intense, loving, and easily heartbroken. Once when I stifled his play in dominoes, he said, "Nonna, you have ruined my wonderful life." Another time when we were talking on the phone, he said, "I love you." I responded in a rather perfunctory way and he said, "Nonna, you don't understand. I love you right now."

A.B. stands on a cooking stool so that he can help me prepare meals. His specialty is mixing fruit salad. When we had our first snowfall this year, A.B. cried "happy tears." Once when he was sobbing at our good-bye, I gave him a ginkgo leaf, and that calmed him down. His favorite word is *hooray*. If we are going out to hunt grasshoppers or on a picnic, he shouts, "Hooray! Hooray!"

A.B. wants to be good, but he has a harder time succeeding than Kate. He is rambunctious, impulsive, and excitable. His parents remind him to make good choices, and most of the time he does. From people in their church and community, his parents hear, "I love all your kids, but Aidan and I have a special relationship."

At two, Claire Annelise has blond hair, which she wears in pigtails on top of her head. She still sleeps with her "passie" and "blanky," but she is already a stand-up comedian. At mealtimes she entertains us by putting Jell-O on her head or making funny faces. She sings elaborate improvised songs in her crib and dances exuberantly to music. When we leave her house, she crawls up to us purring, "Kitty doesn't want you to leave."

Claire is athletic and independent. She's a real sprinter, and last summer our main goal for her was simply to keep her alive. She could be in a street or across the park lickety-split. By now I am not sure I can outrun her.

Her favorite phrase is "I do it." Once she pulled some string cheese out of the refrigerator without permission. When I asked for it, she hurled herself to the floor, covering the cheese with her body in order to save it. I could barely pry her off it.

Jim and I live ninety miles from the children and see them often. Once a month we have "Nonna and Poppa School" for Kate and A.B. We take them to the zoo, the natural history museum, the prairie, and their favorite Indian restaurant for mulligatawny soup. Geographically and emotionally, we are close to my son's family.

Of course, it is more complicated than that. Zeke is the minister of an evangelical church. We call him the "white sheep" of our family. He and Jamie are conservative Christians. I am a mix of Methodist, Unitarian, and Buddhist. As for my politics, let's just say I graduated from Berkeley in 1969 and have become more radical since then. I may well be the deepest-blue Democrat in my very red state. In Nebraska, Zeke and Jamie are mainstream and I am the oddball. Their friends wonder how they can get on so well with us.

We all accommodate. We talk about politics and religion, but we do it carefully and respectfully. I don't swear in front of the grandchildren, and when we are with them we say grace at every meal. Jamie and Zeke put up with our occasional language lapses and my Buddhist altar. Because our families love, respect, and enjoy each other, this actually works, but it is tricky. During the elections of 2008, we agreed on many things we wanted for this country—peace, economic stability, affordable health care, good education for all children, clean water and air, and tolerant and fair policies for immigrants and the poor. We didn't talk about abortion, gay marriage, or gun control.

When we visit, we often go driving to look for animals. At sunset, Zeke takes us to a place where we laugh as we watch hundreds of wild turkeys struggle to fly up and roost in trees. However, Zeke is a hunter and we are birdwatchers. I would about as soon chop off my left foot as shoot a deer, but I respect my son's moral arguments about hunting, and I appreciate that he donates the meat to refugee families. I edit the articles he sells to hunting magazines. I keep quiet when my grandkids tell me they want to go hunting someday.

I am clear about my role. I am the nonna, not the mom. Jamie and Zeke have a right to raise their family the way they want. They have the privilege of instilling their values and teaching their children what they consider to be good and beautiful. It helps that the children are happy, lively, and well-behaved. It helps that we all cherish many of the same things. Still, being a nonna entails opening myself to certain kinds of suffering. I feel great love and responsibility, yet I have almost no control. Like all grandparents, I am at the mercy of my child and his partner.

Being a nonna has given me joy and fresh eyes. My grandchildren are my antidepressants. When I am with them, I laugh and I look. We inhabit moments together. When we see a hummingbird or pick raspberries, I am as happy as they are. Our mutual affection has taught me about pure and nearly perfect love.

One time A.B. went on a father-son canoe trip down the Niobrara River. After the trip I called A.B. for a report. First, he was proud that he and his dad had Magic Markered *Pipher* on all their property, including his Snoopy lawn chair. Then he told me he had almost drowned. He said, "Nonna, when I was dwowning in the wiver, I missed you. I wanted you, Nonna." Of course, he hadn't been drowning. His dad had held him when they jumped into the river and floated through some white water. However, when A.B. shared his story with me, I wanted to leap into the car and drive ninety miles to give him a hug.

As I offer my grandchildren total acceptance, I have extended more compassion toward myself. When I make a mistake or a bad choice, I have learned to ask, "How would I respond if Kate or A.B. did this? Would I be angry at Claire if she were out of sorts the way I am now?"

Mostly this change occurs with small actions. For example, I recently tossed what I thought was an empty can of V-8 juice into the recycling bin, only it wasn't empty and it sprayed juice all over the room. My inner voice called me careless and clumsy, but I stopped it. I resolved to treat myself as kindly as I do my grandchildren. As I cleaned up the mess, I reminded myself that everyone makes mistakes. I asked, "Why should I be exempt from mercy?" These small changes have made my life much easier.

Being a grandmother has given me a window into my own childhood. Jamie and Zeke went to China for two weeks this year and I stayed with the kids some of the time. Kate was my age the year I was separated from my mother. She cried many nights and seemed more needy and less resilient than usual. Observing her sadness and her ways of working with it helped me to understand myself as a lonely six-year-old. Being a grandmother has triggered issues I thought were resolved and given me another pass at figuring things out.

Watching Zeke and Jamie with the children, I've thought about my own parenting. Jamie is a more patient, more available mother than I was. Zeke is a gentle but firm father. I wish I had used the phrase "Make good choices" with Zeke when he was a boy. I wish I had known about butterfly kisses and *The Chronicles of Narnia*, which Zeke reads aloud at night to the family.

On the other hand, now that Zeke is a dad, he has more empathy for what Jim and I were up against as young parents trying to support a family and make our way in the world. As he experiences many of the same frustrations— exhaustion, worry, and irritation—that all parents do, he is more forgiving of us.

I am not the same person as a grandparent that I was as a parent. I have different roles, different responsibilities, and a different perspective. Jamie and Zeke must raise well-behaved, moral, competent, and emotionally sturdy human beings. My job is to simply love those kids for who they are. Just as my grandparents were the great circle of trees around my nuclear family, I am the shelterbelt now, holding back the snow and north wind, providing a cool, shady place in the summer.

I have the great luxury of being easy on the children. As Kate puts it, "Grandparents forget how to spank." My friend's daughters call their grandparents' home "The House of Yes." If they ask, "Can we bake cookies for breakfast, make a tent in the living room, or go buy some toys?" the answer is— well, you know what the answer is. As my friend Regina put it, "I'll be Grandma Chocolate Money."

Traditionally grandparents have given grandchildren time, attention, moral values, and a connection to the great ancestral chain of life. Often they also give children a sense of place. When I think of my sacred sites, the first two that come to mind are my grandmothers' kitchens. I remember their vegetable gardens and fruit trees, the objects on their bedroom dressers, and their yellowed decks of cards.

Grandmother Page gave me a sense that my life was my opportunity to make the world a better place. I was responsible for making good use of my time and my talents. She had great depth and heart, and she wanted me to know everything important that she knew. I learned my values from her. As I've grown older, I've become more sophisticated, but my core beliefs have changed very little. My grandmother knew as much about being good as I do, and she taught me well. She called me "my Mary," and I still remember what it felt like to sit close by her side as she read me stories.

My father's mother, Glessie May, lived in the Ozarks and never had indoor plumbing. No matter what we were doing—pulling weeds, making biscuits, or talking while she did other people's ironing—Grandma Glessie made it a party. She was salty and irreverent, and to say she swore like a sailor would be to insult sailors. Like A.B., she had a special relationship with everyone who knew her. When she went from house to house selling Avon, people would plead with her to stay longer and tell them more stories. Unlike many lively talkers, she was also a profound listener. Even though she died when I was eleven, I remember many of our conversations. Once we talked all afternoon as she dug holes by her tomato plants and buried a small fish in each for fertilizer. She listened to me as if I were a person, not just a child.

Both grandmothers made me special foods. When I visited Grandmother Page, she brought out her jar of fresh molasses cookies. She also knew I liked gooseberry pie and homemade ketchup, and she fixed them for my visits. Glessie picked wild berries and made blackberry cobbler. On her cast-iron stove, she prepared biscuits and gravy, fried perch and hominy grits. Over the years these foods have become sacramental. I'll drive a long way for a piece of gooseberry pie or fresh-caught panfried fish. Like most people, when I think of my grandmothers, my heart grows soft and warm inside my chest. I want my grandchildren to feel that way about me sixty years from now.

Family is bits of DNA on a spiral helix that extends back to the first man and woman. We come from our parents' genetic material, but our bones are built from our grandmothers' cooking and our grandfathers' work in the wheat fields. If we are lucky, in our lifetime we know seven generations of family, from our great-grandparents to our great-grandchildren. We see the eyes of our great-grandmother in our granddaughter. We hear the laughter of our grandmother in our children and their children.

At sixty I have become the link between these generations. As I teach Claire Annelise the names of birds and how to make "smiley face" toast, I remember old ladies in button shoes and black bonnets and men in overalls and straw hats. I play "Peep-peep, little robin" with her when I feed her, just the way Grandmother Page did with me. At night I sing her the same lullaby my mother sang to me and her Scottish grandmother sang to her. Someday Claire will be a great-grandmother singing a Scottish lullaby to a child whom I will never know, but who may still look like me.

Time is everything and nothing. I am aware that I have a finite number of harvest moons, crane migrations, and Thanksgiving dinners before me. This wisdom changes my priorities and reminds me of my place. I am a marker in the long line of women who carried water and nursed babies so that I could be born. I am the granddaughter and the grandmother, the DNA and the storyteller.

One time when I was playing outdoors with the grandchildren, we found a dead mourning dove, most likely killed by hitting a window. I held it by its feet so that the children could look at it from all angles. They walked around it, examining its eyes, its feathers, and its tiny crooked feet. They were curious and dispassionate. They didn't know that the dove's fate would be my fate and later theirs. Their innocence about death protects them, and long may it last. My knowledge of death protects me, too. I am not unsettled by it. Rather, I rest in something deeper than my own life, the great womb of time where all things come and go.

I am honored to write the introduction to this book. I feel passionate about the topic. My favorite questions about any important subject are "What is old? What is new?" All of us writing in this collection are struggling to articulate our ideas about an experience that is simple and complicated, profound and banal, universal and specific. Editor Barbara Graham has woven together stories from many different vantage points. All the stories in this book let us see an ancient relationship from new and nuanced points of view.

My grandmothers cooked on woodstoves and wore aprons and bonnets. They read the Bible in their spare time—and never would have countenanced divorce. The women in this anthology are writers, teachers, and world travelers. They confront different issues from our grandmothers. Even the look of many contemporary families has changed: there are single-parent daughters, custodial grandchildren, divorced adult children, and blended-family and adopted grandchildren. Modern grandmothers often experience great physical separations from their grandchildren, and sometimes great emotional distances as well. Their grandchildren are techno-savvy, steeped in popular culture. Who really knows how to cope with all that?

What has not changed, though, is the power of the relationship. Throughout human history, grandmothers have experienced joy, love, and hope for the future. They have felt the heft and warmth of the baby's body against their chest. From the start of our human experience, there have been rocking, feeding, stories, and songs.

Another archetypal experience we share is a fierce desire to protect. Just as Inuit grandmothers felt this imperative when they walked away from their families onto the ice in order to save the tribe's meager resources for the children, just as the Russian babushkas hid their grandsons under their skirts to save them from the czar's soldiers, so I experience grandmotherhood now.

I worry about what will happen to my well-nurtured, well-educated, art-loving, and bird-identifying grandchildren. When I read them books about pandas and elephants, I wonder if these animals will be extinct before my grandchildren can see them. Even as I put away money for college funds, I fear for our democracy and our ozone levels. As I watch Kate, A.B., and Claire grow up in the twenty-first century, I am as fiercely protective of them as Grandmother Glessie was of me when we foraged for morels or poke greens in a land of copperheads and water moccasins. In the end, we grandmothers have always wanted the same things. We want our grandchildren to grow up happy and safe and to live good, long lives. We want our spiral helix of talents and quirks, bones and wit, to tumble on across time.

MARY PIPHER

PART I
Now You See Me

Age has conferred on me a certain grace.
You're a package I can rock and ease
from wakefulness to sleep. This skill comes back
like learning how to swim. Comes warm and quick
as first milk in the breasts. I comfort you.
Body to body my monkey-wit soaks through.

—MAXINE KUMIN, "GRANDCHILD"

Your Sixty-Year-Old:
Friend or Foe?

MOLLY GILES

Annika at three knows what she likes and doesn't like, and she doesn't like me. "Oma came all the way to Amsterdam just to see you," my daughter Rachel tells her. "Isn't that exciting?" Annika freezes at the foot of the stairs. She has grown into a leggy beauty with hair so long it drifts down the small of her back. But she is still in diapers, I see, still drags a blanket, still has one of those damn binkies in her mouth.

"Hi, darling," I say.

Annika's eyes shift to Rachel.

"Oops," Rachel says to me. "I'm sorry, Mom, I forgot. You'll have to move. You're sitting on Annika's couch."

"Annika has her own couch?"

Rachel nods and gestures to a less comfortable chair. Creaking, I rise. "She likes to have her morning bottle," Rachel explains, "on her own couch."

"She still takes a bottle?" Too late to mask my disapproval, I add, "Where is it? I'll get it for her."

"Nay," says Annika. It's the Dutch "nay," brief and bestial.

"She likes me to give it to her," Rachel explains as she goes into the kitchen.

I bet she does. My eyes narrow as Annika advances head down to claim her couch. She passes me as swiftly as a little ferret, clambers onto the cushions, and stretches out, draping the blanket over her body with two expert flicks until only her ten tiny toes stick out. Her right hand darts to the table, plucks the remote control, and snaps the television on. A brightly colored cartoon from the BBC channel begins to blare. She pulls the binkie out with a pop.

"Mama," she says in a firm voice.

"Coming," Rachel calls from the kitchen.

And in bustles Rachel, my genius daughter, who speaks six languages, has a Ph.D. in genetics, writes for international science magazines, heads a cancer research lab in Utrecht, and is two and a half months pregnant with a second baby. Last night when she met my train at Schiphol, she told me she and her partner, Scott, know they "cannot improve on perfection," but perhaps this new one will be a boy. Scott appears now at the foot of the stairs, tiptoeing across the living room in his long Indonesian bathrobe. His camera is already pointed at Annika, who juts out her chin and gives him a practiced smile before she accepts the bottle of warmed milk from Rachel's hand and plunges it into her mouth.

"Where is dolphie?" Scott sings.

Eyes on the television, Annika thrusts her left hand up. Palmed inside is a small blue china dolphin. Scott snaps the picture, then turns to me and chuckles. "She won't go anywhere without her dolphie."

"Doesn't it break?"

"All the time. But Papa glues it back again, doesn't Papa?" He kneels and kisses Annika's furrowed forehead. She shoves him away. He laughs and kisses her fist. She hits him. I can't look.

"You slept with a sock monkey," I say to Rachel.

Rachel smiles. Her lovely face. All three of my daughters are beautiful, but Rachel, my second, the one who has chosen to live farthest away, has the moon face and full lips of a goddess. "I did?" Her voice is mild. She does not remember her monkey.

I do. I remember everything about Rachel at three. Her monkey, her pillow, her long reasonable sentences. At three, Rachel was toilet-trained, bottle-weaned; already using knife, fork, and cup with ease; able to tie her own shoes, read a few words, and engage strangers with grace. I turn to my granddaughter. "I brought you some presents."

"Did you hear that?" Scott exaggerates enthusiasm, his eyebrows shooting up. "Oma brought you presents all the way from California!"

Annika turns her head on the couch and studies me, the bottle protruding like a platypus snout beneath her assessing eyes.

"Shall we open them now?" Scott crouches, camera poised, ready for the "Annika Opens Presents" shot.

Annika turns back to the television.

"Aw," Scott says. "Please? Pretty please with kafir on top?" He turns to me. "She's not a morning person," he says.

Annika is not a breakfast person either. She sits on Rachel's lap at the dining room table and slowly licks salt, grain by grain, off half of one cashew as the rest of us eat cheese and fruit and sprinkle chocolate, as the Dutch do, Scott assures me, on our hot buttered toast. "Delicious," I suggest, holding out a piece, but Annika turns her head away. During the rest of that day—but who's counting—she licks the salt off the other half of the same cashew. At some point she accepts a small square yellow cracker and eats one corner. "It's funny"—Rachel laughs—"because we're vegetarians and yet Annika has never tasted a vegetable!"

"Aren't you worried she'll get scurvy?"

Rachel laughs again. Annika, bent over her cashew, drily parrots the sound, "Ha ha ha." The child is not without wit. Also, despite the lack of nutrients, she has energy. This day, the first day of my visit, she tours Amsterdam, dolphin in fist, riding Scott's shoulders as we peer into Anne Frank's house, take a barge down one of the canals, and pass through the red-light district on our way to an outdoor café. A whore in a window doing leg lifts waves to her and Annika waves back. Her laughter, when Scott is whipped into an obliging gallop, ripples like a wake of bright bubbles, and even the tall grim Dutch passing us on the sidewalk smile.

That night she agrees to open her presents. She dismisses the lilac tutu I brought ("You used to want to be a ballerina," I sigh to the amnesiac Rachel), ignores the toys and books, but seems to approve of the embroidered denim jacket from the breathtakingly expensive children's boutique in Berkeley. She lets me read to her, and the next morning she allows me to hand her the bottle. I am deeply honored and kneel for a second, as Scott did the day before, to kiss her forehead. She does not strike me.

My visit to Amsterdam is short and complicated by travel. Scott, a computer programmer, has an important project to finish in his office at home, so Rachel and I decide to take Annika to Antwerp, spend a night there, then go on to Paris for a few days. Annika is a good traveler, I am told, but when I see Rachel that morning, I worry. My beautiful daughter stands before me in baggy jeans, scuffed hiking boots, six tarnished silver earrings, and a gauze peasant shirt I gave her eight years ago, when she and Scott first left the States. But it isn't the poverty of what she's wearing that breaks my heart; it's the magnitude of what she's carrying: Rachel is as burdened as a pack animal with an overstuffed shoulder purse and a tall backpack toppling with disposable diapers, Tupperware containers of Cheerios, chips, dried nuts, boxes of fruit juice, baby bottles, crayons, pipe cleaners, stickers, balls, soap bubbles, blankets, several changes of clothes, a canteen of water, four picture books, one parenting book, a box of Legos, three stuffed animals, and a tube of superglue for the dolphin. Ten weeks pregnant and gently rounded already, her brown eyes amused behind the glasses atilt on the slightly swollen nose caused when Annika reared back in her arms a week ago, Rachel squats and holds her arms out. "Sweetie," she coos to Annika, who is sulking in the doorway, head down, "do you want me to carry you?"

"You can't!" I bark. "She must weigh thirty-five pounds!"

Rachel laughs. "Close," she says. "Almost two and a half stone."

I have been told stone. I have been told meter. Annika, who speaks Dutch in preschool and English at home, who knows stone and meter, swivels to glare at me. "Is *she* coming?" she asks Rachel in clear perfect English.

I hold out my hand. "Yes, I am. Want to show me the way to Antwerp?"

Silence.

"Then I'll go by myself."

"It doesn't work to walk on without her," Rachel warns. "She'll just stand there. She doesn't care."

Admirable. I have to respect this child's distrust, her indifference, her serene negativity. It occurs to me that my granddaughter has a stronger sense of self than I do. It occurs to me I can learn from her.

My lessons begin in Antwerp, a city of spires and bony carved carapaces topped with golden cupolas. After we check into the B and B, we head across the cobblestone streets toward the square. At the famous fountain in the Great Market, I begin to tell Annika the story of how the good Brabo killed the bad giant by cutting his hand off and throwing it in the river, but I am interrupted by Rachel's warning, "Mom," and remember that Rachel rejected the *Bambi* video I brought as "too violent." Annika isn't listening anyway; she has seen an enormous trampoline tent set up in a corner of the square. She cuts through the African drummers and the stoners slumped on the steps to zero in on it; Rachel and I follow.

"She's never been on one before," Rachel marvels as Annika clambers up the rope ladder and enters on all fours. At first she clings to the side of the tent, watching the other children, and then she begins to jump. An older boy crowds her, too close, too rough, but she turns her back and jumps away from him. She finds her own corner and outlasts the older boy. She outlasts everyone. But enough is enough. I am restless and hungry, and I want a drink; I look at my watch.

I do not protest when Rachel carries her to the café, where we get a beer and a sandwich; I do not protest when her "dinner" consists of a grape, nor do I protest when midnight comes and she is still not put to bed. I do, however, protest when she wakes up at two-thirty screaming.

"Why is she doing that?" I ask.

"Mosquito," Rachel answers.

"I don't *like* it," Annika screams.

"One mosquito?"

"I don't *like* it."

"She really hates mosquitoes," Rachel says.

Other guests in the B and B rap on our walls as Annika continues to scream and Rachel and I barge around trying to catch the mosquito. At one point we collapse, giggling. Around four a.m. Rachel smashes the tiny menace against the wall. The splotch is red with Annika's blood; she was right to scream; she is allergic and the pink bite on her eyelid is already huge. "It's all right," Rachel says, showing her the smashed bug. "Come to Mama and cuddle."

"I don't *want* to cud-dle! No *cud*-dle."

But a few minutes later she is nestled in Rachel's strong warm arms, sucking her binkie as Rachel kisses the top of her head and sings "The Itsy Bitsy Spider." I sit beside them and, awkward but determined, put my own arm around Rachel. *I* want to cuddle. I have finally figured out what should have been obvious to me from the very first morning: I am jealous. I want my daughter back.

Next morning Annika is swollen and beaten up and out of sorts.

"Where's dolphie?" she grunts.

I had found the tiny wreck of glued blue cracks earlier on the floor and had put it in my pocket. I pull it out now and hide it behind my back.

"Which hand?" I say.

Annika frowns, then taps my right hand; I open it, nothing. She taps my left: nothing.

"Now you see how I was raised," Rachel says.

Just as the lips part to release first the binkie and then the scream I reluctantly hand her the dolphin.

We take the train to Paris, Annika collapsed in Rachel's arms, Rachel collapsed against my shoulder. The flat in Montmartre where we're staying has no elevator, so we climb up five flights of narrow dark stairs. Paint and plaster are scaling off the walls as we pass. Annika's steps are careful; she needs assistance only on curves. At one landing she stops, stares up, and starts to wail again. I follow her eyes to an insect circling far above against a dusty skylight. "It's just a fly," I assure her. "No mosquitoes in Paris." Annika squints at me through her swollen eye; she knows better, and in fact that night, after we have been to Sacré Coeur and have seen the sunset gild the city below, after she has supped on a single *frite* and had a bath and not allowed me to read to her ("That's all right," Rachel says, replacing me on the bed, "Mama will read to you")—after all that, Annika does in fact see a mosquito on the ceiling, and this time I kill it before it lands on her. My reward: an obedient and competent good night kiss.

The next few days are child-centered; we make no attempt to see museums or tourist spots. It's hot and Paris is unbeautiful, sirens wailing, traffic snarled, construction everywhere, odors of dog shit and human pee so strong that Annika crinkles her sharp little nose as we walk.

We go to the Bois de Boulogne, where Annika runs from merry-go-round to swing set to bumper cars. She has a beautiful run, a rhythmic steady joyful pace, hands palm down, braids bouncing in time. She is a delighted hellion, and after a struggle over a before-supper Popsicle—"I don't *want* later! I want *now*!"—and another struggle over which flavor—"I don't *want* red, I want *or*-ange,"—we sit peacefully on a bench under a shade tree. Annika licks daintily as Rachel adjusts the paper wrapping so it doesn't drip. "All done," Annika announces, after a few licks. She takes a tissue from Rachel and carefully cleans her hands, wiping between each extended finger. Her nails are like mine and Rachel's, long nail beds and big moons. "Do you want to throw this in the trash?" Rachel suggests. "Nay," quieter now. I rise and drop it in a nearby bin.

An hour later, at an outdoor café, Annika pushes her untouched cheese sandwich aside, leans on her fist, and in a quiet dangerous tone, says, "Ice cream."

"No," Rachel says, "you just had a Popsicle, remember?"

"*Ice* cream."

"No," Rachel repeats.

All day I've been saying "Don't!" and "Watch out!" and "Be careful!" I've been a gasper and a frowner and, when Annika wailed, a mocker. But now, when Rachel for the first time in three days says no, I hear myself say, "Oh, why not?" I pour more wine. "Let her have it. What's the harm? We're on vacation. Besides, she needs the calcium."

Rachel sighs and I realize that she's been putting up with me the same way I've been putting up with Annika. Rachel the saint. Well—I exchange a dark glance with Annika—no one asked Rachel to be a saint. Rachel calls to the waiter and orders ice cream. Annika, smug, begins singing "Doe, a deer" under her breath. When the tall dish of vanilla arrives,

I pick up my spoon, reach over, and take a big bite. "*Nay!* I don't *want* to share," Annika hisses.

"Tough," I tell her, and take another.

"Do you want me to order some for you?" Rachel asks, her voice weary.

"No," I say. "I've had enough."

Annika smiles at me, smart Oma, and continues to spoon in one tiny contemplative bite after another, her hands around the bowl to keep it from me in case I change my mind.

The next morning I want to buy Rachel new shoes and new underwear and a new blouse and a new purse, but she hates shopping and explains that Annika, in any event, doesn't "do" stores. Rachel has admired my walking sandals, and since we wear the same size, I give them to her; I give her my white tennies, too, and some of my blouses and the earrings off my ears. It's departure day: Rachel and Annika are taking the train back to Amsterdam, and I am leaving later for the airport to fly back to California. I slip out of the flat while Rachel is changing Annika and go down to the corner *boulangerie*; I buy Rachel, who has been having bouts of morning sickness, an apple tart, and then I pause outside a toy store: there is an old-fashioned sock monkey in the window. I go inside.

Back in the flat I make Rachel an avocado sandwich on brown bread and wrap it and the pastry carefully in foil for her trip. "Mama mothers Annika and Oma mothers Mama," Rachel explains as she puts it in her backpack. Annika scowls.

"I have something for you, too," I tell Annika. "Don't worry," I laugh, seeing her scowl deepen, "it's nothing to eat."

I hold my hands behind my back, but this time when Annika, suspicious, taps, I bring my hand out and open it at once. Inside, from the shop around the corner, is a tiny white china unicorn with a fragile silver horn that I knew would please her more than any sock monkey.

It does.

She looks up with a smile so radiant it almost brings me to my knees. She says, "Thank you," at Rachel's prompting, takes the unicorn, and without a pause drops the blue dolphin in my still open palm.

"For me?" That does it. I *will* drop to my knees.

"It's bwoken," she explains, and turns away.

I am sadder after they leave than I remember being over any leave-taking in my life. I wave them off in the taxi, then climb back up the five flights, missing Rachel's calm, tender presence, Annika's dry *ha ha ha*. I laugh, remembering the way she danced to the accordion music outside the cathedral last night, the intent way she colored in her coloring book with her bare toes fanned out on the windowsill, the way she lined her toys up and said good night to each one. I enter the flat ready to throw myself on the bed with heartbreak. But something is already on the bed: the parenting book that Rachel left behind. I pick it up, amused as always by the title: *Your Three-Year-Old: Friend or Foe?* I remember Rachel looking up from it a few nights ago.

"Do you think Annika's a spoiled brat?" she'd asked.

I knew better than to answer. "She's not like anyone I've ever known before," I said, my voice careful.

"Really?" Rachel seemed puzzled. "That's odd. She reminds me so much of you."

Remembering this, I squeeze the blue dolphin, which for

some reason is still in my palm. I feel the tail snap in two. I start to toss it into the trash, then look at it again; it's a clean crack. It can be fixed. Who knows, Annika might want it the next time I see her. I cannot wait for the next time to see her. I wrap the dolphin carefully in foil and slip it into my purse.

How I Got to Be Queen of England

ELIZABETH BERG

When my daughters were four and eight years old, I was eating lunch with a friend named Will. The phone rang, and it was his daughter calling to tell him she was pregnant. "Oh, wow," he said. "Wonderful! Congratulations! I'm so happy!" But as soon as he hung up, he looked over at me and said, "I'm not *ready* to be a grandfather." Will is the sort of man who worries more about aging than any woman I know, and though I meant to offer words of support, what slipped out was "You're nuts."

I think I've been ready to be a grandmother since I knew what grandmothers were. I grew up with only one grandmother, Frieda Loney, and I liked everything about her. She had white porcelain poodle dogs on a chain, positioned just so on an end table in the living room. She wore comfortable shoes that did not pinch her toes and comfortable house-dresses with nary a trace of scratchy slip. She had a pink tiled bathroom with a fuzzy pink rug and toilet seat cover and toilet tank cover. She kept a parakeet on a television tray in her kitchen. Once a week, her six daughters would gather in that kitchen to wash her very heavy, very long white hair, about which she was admittedly vain; and while it dried, she would read their fortunes in tea leaves. Once she read mine and told me that my boyfriend, Bobby, liked me back, which he did not, but oh well. Mostly what I liked about my grandmother was that she was revered. Obviously, there was something to this grandmother business. So far as I could tell, it was like being queen of England, minus the inconvenience of having to wear a crown.

But before I could be a grandmother, I needed to be a mother—and that was swell, too. My children routinely broke my heart, in the good way. When my older daughter, Julie, was three, I took her to a big-box store and told her she could have any doll in the place. We wandered the aisles, looking at this fancy doll and that—the high-breasted, vacant-eyed fashion dolls; the talented baby dolls who did everything short of rinsing out their own dirty diapers. But the doll Julie wanted was one she found tossed facedown in a low bin. It was an ugly doll with a cloth body; weird, half-cloth, half-plastic arms and legs; and a scrunched-up face. There was no wrapping around the doll, and I figured it must be a return. I tried to persuade Julie to pick a doll that looked a little better, one with eyelashes at least, but no, she wanted this one. She pressed it closely to her bosom and said, "I will call her Baby Annie." And right then, I swear, I knew that Julie was someday going to be a great mother. She took the doll home, and the next year, whenever I sat on the sofa nursing her baby sister, Julie sat beside me nursing Baby Annie. She tucked Annie in at night. She carried Annie around everywhere. In the way of children's lovies that end up disintegrating, she loved that doll to death.

After Julie had been married a few years, I began to wonder if she'd decided not to have children. I didn't want to pressure her, even though I'd been sorely tempted, à la Ida Morgenstern, to inquire the day after the wedding if there was any news from the stork. But then one day she called and said she had something to tell me and I yelled, *"Are you pregnant?"* She laughed and said yes, and I screamed and then I cried. She told me it was early, so early, really too early to tell anyone; I must not tell anyone yet. But I told everyone and that is why Julie will never tell me secrets anymore. I was just too happy. Happiness was leaking out of me; it was causing chest pressure similar to a heart attack, and so what could I do? I had to tell my best friend(s). It is true that I did not have to tell casual acquaintances and complete strangers; I admit this. Only I kind of did have to. In the world we live in, any chance to share lovely news is irresistible.

I bought the same book as Julie had, the one that talked about her pregnancy week by week. Up on my refrigerator went pictures documenting fetal progress. At six weeks, the baby was the size of a pinto bean and showed a promising "liver bulge." At thirteen weeks, it was the size of a football. At twenty weeks, it had eyelids, eyebrows, and fingernails, and I said to Julie, "Oh, don't you wish we could just take it out and play with it?" I said "it" because Julie didn't know the sex; she and her husband wanted to be surprised. I was sure I knew, though. "It's a boy," I said with complete conviction, except on the days when I said, "It's a girl."

Julie had asked me to be present during labor, to serve as a coach. Since I'm a former RN, she figured I'd be good to have around; also, I was cheaper than a doula. "But when it's time to push," she told me, "I'd like to be alone with Josh." I said of course. I would do whatever she wanted.

On the plane from Chicago to Boston, I sat looking out the window thinking that my baby was going to have a baby. It was an odd, exhilarating, Russian doll type feeling. And I thought, too, that although the baby was going to be born to Julie, it would also be born to me. Because I was *the grandma*. As soon as I got home, I was going to buy a parakeet for my kitchen.

I closed my eyes and tried to imagine Julie in labor, but all I could think of was myself in labor with her. I saw again that little room, saw the heavyset nurse coming in to increase the pitocin drip, for which I wanted to smack her. But I was good; I didn't swear or even moan much. When the doctor asked if I wanted anything for pain, I roared, "No!" I got through the pain; I exulted in the delivery; and when Julie's father and I brought her home on a beautiful autumn day, both of us admitted we were stunned that they'd let us just *have* her like that. I recalled her being in the car seat in back, and as we passed a war memorial, my husband turning around to say, "We don't believe in war." I think that's when it really hit me that we were her *parents*, responsible for her in every way. I remembered her learning to walk, losing her two front teeth, playing board games, shopping for a prom dress, graduating from college, walking down the aisle to meet her beaming groom.

On the day the baby was due, there was no sign of labor. Julie, Josh, and I went out to dinner, and while Julie was eating she felt a pain. Hooray! we thought. This is it! We finished dinner, we went for a walk, and the pains went away. At home, Josh and I sat on the couch watching television and eating M&Ms, exhorting Julie to walk up and down the stairs to get that baby *going*. "Faster," I said, then held out my hand for more brown ones.

The next day, while the doctor was giving Julie a treatment to soften her cervix, her water broke. She was told to move around a bit until the pain got more, uh, interesting, so we walked up and down the hall. Like me, she wanted to have natural childbirth, and she was happy that so far the pain wasn't too bad. And then it got bad. She moved to the birthing room, and the nurse brought in a beach ball for her to sit and rock on. She sat, she rocked, she moaned, and after a while her eyes got the glazed, distant look that animals get when they're in pain. In one small part of my brain, I was thinking, *Well, this is it; this is good and natural and necessary; this is what she must go through to deliver.* But mostly I was thinking, *Stop it! Leave her alone! Don't hurt her so much!* The contractions were intense and coming right on top of each other, and after a while Julie decided to get an epidural. And let me tell you: within minutes, she had left the medieval torture chamber and was bantering with the nurses, telling jokes, making delightful conversation with her husband. It was as if she were at an oddly intimate cocktail party where every now and then someone came and had a really good look up her dress.

Although the good part of an epidural is that it takes away the pain, the bad part is that it slows down labor. So I went back to Julie's house to sleep and to take care of their dog, Wrigley. In the spirit of celebration, I gave him extra food. Then I gave him some scraps. Then I invited him to spend the night on the bed with me. I fell into uneasy sleep, hopeful that I wasn't going to miss anything.

Early the next morning, I raced to the hospital and arrived just in time for Julie to push. She said, "Mom? I know I asked you to wait outside, but I'm kind of scared, so would you stay?" To say that I felt honored would be engaging in the fine art of extreme understatement.

So while Josh stood at Julie's knee, I stood at her head, watching her turn bright red every time she was told to push. I looked down at her young woman's face and I saw her two-year-old face as she sat on the floor next to me while I was being interviewed for a job. I hadn't been able to find a sitter and the woman told me to bring my daughter along with me. The interview went on for some time, and the woman kept looking at Julie quietly playing with a few toys and saying, "She is such a *good girl!*" And I said I knew it, with a kind of amazement. I was aware that it wasn't our fantastic parenting that had created such a sweet child; she just came that way.

Anyway, the good big girl pushed and her face turned red and blue veins bulged at her temples, and Josh saw a bit more and then a little bit more of the baby's head. And then a bluish-white body came sliding into the world, facedown. I recall the moment as being profoundly quiet, though I know it was not. Then someone said, "Turn it over!" because we all—mother, father, grandmother, nurses, doctor—were anxious to see what sex it was. And when the baby was flipped, I saw Matthew Sumner Krintzman, a live baby, another human thrust suddenly onto the planet where a moment before there had been no such being. I saw that he had curly hair like his father, and that—was it possible to say this so soon?—he looked *exactly* like his father. I saw my son-in-law's hands fall to his sides and his shoulders slump and his head drop and I saw him weep with the kind of joy that is so all-encompassing the body cannot contain it and, in fact, seems to break with it. I imagined him thinking: *Look what we did. Look at that. Look what we did.* I saw my daughter take her baby to her breast in the same unequivocal way she did with Baby Annie. It was a movement of glorious strength and beauty that announced, *I am his mother, he is mine, and I am going to take care of him every single second of my life.* And again, I know there were sounds in the room, but my memory plays that scene back to me in absolute stillness, as though we were all underwater, yet with the sun shining through the high hospital windows. Absolute quiet, as though we were witnessing a living sacrament, which of course we were.

I had my moment of holding the baby, of staring down enraptured into that calm little face, into those shiny new eyes, so wise-seeming, so connected still to that vestigial home, and then I called everyone on my list. I said it's a boy. I said he looks exactly like Josh. I told everyone his name, which had also been a secret kept even from me—for obvious reasons. I tried to impart the wonder of all I saw, the privilege; but I'm afraid I'm not equipped to articulate such a thing. Who would be? I saw my daughter give birth to her son, and I was crowned.

On the day I saw Matthew delivered, I learned something. I learned that he was not born to me or even to his parents. Instead, we were born to him, as each of us took up our respective roles. For me, there was another feeling, too, a mix of gratitude, awe, hope, protectiveness, and a dazzling awareness of continuity, which had been hinted at in my head but now was fully realized in my heart.

I don't know if my grandmother felt the same way about her babies having babies. We differ in so many ways—she was English and reserved and did not believe in overpraising a child or grandchild, whereas I want to call the Associated Press after every one of their accomplishments—say, a good burp after nursing. Frieda Loney did not pull you up onto her lap and squeeze you and cover you with kisses; she did not exuberantly read picture books to you; she did not take you outside and point to birds, or sing to you, or put her hand over her heart and melt when you spoke your little toddler sentences. Yet somehow, though she never said the words, you knew she loved you. Her prize possession was her charm bracelet, which was heavy with little silver heads, one for every one of her children and grandchildren and great-grandchildren, and she took that bracelet off only to bathe.

Sometimes I imagine my grandmother back in her kitchen, sitting on a chair with a towel draped around her shoulders, her silver hair spread out to dry, a teacup in her hand. I stand before her, my daughter beside me, my grandchild in my arms. My grandmother turns to me, and in her mild blue eyes I see an acknowledgment of something she cannot articulate, either. She turns back to telling people's fortunes, and though she is smiling, I know it's not at them. I adjust my invisible crown and take it from there.

What Counts

BEVERLY LOWRY

The first time I saw him he was seven. It was Christmas. He was flying in with his mother and my son Colin, from San Jose to Austin. This was in the days when we could still meet our people at the gate when they landed and see them off when they departed. I'd left home early—we lived twenty-six miles from Austin—and arrived in plenty of time. Waiting as the plane taxied from the runway to the gate, I felt my heart go into a serious scramble, and I was as fidgety as if on a blind date.

It was 1987. My husband, Glenn, and I hadn't had the heart to celebrate Christmas for three years, since the sudden death of our other son, eighteen-year-old Peter. Now here came this new boy into our lives.

Could we tell a seven-year-old boy we were still too sad to remember the past and do Christmas? Would he expect Santa to come? Would he even like us?

His name, I knew, was Brandon, and Colin was in love with his mother. The three of them lived in Santa Cruz, California, where Colin and Andrea had gone to college. Colin had told us about Brandon: how the first time he invited Andrea over for a meal, she let him know that if she came her son would, too—that they were a package deal.

For that occasion, Colin had made a special dish, chicken with yogurt, which Brandon, he reported, had turned down flat.

By the look on our son's face when he told us this story, we knew this was not a casual romance, and that he already loved the boy as well as his mother. We knew that Brandon's biological father wasn't much on the scene, and even though Andrea and Colin hadn't yet moved in together, they were a family. We also knew that if Andrea wanted him to take on the job, Colin was willing to be a father to Brandon, or anyway to try. I wasn't sure how Brandon felt about this. A few days into his first visit, the river in front of our house flooded, and a man drowned in his car. Brandon and I stood on the deck talking together about the boy whose father had died. "It's terrible when you lose your father," he said. "But if your mother dies you lose everything." I realized then as long as he knew Andrea was there, he was fine, no matter whether his father was biological or a volunteer.

When the flight's arrival was announced and the agent unlatched the door, the boy burst out, as if propelled. I'd seen pictures, so I recognized him; but I think I would have known who he was anyway. Once he turned the corner he barreled down the ramp, arms out for balance as he stomped his way forward at a headlong, all-out tilt. In his left fist he clutched the ear of a white bear, nearly as tall as he was. The bear's head flopped as its back paws dragged on the ground.

Headlong was how he aimed himself toward me, as if he knew which one I was and how hard I was hoping. And headlong my heart went up to him; both of us were holding nothing back.

Colin and Andrea came several steps behind, watching Brandon, watching me. When he got to the bottom of the ramp, he did not slow down or pause to think what to do next. He rolled straight into my arms. I could not believe it. Had his mother told him to do it? Had Colin? Had they said to him, "It will make her really happy if you go fill up the space in her arms where a different boy used to be"? I don't think so. It was how he was and how much I wanted him.

I had a grandson. From the first, he called me "Bev." I am still Bev to him. Not for a second did I think of him as a *step*-grandson. He knew me from the beginning as his grandmother. Andrea's mother was still alive then, but she died a few years later, and Brandon didn't see his paternal grandmother much. But we didn't think any of this out; we didn't count up to figure out how many grandmothers a boy needed or deserved. In the end, blood counts, but not as much as love. These many years later nothing has changed.

A compact guy with intelligent blue eyes and a forehead that curled often—still curls often—into a ponderous frown, he had gelled his blond hair into high stiff spikes, giving him a look of surprise and readiness. He was up for whatever awaited.

I scooped him into my chest, him and the bear together, and said to myself, "I'm having this. Oh, yes. I'm having all of this I can get."

Then Colin was there, and the love of his life, Brandon's mother.

Peter's death had come like a shot in the night. He'd been hit by a vehicle—car? pickup truck?—on a dark country highway in the middle of a September night. He was buried in the town cemetery not far from where we lived—on the San Marcos River in Caldwell County, Texas—beneath a black marble stone saying "Loved. Missed." By the time Brandon came into my life, I had pretty much given up creating scenarios that would explain what had happened to Peter that night, even though any explanation seemed preferable to what we had, which was a mystery that would never be solved. But mystery was what we were left with.

I'm sure I never thought of Brandon as a replacement for my dead son: how can one boy possibly take the place of another? But I think other people thought I might be hoping for just that. Later, I found out that Colin had explained to Brandon about Christmas and Peter and our not marking the day. But at the last minute, I'd relented. It wasn't fair, I thought, to ask a child to come for Christmas and not do anything. And so without telling anybody, I tied red ribbons on the branches of the ficus tree in the living room and put wrapped presents beneath its potted trunk, and when we got home from the airport, Brandon's eyes went wide at the sight.

"Colin said we wouldn't have a tree!" he exclaimed.

"Well, it's not exactly a Christmas tree," I said.

"Yes," he said. "It is. "

We stood and looked at it, and everybody knew that if not for Brandon there wouldn't have been ribbons, but nobody said anything.

During that first visit, what we did, my grandson and I, was what is called "bond." We laughed and joked together, and watched the river recede from its flood stage. We *played*, as if we were the same age. With Colin and Andrea, he came back to San Marcos as often as possible, and in the next couple of years, having studied movie techniques from FX magazines, he became a kind of an underage special-effects expert. When Colin and Andrea went out for the evening, and after Glenn went to bed, Brandon and I often watched movies. He liked horror movies. They scared me, but in truth, I would have done almost anything to hold on to his love and the connection between us. So I agreed with his selections, and we watched Freddy Krueger's nighttime slaughters and sometimes Michael Myers's. And when the screen ran with blood, I would slide from the couch to the floor with my hands over my face.

"It's okay, Bev," Brandon would say. "It's not real blood."

And he would explain how the moviemakers had created the gore, what the blood really was, the eyeballs, the trailing entrails. Once, we watched a movie of my choice, a modern-day romance. When a fairly obvious sex scene came on, I glanced sideways at Brandon, who without saying anything had placed his palm flat across his eyes about an inch from his face. I didn't let him know I noticed, but simply said I didn't like the movie much, did he? He said not really and we went back to Freddy Krueger.

At some point, a friend told me that people who cared about me were worried that I was getting too carried away with Brandon, giving too much of my heart to him, when who knew what would happen between Andrea and Colin. My friends had seen me through terrible times after Peter's death, and now here I was smitten with a new boy.

Was that smart? What if Colin and Andrea split up, then what? I'd be left to grieve once again.

I listened to whatever my friends and family told me, especially in those days when I couldn't quite pull a dependable sense of self together. And so I thought about what my friends said, and then I took Brandon aside.

"Okay, Brandon," I said to him. "We don't know what will happen with your mom and Colin, right?"

His brow furled, not in worry but contemplation. "Right," he said.

"They could live together the rest of their lives, they could get married, or . . ."

Deeper frown.

". . . they could break up. Right?"

"Right."

So I told him I would be his grandmother for as long as he wanted me to, whatever they did, however long they stayed together—or did not.

We would have our own pact.

He agreed to be my grandson under the same terms. And we shook on that. And nothing has changed in the twenty or so years since.

In that many years, all families go through a great many changes: death, divorce, accidents, birth, loss, slippage into one kind of destructive behavior or another. Our family is no different. There have been hard years and good ones. Colin and Andrea married, and then after a number of years separated, and then put their marriage and their love back together again. They had no biological children. Brandon represents us in the next generation. He is our boy.

In all this time, despite some cataclysmic events in my life and his, our vow has lasted. My friends have infant grandchildren. Mine is grown, with his own life to live, separate from ours.

In the spring of 2006, I moved back to Austin, into the same neighborhood as my son, my daughter-in-law, and Brandon. I didn't plan to move that close to them or to horn in on their lives the way that I've seen some parents do. The house came up; I loved it; I wanted to live in Austin; I rented it. As it turned out, nobody feared the proximity or the possibility that his or her privacy would be invaded. We live close, but apart. Brandon is a grown-up, with his own life. We spend time together when we can. I am especially fond of throwing family dinners on Sunday evenings, when the four of us gather to tell stories, eat a great deal, and talk about whatever we're up to. When I am away from home, commuting to a job or traveling on one kind of adventure or another, I leave my car with Brandon. He's good at fixing things. I am not. When he comes over to help out, we talk over a world of subjects. I give him books. Sometimes we walk his dog together, down the hike-and-bike trail near my home, along Lady Bird Lake.

Among his many talents, Brandon is a gifted metal sculptor. During the fall after I moved to Austin, I spied a tree he'd made from scrap iron in Colin's backyard. A sapling with no leaves, it was about five feet tall and was just sitting there, leaning against the garage. Turned out that Brandon had made it on commission; its slim branches were to be used as hooks on which to hang hair extensions in a beauty parlor. But the tree was too large for the beauty shop, and I bought it instead and put it on my front porch.

That year, my two brothers and I celebrated our first

family Christmas since before Peter's death. My brother David came with his wife, Gwen, from Houston; Eddy flew in from Seattle with his wife, Anne. Before they arrived, I bought three strands of purple and white lights from Target and strung them on Brandon's tree. For ornaments, I used old jewelry and trinkets gathered from drawers: single earrings, gaudy bracelets worn once, an old watch which hadn't worked in years, but which for some reason I couldn't throw away. Beads, colored ribbons, souvenirs from trips.

Over Christmas dinner I reminded my family how a few years before, my niece's daughter, Micheala—who was then about four years old and who lives with her father—had visited us at David's home in Houston. Brandon was there, too. My brother does not have biological children, but his wife, Gwen, does. David is very much a grandfather to Gwen's grandchildren, some of whom were at the table that evening.

When we sat down to eat, Micheala spoke first. "Now who," she asked, "is the mother of who, here?" We looked around, thinking of the various ways we were all connected, beyond blood and genealogy, and we laughed and said we were all mothers and daddies and children of us all. Micheala didn't seem entirely satisfied with that, but in time she seemed to understand.

After the holidays were over I left the purple and white lights on the scrap metal tree for several weeks. When I took them down, I put them in a box with the earrings and the beads.

Brandon's tree now takes it place as a permanent fixture on my front porch, sitting to the right of the front door, between a metal guinea hen from Zimbabwe that I bought at Eastern Market in Washington and a bright red American Flyer sled that I found at a yard sale in Buffalo. The guinea hen requires no corn; the red Flyer will never again slide in snow; Brandon's tree needs neither water nor raking. It will serve as my Christmas tree from now on—or at least until as far into the future as I can imagine.

Nana

ROXANA ROBINSON

During the years while my daughter was growing up, each time I took a trip without her—as the airplane struggled to lift off, as the engines strained and the wings tilted alarmingly toward the earth and the landing gear groaned fatally—I gripped the armrests with white-knuckled fingers, wishing from the bottom of my soul that I had never come on this stupid trip, and anguishing over the thought of how in the world my daughter would manage to grow up without a mother.

While she was small, the thought of her grief was unbearable and made my heart race with terror. When my daughter reached eleven, the thought was still terrible, but I knew I was no longer quite so essential, and I began to hope she would survive. At eighteen, I wondered, in my heart of hearts, if she might actually be happier without me. When she was about twenty-one, I stopped gripping so hard—though not altogether.

When you first become a mother, your child becomes the center of your gaze. This is biology at work, survival strategy: human babies need more care than any others on the planet. So this is how you start out together: her helplessly dependent, you fiercely protective. For years, as she is growing up, you are wholly responsible for everything, and whatever goes wrong is your fault: the time she got that terrible infection and had to go to the hospital, the time you were late and the non-English-speaking babysitter walked out and left your three-year-old alone in the house; the time in seventh grade with those awful girls; the time the horse kicked her. To say nothing of the times when you were mean instead of kind. All these things would not have happened, as you well know, if you had been a better mother. You should have prevented them. They will still wake you up, years later, with a dark stab of guilt: there are things for which you will never forgive yourself. Because long afterward (forever, in fact), you will continue to carry your child as you did in the months before her birth. She is still there, just under your beating heart, a constant beloved presence, burden, and delight.

It's a deep connection, between mother and daughter. So when all my friends told me that being a grandmother was "the best," I wondered. What could be better than this? My friends shook their heads. "Whatever you expect, it will be better." Everyone loves being a grandmother. What is it about this job that's so great?

I was curious and eager to find out for myself, but this is a job you can't apply for. Whether you get it or not is entirely dependent on someone else. Your qualifications have no bearing here.

My daughter is my only child, and that makes me think of the old adage "Don't put all your eggs in one basket." If you have only one child, this is just what you've done, both literally and metaphorically. This is where all your maternal energy and intensity is focused, and it's where all your bio-logical information is stored: this basket matters deeply.

Two years ago, my daughter (also Roxana) was married, and I began turning into an old adage myself, wondering when she was going to have a baby. Isn't this what old women do—aren't they always asking when younger ones are going to have babies?

I didn't feel particularly old, but I suddenly understood why they do it. As a mother, you too are part of the biologi-cal clock; its steady tick reverberates within your conscious-ness as well. My friends and I ask this question all the time about each other's daughters: "When is she going to have a baby?" It's a question we can say out loud, unlike the one that precedes it: "When is she going to get married?" Those questions are taken from the same text. We're asking if our children will enter into the dance of the future, if they'll take those opening steps that lead to the next generation.

This too is biology, ingeniously at work through the emo-tions: these questions are intensely important, and when we hear about a wedding or a baby, delight fills us. This sudden upswelling of happiness has something to do, of course, with the particular love that you feel for a particular child, and also with something larger, more encompassing—the long steady beat of life.

One evening last summer, my husband, Tony, and I were about to go out to dinner with Roxana and her husband, Danny. We were all in the living room of their apartment in Greenwich Village, getting ready to go. My daughter, stand-ing in front of the bookcases, pulled on her sweater, then turned and said she had something to tell us. Her voice was annunciatory and proud. It was the look on her face, really, that delivered the message, and the room lit up with joy. Of course they'd had their earlier private moments of joy; we multiplied this by the length of another generation.

That was my first moment of grandmotherhood, I suppose—seeing my daughter so fresh and radiant, making her announcement, her still slim body holding its secret.

During her pregnancy, I watched Roxana become fuller and rounder as she moved toward The Day, taking on the peaceful beauty of women who are, literally, full of life. Now everything was focused on The Day. She told me her plans: a midwife, in a hospital. She was taking Lamaze classes in natural childbirth. She was using a doula, who was also her Pilates teacher. What, I wondered, was a doula? Explanations didn't entirely help: it seemed that the doula offered something part spiritual and part physical, but it wasn't clear to me exactly what.

One day we received an e-mail with a mystifying attachment: the sonogram. This is the baby, we were told; here is her foot, there her head. We could make nothing of these amorphous outlines. It was exciting, but also somewhat unnerving; it seemed to me too intimate for us to see. I felt I shouldn't know what she looked like now, before she was ready to be seen, while she was still dreaming, while her brain was still forming, while her world was liquid.

But it was extraordinary: she was there. She was real.

And she was a girl.

They'd chosen her name, but wouldn't tell it. My daughter said, "If you tell people the baby's name after it's born, they say, 'Oh, what a great name.' But if you tell them before, they say, 'Oh, don't name her that. We had a dog named that, and she bit everyone.'"

Of course she was right; still, I was dying to know. Sometimes I asked her outright.

"Is it Melchisedic?" I asked—Sarah Crewe's pet mouse in *The Little Princess*.

"It *might* be Melchisedic," she said, laughing.

As the due date approached, Roxana was more and more enormous, the baby so demandingly present that each day the birth seemed imminent. But there were some false starts, and by the date itself Roxana announced that she'd given up hope. She'd decided that pregnancy had become a permanent condition.

The next day she went into labor, very early in the morning. All day I waited near the phone as the hours dragged past. Danny called periodically. The doula was there, I was told. The mysterious doula! What was she doing? She was making tea, buying groceries. She was coaching my daughter's labor: then I began to understand. Midwives encourage you to spend most of your labor at home, so now the presence of the doula, with her deep intimate understanding of the body, made sense. She stayed all day. I spoke to my daughter once or twice, but she was in a removed and distant state. She was being taken over by the life of the body. She herself, her own consciousness, was becoming submerged in it, in this mysterious force, with its violent paroxysms, its urgency, its own interior logic. She was deep in the center of the current, too far out for us to reach, and she was headed for the falls. All of us were helpless on the banks, watching. All during the pregnancy we'd talked about the birth, every aspect of it, but the thing we didn't mention was that birth is perilous. It's very close to death. The two things move terrifyingly near to each other, like two huge planets. Their conjunction is unthinkable.

That evening she was still in labor. She'd been in to see the midwife, who sent her back home. As I got into bed that night, I was suddenly sick with fear, terrified by all the things that could go wrong. Roxana had told me one day about how the baby's head must turn and twist and bow and straighten during the birth. I hadn't wanted to listen, to visualize it—the chances of something going wrong seemed greater if I dwelt upon it. Now the risks seemed too immense, too dangerous, to consider. And I was helpless, I could do nothing to protect her. All I could do was whiten my knuckles and grip, afraid again for her, but this fear was different: it had nothing to do with me. It was only her. My daughter was struggling in this wild current; it was she who was braving those rapids, alone in the frail craft of her own body.

The following day she was still in labor, but now in the hospital. I sat waiting by the phone, biting my nails and jumping at every sound. Danny called every few hours. In the late afternoon, the phone rang.

"Hello?" I said breathlessly.

"Hello, Grandma," Danny said.

"Oh," I said. I was stunned. A stillness spread out around me. My eyes filled. I couldn't think of the next thing to say. "She's here?" I asked stupidly.

"She's here," he said, "come and see her."

My husband was due home shortly, and we were meant to be at a black-tie dinner at the opera in an hour.

"We'll be there in twenty minutes," I said.

We arrived in our evening clothes.

They were still in the delivery room, which held a bed, a chair, and a high padded table. It hadn't been cleaned up and was still unkempt, echoing with urgency. The bed was pulled out from the wall; the sheets were tumbled. On the floor was a smear of blood. My daughter was in a hospital gown; a transparent oxygen tube was taped to her nose; there was an IV stand by the bed: frightening reminders of the passage she'd just made. I didn't want to look at them, but my daughter was smiling—beaming, in fact—and there was something else to look at. There was the baby, wrapped like a loaf of bread, in a striped tea towel.

She'd arrived.

She was strange, glowing brick-red from the compression of the birth canal, from her passage from the other world. She was full of blood; she was weighty, over eight pounds, and gravid with life.

Her hair was thick and black, thatchy and damp. Her cheeks were full and pink, and her eyes—oh, her eyes. They were open and liquid, an indescribable color, neither blue nor brown—the color of new. Her gaze was mysterious and calm. She had never seen anything before this room, these faces. This was the world, where she would now live.

"What's her name?" I asked.

"Lucy," they said.

It was perfect, a jewel of a name.

"And what do you want to be called?" my daughter asked me.

"Nana," I said. This was not what I called my grandmother, but what we called my mother's favorite cousin, who was also Roxana. The baby and I each had a new name, as of course did my daughter: she was Mama.

"That's your Nana," my daughter said to Lucy, who gazed at us thoughtfully.

The thirty-six hours of labor were now behind us. The oxygen tube, the IV stand, the bloody smear were all irrelevant. I watched Lucy in the arms of my beautiful daughter, who was now a mother, and also still a daughter, just as I was still a daughter, and a mother, and now a grandmother. This was part of the dance, these were the steps to the future.

Lucy, radiant and glowing, is the future. And she's mine, in a way, though of course she's much more my daughter's. But she's also mine, just as my daughter is mine and as I am hers, as my mother is mine and I am hers. We belong to each other, linking past and future. As Virginia Woolf wrote, "We think back through our mothers, if we are women." It's our mothers who teach us how to live in the world. And we think forward through our daughters, if we are mothers, and beyond them, through their daughters.

"Would you like to hold her?" my daughter asked—an unthinkably generous offer.

I took Lucy in my arms: she was glowing with warmth. I touched her bare shoulder. It was the color of terra-cotta, and silky, unimaginably smooth; it had never been touched before now. She looked up at me with the preternatural gaze of the newborn: wise, quiet, sibylline. Her mouth was wide and delicate, the line of red lips perfectly distinct. Her black hair stood up wildly, like damp fur. Her nose was brief and curved; her eyelashes were long, dark, and fine. Her eyebrows were high and faint, the barest of brushstrokes. She was so new. I could hardly bring myself to hold her, she was so important; I could hardly bear the thought of giving her up.

I could see that her arrival—that time in which I was powerless to help my daughter anymore—was the end of one thing and the start of another. From now on it will be my daughter's turn to grip the armrests. This is, actually, a relief: I couldn't bear to go through it all again—the hospital, those mean girls. But here, for all those years of gripping, is my reward: Lucy. She's my retirement gift, the platinum gold watch for being a mother.

Here is a baby for whom you don't have to grip the armrests, whom you can adore without being responsible for everything that goes wrong. You aren't in charge, so nothing will be your fault. It's like being told you no longer have to eat vegetables, only dessert—and really only the icing.

This fortunate position—the one you couldn't apply for—is one you can't lose either. It's yours for life: this will always be your daughter's daughter. These two will always be yours, and you, theirs. I'll always be her Nana. Maybe this is biology at work once more: it seems now that this is just what I've always wanted.

Now You See Me,
Now You Don't

LYNNE SHARON SCHWARTZ

From day one, she stares right at us. We flatter ourselves, thinking, *Already she's interested in us!* But the books say she barely distinguishes us from the pictures on the walls or the furniture. We persevere, stay nearby so she'll know us. When she does start to distinguish faces from the pictures on the walls and the furniture, we want our face to be one of the important ones. (After her parents, of course. No envy or rivalry there. We know what their love feels like, that love fraught and agitated, doused in anxiety.) Soon she distinguishes us, for sure. She's happy to see us. When we appear at the door, she has an inkling of what to expect. Because when we're left alone with her we let her see our intimate face. We hide our face in our hands, then show it. Look, I'm here. Now I'm not here. Here, not here. And she laughs uproariously.

We talk to her in our intimate voice. We sing to her. And we discover that she's musical: a born music lover, like us. She looks nothing like us, but she has the music. We sing to her with our best, our secret voice, a voice dense with emotion that we're shy about showing the others, on the rare occasions when we do sing in front of others. And she loves our singing, as no one else in the world does—there's no reason why they should. We sing and she listens, rapt. It started, this singing, as a way to quiet her when she was fretful, but soon it became our private thing, what we do together. When she can stand up, she dances. We find music with a strong beat and she bounces up and down, little ballet pliés. Over the years we've often danced alone in the kitchen, holding a mixing spoon, and now we have someone to dance those silly dances with.

Now when we appear she looks at us the way no one does anymore, and maybe no one ever will again: Oh, it's you. You intrigue me. Singing, music. I want to know all about you. What else is there, her eyes (sometimes gray or green or blue) ask, besides the music?

Well, I've got a few other things up my sleeve, but she's not quite old enough. I'll wait until she's ready—as long as I can. I used to think at this point I wouldn't learn much more, anything truly new, that is. Not so. She's something I don't know at all, something left to discover. As she discovers me. Together we're engaged in an endlessly intriguing mutual scrutiny. And while we're at it, I'm winning her confidence, so if she ever hears the music of the spheres, she'll tell me what that sounds like.

Being a grandmother. What to say about a subject so strewn with clichés and sentimentality that it's as daunting as a minefield? I once heard the writer Grace Paley tell a group of students that the old saw *Write what you know* was too simple-minded. Rather, write what you don't know about what you know. She was right. There's no thrill at all in setting down what we already know, or only an accountant's thrill, a cartographer's thrill. For instance, that the grand-daughter is perfection, the most remarkable child that ever lived, and so on. However true, there's nothing there to dis-cover. And to write is to discover.

When the platitudes are swept aside—freedom from re-sponsibility, from the need to discipline, to civilize—we're left with a peculiar late-life love affair. To understand its potency, you have to ponder love affairs in general, because this one is similar in its inner dynamics, even if the love object is a fraction of your body weight and can't yet con-verse, let alone eat properly. And the erotic charge is unde-niable, the longing to see the child, to be with her, to look, to touch. When that longing is fulfilled comes the age-old state of mindless bliss.

Indeed, the kind of love this new one most resembles is that most universal and best-documented of genres, teen love: the same giddy absorption, the same loss of all sense of proportion, the same transcendent idiocy, when a mere glance from the beloved in the school cafeteria could send us into fluttery spasms. Anything more emphatic brought rampant joy—until the inevitable crash.

I never longed to take that high ride again: to tell the truth, I'd never enjoyed it all that much. I'm not a sucker for romanticism, and I'd rather be mildly tipsy than blind drunk. Fortunately this reincarnation of crazy love offers the adoration without the agony, which was tangy, certainly, but toxic.

All that, though, is still the known part. Beyond the known is a state of being that's mysterious and unsenti-mental, even a bit scary in its utter irrationality. There's something suspiciously viral about the condition: relentless, forceful, and all-consuming. Those it strikes feel helpless, stupefied, even stupid in their immersion. Before it struck me, I'd listened—patiently, indulgently—to others in their blithe affliction. I'd never be susceptible, I thought. I knew love—infatuation, passion, devotion, the whole business— inside and out; I wrote the book—lots of them, actually, about the ways we link or entwine or hook up. No variety of attachment could subjugate me.

That it could was something I didn't know.

The love grandparents bear to grandchildren is viewed sentimentally as the most pure of passions. But all love affairs have their source in self-love, and this one is no exception. Beneath the selfless grandmotherly devotion, I suspect, lurks the same self-serving quest as always. The allure of love is being seen. Even more, being seen anew. Seen right. We love the person who sends back the most flattering reflection, whose vision of us fits most precisely with our own—cut from the same cloth, and congruent. On more lasting acquaintance, that perfect fit may not endure, just as our most cherished clothes tend to fit less well over time, as the body, that notoriously unstable landscape, shifts and betrays. It might happen that we have to go seeking an entirely new outfit. (Though that won't happen with the grandchild, I'm quite sure.)

Like so many perturbations of the heart, what makes this one interesting and worth parsing is, precisely, its impurity. The wonder of the grandchild is that she sees us with fresh eyes, offering a thrill to the ego. Eyes that couldn't be fresher—they've hardly seen anything else. She's an empty mirror on which we can flash our best self, see it registered and flashed back. A perfect reflection: she doesn't know enough to make judgments or be critical.

Of course, like any newborn creature, the grandchild is not a blank slate. Anyone who's ever observed the visible nuances of heredity knows that. But she's blank as regards her impressions of us. In that way she differs from everyone else in the world, all the people we know who've already formed their impressions and opinions. And we needn't worry about whether she'll love us back. Of course she will. Fresh as she is, she doesn't know enough not to. (In that sense we may be taking advantage of her innocence, but it's a quite benign exploitation.) This, then, is the only relationship in which we loved someone infinitely and hadn't a worry in the world about whether the other would love us back.

But what about our own children? Didn't we assume they'd love us back? Yes, but that certainty was so clouded over by the intricate fears involved in raising them that we couldn't enjoy it with anything like the abandon we feel now. So. Reluctantly, inevitably, we near the tangle shrouding the mystery: to think about grandchildren, we have to think first about children. Immediately the bright subject flickers and darkens; the plot thickens; complexity looms. Grandchildren are simple; children, not in the least. Ours are grown now, and have impressions of us and opinions galore. So many that they've lost interest. Who wouldn't?

Our memories of them as small children are vague, alas, made blotchy by old panics at every stage, panics that blurred our appreciation like smudges on a camera lens. It was terrifying, actually, to grasp that they would be forever with us, part of us to death and beyond. It was our job to civilize, socialize them, and what young creatures wouldn't harbor less than beneficent feelings for those charged with curbing their appetites and impulses? They thought we were all-powerful. How could they know we were frightened all the while, frightened of them? What would they think of us, how would they judge us, would they ever forgive our civilizing duties and come to love us without reservation? Even more, would they care to know us? Their relation to us was an existential conundrum: we made them; at times they felt like our possessions. And yet our task was to free them from us. How could we own them and also free them?

For their part, they thought about us both too much and too little. They'd forget us at the oddest times, just when they ought to be remembering us—say, when they would disappear overnight and forget to call. Quite forget our existence, and we'd have to go hunting for them, reminding them who we were and where they belonged. Yet at the same time they thought about us too much. We're not so important, we wanted to say. Go ahead and do as you like and stop worrying about what we'll think. We won't think anything. In fact, we'd be very glad to think about ourselves for a change. We fretted over them and they fretted over us, but never at the same times and in the same ways, never in harmony. And sometimes we'd catch each other fretting and send, mutually, a sympathetic, rueful glance of complicity, as if to say, Will we be locked this way forever?

And then at some point we released each other. At some point in young adulthood, they stopped fretting over us, stopped referring to us in their heads at every critical moment. They lost interest and left us behind. And we, who are constitutionally unable to lose interest in them, we, for whom the children are and will be forever a source of fascination because they're ours—and as well as we know them, we still can't predict what they'll do tomorrow—we must paradoxically rejoice that they've outgrown us. We must accept with good grace that we're no longer objects of any interest. We're what they've put behind them. We're simply too well known. There are ways, to be sure, that children don't know their parents at all. But in the long run, those ways don't matter. In the ways that matter, they know us all too well. They've gotten to the bottom of us. They find us predictable.

But to the new one, the grandchild, whom we did not produce and whom we do not in any way possess, we're new. We interest her. And—bittersweet gift of mortality— we won't live long enough for her to get to the bottom of us. Meanwhile, we can inscribe the precise image we want recorded, in perpetuity. We can show the self—our self that no one else would care to see. So we murmur secrets, we sing, we dance. We wait. We assemble our gifts for when she's ready. Some of them are even our own books.

Raising children and writing books. Those are the two endeavors I spent my life on. They've been my education, the process of making a niche for myself in the world. Of course there's been all the rest of what constitutes a life, including love, the grown-up kind. That was an education too, but it was something I learned with another, while the books and the children were what I had to learn alone. Many more books than children: children take more time and work. And the two endeavors were always in conflict, always attended by guilt and doubt. Each seemed to detract from the other. When I was writing, I felt it was time I ought to be giving to the children. With the children, I felt it was time I ought to be giving to the writing. I never figured out a satisfactory balance, and eventually I learned to live with that incessant tug-of-war.

I felt at times, guiltily, that if not for the children, I might have written more, and better. At the same time I grasped that if not for the children, I might not have had anything to write about. Not that I wrote exclusively about child rearing or family life, not at all. What I did write about perpetually was the evolution of character: what it means to become and remain a human being; what it feels like, here and now, to be the enigmatic, flawed, mortal, relentlessly self-conscious creatures we are, struggling constantly between the world within and the world without, mediating between what we are and what we yearn to become, what the world will permit us to become.

None of this could I ever have understood without the children, without watching their astonishing transformation from know-nothing frangible infants into something resembling . . . me. In that sense the children gave me my writing life, my raw material, and I'm grateful.

I observed the genetic code unfolding and marshaling its forces, preparing to collide with circumstance and destiny. I gathered data on what shapes human nature as it undertakes its delicate negotiations with the world, and this ramifying human nature and these worldly transactions became my subject. But I couldn't watch with the kind of thorough and dedicated attention such researches deserve, because these were, after all, my children: I had to feed them and clothe them and see that they didn't choke on buttons or put forks in electrical sockets or run out into the street under the wheels of a car. And when one did run out into the street in front of a car and I ran out to grab her, I realized instantly that the old cliché about mothers is true.

The clichés about grandparents are true too. Yes, we're more relaxed, less anxious and burdened; we can delight in the grandchildren with abandon. Except that it's not the delighting part that absorbs me. Sure, that giddy, adolescent high is a blessing right up there with the best of life's intoxicants, but being ineffable, it doesn't bear analysis. What does is the intense, focused concentration on the process of becoming human, embodied in the grandchild, who metamorphoses into a person right before our eyes, a live documentary in slow motion.

When I point to my hand and she points to hers, right in front of her, that's simple to understand. When I point to my nose or eyes or chin and she points to hers, how does she know? How does she know she has a face that's the same as mine? She's too young to grasp what mirrors are for. When I spoon food into her mouth and she tries in turn to put the spoon in my mouth, how does she know I eat the way she does? How does she know she's one of us and not one of the very plump rabbits her parents keep in a cage in the living room, and who are closer to her size than I? What encoded pattern helps her deduce we're the same, only on a different scale? She must figure out that resemblance trumps size as a criterion of species identity. And then she thinks: I eat, so this bigger version must eat too. Once she gets that straight, her next step is: I laugh, I cry, so she must laugh or cry too. She discovers the concept of our common humanity. A little later, though, she finds that "I want" and "She wants" are not always the same thing; they might be antithetical, and so she's got to fight for what she wants. Yes, we're the same, we share a common humanity, but our interests are not always the same. She grasps the primal flaw of human society already, and she's not even two years old.

These aren't questions that can be answered by experiments with rats and mice. They're not questions that can be answered at all, only lived with and incorporated into our ever-shifting mosaics of who we are and might become. We observe and brood over the givens and then piece them together as imaginatively as we can. This time around, with the grandchild, I observe with no conflict at all. Love and work conjoin. My heart may be in thrall, my spirits buoyant as a teenager's in love, but my head is clear.

Clear enough to wonder, for instance, why she finds playing peekaboo so funny. From quite early on, there was that burst of knowing laughter if I covered my face with my hands, then revealed it. There's the element of surprise, of course. But her life is full of surprises: doors open and people materialize; buttons are pressed and lights go on; music and pictures appear. Nearly everything is a surprise to one so new. Only the hiding and showing are so uproariously funny.

Beyond the question of where a sense of humor comes from, what does she intuit about "here" and "not here"? After all, it is the duality we struggle with from birth to death in countless formulations. Love, work, money; courage, power, ambition, and confidence: all these crucial components of our lives have a way of appearing and disappearing—being "here" and then "not here"—in baffling, even frightening alternation. The ultimate guise that duality takes on is the "here" of birth and the "not here" of death. Could she have some notion that our game is emblematic of the life process? Is she laughing at the succinctness of the gesture: now I'm here, now I'm not? She can't possibly know that just as she recently arrived out of nothingness to be so vividly "here," just so I, merrily making only my face disappear, will in time vanish totally to the "not here." But I know. Nevertheless, I laugh with her, a laughter tinged with that knowledge, making the game more precious, the time left to play more precious, the laughter itself a kind of whistling in the dark.

If You Knew Harry . . .

SUSAN SHREVE

Harry is not my grandson. Theo is. But Harry figures in my learning to be a grandmother—a process that began with my name several months before Theo was born. My own children had two grandmothers, both of whom were called Nan. My mother got to pick her name first because I was her daughter, and so my mother-in-law decided to be called Other Nan. Nan and Other Nan. I wanted to avoid that confusion. The new baby already had Nanna, my son-in-law's mother, and Tante, my ex-husband's wife, and a large family on both sides, all named except me.

I was not a young grandmother-to-be. I was older than my own mother had been when my first child was born and certainly old enough to be a grandmother, but I wanted my own name, nothing generic. I believe it was less a question of holding on to a disappearing sense of youth than choosing a name that would indicate my particularity to this child already rich in grandmothers.

I chose Sooz.

When I divorced, my children—with the exception of Elizabeth, who is the daughter who was pregnant with Theo—had stopped calling me Mommy in favor of Sooz as a declaration of independence and probably punishment.

"Sooz is not acceptable," Elizabeth said. "You need a grandmotherly name that reflects who you are to this baby. How about Grandmommy?"

Grandmommy, I thought, *is too long—although the shortened Mommy would do. Other Mommy? Mommy number two?*

I had the usual expectations from stories I'd heard from friends—how blissful to be a grandmother, how delicious to be the beloved, uncritical figure in a perfect relationship unencumbered by the problems of discipline, earning by seniority all the pleasure and none of the responsibility for the child.

But I didn't exactly share their sentiments.

Theo Oliver Greiff was hard won, like the babies of many mothers today caught in that purgatory between heartbreak and joy that accompanies in vitro fertilization. I followed Elizabeth's pregnancy with the same obsessive intensity as I had my own. I listened to the report of every detail, day to day, week to week, and traveled as often as possible to New York City, where Elizabeth lived, and examined the sonograms for signs of familial resemblance in the floating boy, almost as if I were the pregnant one.

I didn't want to miss a moment in this child's becoming.

On the day he was born, we—my son-in-law, Rusty; his mother, Nanna; his father, Poppa; my husband, Tim; my ex-husband, Grandpa; his wife, Tante; my younger daughter, Aunt Kate; and me, *best in show, the blue-ribbon grand-mother-to-be*—gathered in the waiting room at the hospital dressed in scrubs: a green cotton uniform to show that we were on the same team. In that crowd of family, it became clear to me that Theo was going to have a lot of intimate relationships to negotiate.

Or, more to the point, I realized I'd better find a name.

When Kate, the youngest of four, was seven, my mother died. She had been the perfect Norman Rockwell figure of a grandmother—pretty, cozy, fleshy, with an ample bosom, endless patience, a quiet, mysterious, childlike way about her and complete, simple delight in being a grandmother. She wasn't well enough to take care of my children alone, but she could sit for hours with Porter, my older son, for whom she was a confidante; play dress-up with Elizabeth, who wore her high-heeled shoes, her wigs, her makeup, her silky skirts dragging the floor; play house with Caleb and Kate; and tell stories to them all. But they were her grandchildren and there was no confusion in her mind, no interest in taking them on as hers to raise, neither the stamina nor the desire.

I wish I could say that I shared her clarity about the role of grandmother.

When I first saw Theo, he was minutes old and I was alone, having gone to the nursery before the rest of the scrub team. I looked through the glass where the nurses were checking him. His tiny fists were tight, his body was taut, and he was watching, watching, although he could not have seen that I was there watching him.

Hope was Theo's first gift.

What a grandparent knows that a parent does not know are the years of small failures, of wishing you had been this kind of parent instead of that kind, of decisions made and revisions tried, then the slow, inevitable, terrible, wonderful breaking away. As new parents, my husband and I had been determined not to make the same mistakes our parents had made. We would follow a path of our own devising, avoiding the pitfalls because we knew what they were. It was possible, we believed, to raise happy children in a happy home.

I should put in perspective what I was expecting. I grew up in a quiet, orderly house with one brother, two parents, one grandmother for six months each year, one dog, no cats. My small family had left the Middle West in the 1940s for Washington, D.C., a transient city where we had no connections, where the people we called aunt and uncle were neighbors, friends of my parents, parents of my friends. They were slim pickings for kin, and I yearned for a tribe.

Books about big families were my favorites—*Cheaper by the Dozen, Life Among the Savages, The Moffatts, Little Women.* I loved to go the houses of friends, cheerful, chaotic houses where there were many children and the noise level was high: basketballs pounding in the backyard, babies toddling around the living room, young girls making chocolate chip cookies in the kitchen, loud music soaring from the basement.

And so I began practicing for motherhood at an early age. I had a closet where I kept my dolls and their clothes. I was the mother of these dolls, some of them adopted, many of them orphaned in my imagined life for them. I hid them in the closet for privacy. And at night, before I climbed into bed with a book, before my mother came upstairs to kiss me good night, I'd go into the closet, change my dolls into their pajamas, kiss them good night, tell them a story. "Good night, my darling children," I'd say, as my mother said to me.

I wanted a big family when I grew up and that's what I got.

But then, when my children were eleven, thirteen, fifteen, and eighteen, I separated from their father. We had been together since we were sixteen years old. It wasn't the end of our family or the end of our friendship. But it was the end of the promise we had made to our children for a forever kind of happy family.

Theo was a second chance, a new baby with whom to start over.

Elizabeth was almost two when our third child was born, and since her older brother had lacked enthusiasm upon her arrival, I expected the worst. As it happened, she was simply a mother-in-waiting, delighted to have the next two children as her own to instruct and protect, so much so that I sometimes wondered, especially as they all grew older, whether she thought of herself as necessary, more competent than me, cooler in a crisis, better equipped for motherhood.

With this in mind, I was vigilant about my new role. In the first three weeks of Theo's life I became my daughter's lady-in-waiting.

The first rule I made for myself as a grandmother was to follow my daughter's rules. This is not to say that I didn't have opinions or that I didn't express them. But I knew I'd be much more likely to have Theo to myself if Elizabeth trusted me, and I was willing to do just about anything to gain favor as a responsible, dependable, dutiful grandmother.

By luck, Elizabeth is not a young woman with a long list of musts: must not eat this or that, must not do this or that, must not say such and such, must not be allowed to go here or there—although I shudder to think that I actually *spanked* a child, which is certainly a *must not* for this generation. I also allowed the word *stupid* to be said in my household and cookies to be served with chocolate milk, and I am bowled over to think that so many children of my generation survived without padded car seats or in a playpen, as mine did, traveling unfettered in a mesh box in the back of our van.

I had my own secret plans for Theo, made possible by my role as lady-in-waiting, and I imagine these plans were uncommon among other women my age. I simply was not done being a mother of babies, even though I was sixty-four years old, with four grown children.

Theo is not the only child whose mother I've allowed myself to be mistaken for. When I traveled around town doing errands with my brother's baby, Benjamin, I never corrected people who stopped to ask, "Is he your first? How old? How adorable!" I did wonder, though: Did I wish I were still in my thirties or early forties to legitimately lay claim to this baby? Did I long for more children to last me into old age? Was I so locked in a harness of immaturity that I couldn't move gracefully into my fifties? Was I crazy?

And now here was Theo, this beloved boy bursting like a meteor into my late middle age, and he was mine! Well, more or less mine.

I had a full agenda. In New York, I would take him to the Museum of Natural History, to the children's bookstore downtown, to FAO Schwarz. I would take him to Washington when Elizabeth stopped nursing and he could spend a month or so with me, then to London when he was older. With Theo I would do all the things I'd been too busy to do with my own children. I'd be the disciplinarian I had never been; the quiet, patient observer I had never been; a member of the club of sacrificial mothers with ponytails and aprons baking sugar cookies—a club to which I had never belonged but had loved to read about in those books out of childhood.

Nothing bad will happen on my watch, I told myself.

But I didn't remember what a whole day with a child was like. The first day I had Theo to myself in New York felt like a month. (This, even though with my own children it seemed as if the whole of their childhoods from start to finish had been over in a heartbeat.) We played ball and dropped by the sandbox at the playground. We went to the Museum of Natural History, then rode the carousel in Central Park and, fearing that Theo might slip off the horse, I wrapped my arms tight around him—and together we slipped off onto the rotating wheel.

I skipped the description of the carousel ride when I returned Theo to my daughter. "He was wonderful," I said, taking off his jacket and hat. "Smiling his great big smile at everyone who peered into his stroller."

"Hmm," Elizabeth said when she picked him up. "He seems to be missing a shoe."

"A shoe?" I asked, completely unaware that Theo had spent the afternoon with only one shoe. "It must have dropped off in the museum."

"Did you put the A and D ointment on his diaper rash?" she asked, scrambling through the diaper bag.

"Of course," I replied. "I changed him at the coffee shop." And then I remembered that the A and D had dropped out of the diaper bag and I'd forgotten to pick it up when we left in a hurry because Theo was crying his heart out.

Almost thirty years had passed between my last baby and this one, and I was foolish enough to expect the full measure of motherhood to dust my shoulders like snowflakes once again.

On Elizabeth's refrigerator there are photographs of her brothers and sister, Rusty's brother and sister, their children, all six grandparents, and some great-aunts and great-uncles—a collection of people who live in Boston, Chicago, Los Angeles, Indiana. Most mornings, when he got old enough to recognize everyone, Theo went to the fridge and named us one by one. His people: "My Aunt Katie. My Nana. My Grampa. My Tante."

"My Soozie." Despite Elizabeth's initial reservations, the name had stuck.

During our long walks around the Upper West Side before Elizabeth and Rusty moved to Washington, I would talk to Theo about this and that, prefacing each sentence with Soozie: "Soozie is taking you to the penguins at the Central Park Zoo. Soozie is getting you a muffin. Soozie and Theo are going to the Museum of Natural History. Soozie, Soozie, Soozie . . ." until one afternoon as I arrived at their apartment, he looked up from lunch with his adorable smile.

"Soooooooooozeeee," he said.

The collection for which I am writing this essay is about grandmothers, not grandchildren, and I have to remind myself not to succumb to the effusive language of a new love affair, to stick to my own role in this story, which is both more complicated and less pure than Theo's. And though as

I write this Theo, now four and a half, has two brothers—Noah and baby Isaak—it is Theo who has been my principal adviser, my first instructor in the art of grandmothering.

The summer he turned one we were in Massachusetts on holiday, all of us, and I was sitting on a couch watching my assembled family eat breakfast as tears of sadness or loss—or was it change?—gathered behind my eyelids.

Theo had been walking fast back and forth across the wood floor, and suddenly he climbed up on the couch and pressed his small, warm body against mine. And remained.

I do not know when empathy begins to develop in a child, but I have read that there is evidence of it in the first three years of life. Call it accord, harmony, or identity with another person; it is at the core of human connection and feels to me as if it ought to come of a life longer lived. I did not expect to find empathy in so young a child, for whom life is new and, rightly, self-centered.

So what a generous surprise to discover it in the soft silence of this child just turned one! At that moment, I took on the unassigned role of guardian of his tender heart.

I lifted him up, swinging him around and around, kissing him all over his face. "Thank you, thank you, Theo Oliver Greiff, my adorable," I whispered in his ear, as he struggled to be put down on the floor so he could continue running back and forth across the polished wood.

Now, nearly four years later, I watch my daughter with three small children, happier than I've ever seen her; and I remember that sense of size, of actually expanding to include new lives. She is a giant with these children in her charge, capable of holding up the world.

I suppose I wanted to feel that way again. To start over like some of the men I know—new wife, new set of children, new life. Not bad.

But not necessarily good either. The tears to which Theo responded were tears of recognition that my life had changed and it was time for me to own up to it.

Years ago, when I was in college, I met a mother of three grown children, an artist, unusually independent-minded among the women of my mother's generation. I met her only briefly, on one memorable visit, and never saw her again.

"I want to be a mother," I told her when she asked about my plans for the future. I was thinking of all those dolls, all those books I'd read, a child of the 1950s, ready to marry, to take my husband's name, to have a family.

"Good idea," she said, "as long as you know that from the moment a baby is put in your arms, his wings are growing and it's the wings you're in charge of protecting."

I knew intuitively even then that it would hard for me to stick to protecting the wings.

But life has a way of surprising us, fast-forwarding before we know exactly where we are or how we got there. Suddenly I was a *grand*mother. It came on me like a condition, a sense of being, and I no longer wished to be the mother of young children. I felt free and excited with the thrill of adventure that comes with the beginning of a new story. I was who I was—the mother of grown-up children with children of their own, happy to be a grandmother. I no longer imagined myself pushing a stroller to the playground hoping the other mothers would think of me as one of them.

They wouldn't, of course, and that was fine. I wasn't up to that job anymore, only the one I'm lucky enough to have been given.

Nevertheless, some patterns of thinking get stuck and are difficult to get unstuck. Which brings me to Harry.

It was an autumn evening last year, still warm. The windows were open, and a soft breeze was floating across Theo and me as I read to him, both of us squished into the corner of his bed. Stories are central to my relationship with Theo. "I'll tell you a story" or "I'll read you a story" stops him in his tracks. This evening I was reading a new book in which there was a minor character named Harry.

"Did you hear about Harry in that book?" he asked.

"I did hear about Harry," I said. "He's four years old."

"I have a friend named Harry," he said.

I knew Theo had a friend named Harry, a best friend, an enchanting, witty little boy with freckles whom he loved.

"How great!" I said to him. "You're very lucky. I wish I had a Harry in my life."

Theo looked at me with a combination of concern and disapproval.

"But Harry is not in *your* life, Soozie," he said, folding his arms across his chest, assuming a posture of self-protection, as if I were after little pieces of him that he didn't want to give away. "Harry is in *my* life."

"I suppose you're right, Theo," I said, kissing him good night. Then I turned out his light and walked quietly downstairs where his mother—who is well acquainted with the real Harry—was waiting.

What I Want to Be When I Grow Up

VIRGINIA IRONSIDE

When I was five I wanted to marry my father. When I was ten I wanted to be an opera singer. At fifteen I started looking for Mr. Right. And though at thirty I thought I should (note the *should*) become a social worker, that idea lasted only a month. Then round about forty I realized I must be a writer, simply because I'd written so much. At sixty—despite everyone's saying, "Never give up hope; never say never!"—I knew there was no Mr. Right. That's when I discovered exactly what I wanted to be at last.

A granny.

What was so peculiar was that no one had alerted me to this possibility. It was as if I'd gone to the careers mistress at school and she'd given me millions of options, but failed to mention that at some point in my life—if I played my cards right—I could become a grandmother. Meanwhile, all my friends were so busy predicting the arrival of a knight in shining armor that they failed to mention that the particular knight who was to capture my heart was not a tall, chiseled-faced, nattily dressed man but rather a small, red chap with a squashed-up face, in nappies.

Many of my friends think my devotion to being the perfect granny is idiotic. They tell me to "get a life"—as if I haven't already got one. They tell me I'm mad every time I put off going to see some ghastly Shakespeare play at the National in order to babysit. "He's asleep, for Chrissake!" they say. "They could get anyone to stay with him! Why *you*?" But I would rather sit downstairs in a quiet house listening to my grandson's regular breathing on the monitor for hours on end than see some self-serving actor enunciating his socks off as Hamlet. I'd rather know, if my grandson wakes, that someone who loves him will be there, instead of a spotty sixteen-year-old who would stuff a bottle into his face while continuing her mobile phone conversation. Just pottering about aware that he's upstairs sleeping, his small fingers stuffed into his mouth, gives me a glow that pervades until the next day.

Even my friends who enjoy being a granny offer an unpleasant caveat. "What's so lovely about grandchildren," they say with a knowing wink, "is that you can hand them back to their parents at the end of the day."

Oh, really? Maybe for you, I think, but often after I've said good-bye my eyes are clouded by tears as I drive home.

So how did it start, this new career?

Like all mothers of an only child—and a son, at that—I'd sensibly put the idea of grandmotherhood out of my mind. I believed that the chance of my son's ever having children while I was alive was so remote I couldn't even contemplate it—even though he was just thirty-two when I turned sixty. Besides, I reasoned, if he did get someone pregnant, she'd probably be some ghastly mistake he'd met at a club, and there would be no chance of access, only monthly bank drafts. Or, if he did fall in love, it would be with an Australian and they'd emigrate and never be seen again. Or he'd get together with someone with a great, groaning family and I'd be allowed only a peek every other year. Best not to hope at all.

Then he rang and told me his girlfriend was pregnant, and the feeling of delight I had was overwhelming. All the pent-up longing and relief and joy came bursting out like a great golden cloud. And I can tell you, golden clouds don't come my way that often. On the rare occasions when they do, my jaundiced eye turns them into sensible dust before they've even opened their mouths to say hello.

So, inevitably, after the initial delight, the joyous anticipation began to wane and the idea settled, as usual, into my fairly gray landscape. When I was shown the scan, I have to admit I couldn't make head or tail of it, let alone "him."

"Look, Mum, there's his head and his little legs," my son said proudly, leaning over what looked to me like a black-and-white reproduction of a Jackson Pollock painting.

"Oh, er, yes," I replied. It looked rather like those photographs that newspapers show when someone discovers the face of Christ in a potato chip, or the sign of the cross in a cloud.

"You can't see it, can you, Mum?" said my son withering-ly. "Look! It's obvious!"

It wasn't obvious, and even on the day my grandson was born I was alarmed, on visiting the hospital, to find that far from falling for the baby straight away, I found him an in-comprehensible little red, wriggling thing who looked, to my eyes, like a cross between a very small alcoholic and a rat.

But then something happened. I met him a few more times at home and I held him in my lap. His funny little bottom fitted into the palm of one hand, while his head fitted into the palm of the other. I stroked his head. The smell of him, his disapproving expression when he slept, the delicacy of his skin, the lightness of his little body—he was too much for me to resist. This little charmer jumped straight into my heart.

Sometimes I wonder if the seeds of my career hadn't been sown years and years before, with my own grandmother. She was my lifesaver. She lived below us in our house in London, and when things got too tense within my parents' loveless marriage, I would go downstairs and find her in her cozy sitting room, eyes twinkling, full of jokes and love. It was as if she'd nothing to do all day except sit downstairs, waiting for my arrival. She had a magical cupboard stuffed with toys and board games like Snakes and Ladders. During hot summers we'd sometimes take a picnic out to the park and eat sugar sandwiches as a treat. And since I was a lonely only child, each year I looked forward to the week my grandmother and I would spend at the seaside, just the two of us. We'd take bags of plums down to the beach each day and, in the evening, visit the funfair down the road. I still remember the sound of the waves mixed with the music from the merry-go-round and the screams from the Big Dipper. Whatever ride I went on, my grandmother was always waiting for me at the end, eyes bright with excitement: "Was it *very* scary, darling? Was it fun? You're such a *brave* girl!" When I was older she would buy tickets to musicals and the theater, taking me to see old vaudeville stars and singing along with the old songs.

Now a granny myself, I'm astonished to find myself behaving like her. I love rediscovering *The Cat in the Hat* and *The*

Very Hungry Caterpillar. I dig up recipes for peppermint creams and cheese straws. I search out information on the Internet about how to rear tadpoles. I collect bits of sweet wrappers, feathers, and colored straws so that we have enough material for collage and painting sessions when my grandson comes to visit. I can't see a picture of a cow without saying "Mooooo" or a dog without saying "Woof-woof!" This little boy has even got me knitting. Pairs of socks! Hats without seams! Sweaters! And though I haven't made a single gingerbread man since his father was very young, I am now baking like mad. My grandson stands on a chair dressed in an apron cut out of an old plastic bag with a giant wooden spoon in his hand, while I pour the ingredients into an enormous bowl. He stirs erratically, covering us both with flour, stopping frequently to lick the spoon.

Strangely, when I had my son more than thirty years ago, I wasn't nearly so taken with life with a toddler. I remember sitting in gloomy playgrounds staring at my watch and thinking that I would rather be dead than spend another minute there. I remember the sheer grinding misery of getting up morning after morning, at the crack of dawn, to give the screaming child his breakfast, not to mention the endless, deadly days of shopping, freezing parks, broken sleep, and minced-up meals, the feelings of rage, resentment, and hopelessness that dogged me every day, every week, every month. And when he cried, I'd be tortured by feelings of being a bad mother who never should have brought him into this cruel world.

But when my grandson was tiny, I couldn't wait to get him into his stroller and down to the park. With him I could stand for hours by the duck pond, laughing at the antics of moorhens. When he fed the birds bread, I admired the way he knew exactly when to open his tiny fingers to release the crumbs in the right direction for the ducks.

What is so immensely rewarding and fulfilling about being with my grandson is that my love for him is pure and clear, unclouded by all the guilt, panic, and anxiety I felt with my own son when he was tiny. I don't have that sense of "Oh, Lord, he's tired and listless; he must hate me" or "Oh dear, if I do this or that it will ruin him for life." If by chance my grandson suddenly starts crying or yelling his head off, I'm guilt-free. Experience tells me that his fears are only tiny clouds in a fundamentally blue sky, and they will, with enough kisses and cuddles, pass.

Now I'm not saying that sometimes when I've looked after him, I haven't felt slightly anxious. I don't have the same confidence with him as I did with my own son, simply because he isn't mine. There was a moment when his chubby leg got stuck in the bars of his high chair. I'd laid it on the floor and, with cushions and other bits of furniture, created a baby's assault course for fun. But then he got stuck and there seemed to be no way to free him without either breaking his leg or sawing him out. I was paralyzed with terror. Eventually I managed to ease him out, with no visible marks. But the fear of something happening to him on my watch never leaves me. When there is nothing to fear, I invent something: "What if I were accidentally to push his stroller out into traffic and his legs got amputated by a passing lorry?" I forever go over the scenario. What would I say when his parents came home: "I'm terribly sorry, but I'm afraid he's . . . legless? . . . dead?" So far, however, he's survived. And the pleasures of grannydom have far outweighed the anxieties.

Not for me the cringing cries of "Don't call me granny!" I have friends who, fearful of the label giving away their age, insist on being called by their Christian names. Another demanded to be called "Glammy"—but not for me such euphemisms. I'm a granny, and I want to shout it from the rooftops. I even put up with the appalling "Gaga" that my grandson called me for a while.

"Do you think," ask my friends, "that it has anything to do with genes? That you're programmed to feel this way because you like to think of your great genes being handed down to future generations?" Not a bit. In my own case, I always thought it would be preferable if my genes stopped reproducing as soon as possible. But seeing them mixed with my son's girlfriend's genes, I have altered my opinion.

Now that my grandson is three years old, I have realized that the nicest words anyone has ever said to me are not "I love you," but what my grandson said the other day when he crept into my bed at five in the morning, claiming that he had woken early because he'd had a "deem about piders."

"Granny? Granny?" he said when he'd finally managed to wake me up. "I got good idea. You go down the end of the garden and be monster, and I get my sword and I be knight and come and kill you!"

And amazingly, I found myself, in the early morning darkness, in my dressing gown and slippers, hiding behind a tree as my grandson charged down the garden roaring toward me, plastic sword in hand.

As I growled and raised my hands, making clawlike threats, I knew at last that this was what I had always wanted to do when I grew up.

PART II

Through the Woods

Remember, as far as anyone knows,
we're a nice normal family.

—HOMER SIMPSON

Facebook Grandma

RONA MAYNARD

On my desk sits a photo of a boy with mischief on his mind. My grandson Colsen, age eleven. With his goofy grin and cocked head, he seems to be thinking about one of those endearingly dumb jokes that are part of children's secret language. He looks nothing like me or my husband, or even like his father, Ben, my first rascal and only child. His resemblance to no one but himself pleases me. It suggests the man he'll be soon enough, a man of humor and spirit who will carry a little of me into the world.

I don't keep a copy of this photo in my purse, to many people's surprise: the mailroom guy at my former job, the owner of my local deli, my breeze-shooting seatmates on planes. They can't understand why a woman with a grandchild would not want to show off his photo to the world. Isn't doting every grandmother's time-honored privilege? I'll pass, thank you. To me Colsen's school portrait, and the memories it evokes, are too personal a pleasure for sharing with strangers. They would see just another sixth-grader with freckles and slightly buck teeth; I see a boy whose unexpected birth rearranged my entire mental landscape and unearthed, by degrees, an attachment that both echoed and deepened my love for his father, another unexpected baby.

Both babies arrived amid other preoccupations—Ben

when I was a full-time student and anxious new bride of twenty-two, Colsen early in my tenure as a magazine editor, just after my forty-seventh birthday. Both times I stumbled into an awesomely complex transition years ahead of my friends, leaving me to grapple alone with the puzzle of modern motherhood. I was the first to scour the city for trustworthy day care, the first to be accused of neglecting my child because I held a full-time job, the first to come home from a vacation and find that my teenager had held a drunken bash so rowdy the police had come to our door. I worked it out by trial and error, often fearful that I must be falling short as a mother.

When Ben grew up to be a generous-hearted young man, it seemed that I could finally relax. Then one April evening, he dropped by for pizza. He was twenty-five, just starting out in his career. When I asked about his girlfriend, Ben flashed an odd little smile, equal parts dismay and delight. He put down his fork as if he'd been waiting to get through this moment and came straight to the point: "She's pregnant. We're keeping the baby."

I was about to become a modern grandmother. What would this mean? And who could help me rise to the occasion?

No one in my circle, that was clear. My friends were still doing carpool duty and laying down the law about curfews. The grandmothers I knew were ten years my senior and retired, or soon to be. While I worked long hours, they spent the afternoon mini-golfing with the grandkids. The women in my family made even more unlikely role models—my mother, whose boundless affection for Ben had a troubling flip side, harsh judgments of me for working; and my ferociously competitive grandmother, who seemed to love me less for myself than for her own reflected glory. Grandma's glass-topped coffee table served as a trophy case for stories and drawings by my sister and me. Her conversation circled endlessly around our latest adorably quotable sayings. She brandished our achievements, real and imagined, like a shield against the boasts of other grandmothers. A Jewish immigrant from Russia, with few years of schooling and a lifetime of grudges against those with more money or social position, she counted on us to prove her worth. When she pressed me to her corseted bosom, I would crumple like one of the hand-embroidered linen hankies nestled in her big black purse.

Where was the confident, youthful grandmother I aspired to be? Clearly, I would have to find my own grandmaternal style. Eleven years later, I've more or less done it. But there are times when I still feel out of step with social norms, like when I check out the "contemporary" birthday greetings for grandmas at my local card shop. Here's one: "Top 10 reasons kids need a grandmother." First reason: "Who else would even think of bragging about you to a stranger?" (Obviously, not me.) Next reason: "Moms don't always respond positively to 'Can I have that? Can I? Can I?'" For the record, I'd rather eat a bucketful of Legos than give in to a tantrum in the toy department.

Suppose I could create my own birthday card about the reasons why a kid should love a grandma like me. Instead of Doting Grandma, I'd feature Subversive Grandma: "Nobody else would have the bright idea of buying a *Blazing Saddles* DVD so you can split your sides at the bean-eating scene." Next up is Gourmet Grandma: "She knows you'll never get to taste truffled gnocchi at the best trattoria in town if you insist on chewing with your mouth open." And how about Pilates Grandma? "She's in better shape at fifty-eight than she was at twenty, so why worry about getting older?" Closest to my heart is Truth-telling Grandma: "She'll give you the scoop on the outrageously naughty stuff your dad used to do as a kid." Mini-golf is all very well, but only I can tell the story of how Ben was once caught stealing coins from a wishing well with a magnet, or how he wept the day thieves stole his bike.

In the first photo ever taken of Colsen and me, I'm perched on the edge of a sofa, holding the newborn at arm's length as if he were a fragile and unlikely gift—an antique soup tureen, say—that I'm terrified of crushing. I still wear the uniform of my student days, a black turtleneck and tight jeans. People have been telling me for months that I don't look old enough to be a grandmother, and this usually makes me smile. I'm not smiling in the photo. Though I always figured I'd have a grandchild someday, I'm not ready to assume the mantle of an elder.

I remember that December afternoon, the parents arriving at our door with their rosy princeling and his carload of paraphernalia, like a thrilling but complicated present with many accessories and no operating instructions. On their flushed faces, joy collided with weariness. They looked shockingly young. How would they cope?

I'd been listening to Handel's *Messiah*, as I always do around Christmas. "For unto us a child is born, unto us a son is given." Although I'm not a Christian, those lines have always stirred something powerful in me, a conviction that parenthood should not be a lonely ordeal but a commitment undertaken with encouragement from those who know the pitfalls and rewards of the journey. That's what I hoped to provide. My mother would have said pretty much the same thing when Ben was born, another December baby. With the best of intentions, she set out to help me. As I saw it, she usurped me.

My mother flew through a blizzard to welcome her first grandchild. Her plane barely made it to the runway. Still in her snow-covered coat, she folded our newborn against her shoulder and exclaimed at his beauty. Those blue eyes! That exquisitely shaped little head! I hadn't yet done much exclaiming myself; the rigors of drug-free childbirth had worn me out. Within a day or two, my mother preempted me again. Dancing Ben around the living room, she said, "You know, I really do love him." Wasn't that what I should be saying? I wanted my mother to love my baby; I just couldn't bear the thought of her love surpassing mine. I needed time to fall in love with my child—not that I dared admit it. To tell the truth would have been to confess my failure as a woman.

Even though my mother quoted Dr. Spock—"You know more than you think you do"—her fervor sent a different message: *I'm the expert in this family when it comes to nurturing a child.* So she was in the eyes of the world. She wrote articles and books on child care and for a time hosted a Canadian television show on parenting. Although she had hoped for a full-time job as a professor, she couldn't leap the barriers of her time. So I became the first briefcase-toting mother in our family, and this eventually made us rivals, not simply for the right to fulfill our ambitions but also for the less obvious prize of centrality in Ben's life.

From Ben's perspective, my mother was the ultimate grandma. He called her "Das," a baby name she liked for its jauntiness. The two of them forged a special bond during weekly overnights at her house, when she would let him have his fill of apple juice and homemade chocolate cookies. Yet I detected a reproachful edge in her attentions. Ben once returned from her pleasure dome with such excruciating stomach pains that I had to rush him to the ER. "You overdid it," I told my mother. "Indulgence is my role," she insisted. "Someone has to put Ben first." The old story: by pursuing a career, I was neglecting my child. If she had been my only critic, I could have shrugged off her chiding. But working mothers like me were a suspect breed in those days. Every time my son landed in the principal's office for some misdeed, I got a lecture from the teacher: "He needs more nurturing."

I chose to have no more children. Why expose another kid to my slapdash mothering—same old peanut butter sandwich for lunch every day, no one home to greet Ben after school? He had a habit of losing his key, so we kept a spare in a plastic box tucked under the porch.

Years after he became a man, I couldn't quite shake the feeling that my son had thrived in spite of me. That started to change when I first saw Colsen in his arms. Ben needed no assistance with burping or diapering, and thank goodness: my skills were decidedly rusty. He embraced the humblest devotions of parenthood with a confident tenderness that seemed nothing short of a marvel. I remembered the days when fathers used to talk about "babysitting" for their own children. My husband had been such a father, loving but far from hands-on, and this used to be a sore point between us.

Yet together we had raised a different breed of father for whom the very essence of manhood was caring for a child. Surely I deserved some of the credit. Along with my relief came gratitude that I could tell my son what my mother had never told me. "I'm proud of you," I told him. "You're a natural father. You've put your feckless parents to shame."

Ben's fatherhood proved that my love for him had never been deficient. I had to ponder the gift of this knowledge before I could make room in my heart for another blue-eyed infant boy. I was babysitting one night, hoping I could lull him to sleep without phoning his parents for advice, when I put on a suitably gentle CD: the layered, life-burnished voices of Emmylou Harris, Dolly Parton, and Linda Ronstadt. "To know, know, know him/Is to love, love, love him," they sang. It was as if I'd never heard that song before. With Colsen against my shoulder, I chimed in and danced around the room.

There's a question people always ask when I first mention my grandson. "Does he live nearby?"

Not anymore, I explain. He lives with his mother in a small town several hours from our Toronto home. His parents parted years ago, and Ben is now a long-distance father. There's lots of driving for everyone, but we make it work—a modern family, pulling together for Colsen's sake. Next question: "How often do you see your grandson?"

He visits every couple of weeks, I say. We take him swimming; we play Monopoly. Sometimes we spend the night in his picture-book village, a perfect place for a kid to go biking down broad, shady streets that have scarcely changed in decades. His maternal grandmother owns a pub on the town square, and Colsen has the run of the place. When we make the trek for dinner, we find him waiting for us at the table in the window. He has set our table like a pro and can't wait to fill us in on the daily specials.

One last question, posed in tones usually reserved for a grave illness in the family: "Isn't it hard for you? Don't you miss him?"

If Hallmark made cards for long-distance grandmothers, a fistful would have come my way. But missing is not the right word for the fleeting, irrational spasm of anxiety that sometimes overtakes me in the winter, when drifting snow surrounds Colsen's village and a month might go by between visits. I picture Colsen at the pub, his second home. I envy his other grandmother for having him under her roof; she lives upstairs, where he has overnighted countless times. When he hears the word *grandmother*, is her face the one that instantly comes to mind? Am I a vaguely pleasing afterthought? I have to remind myself that we are not competing for an Olympic medal in grandmothering. We are simply two women who treasure him in our different styles. He is blessed to have us both.

To be honest, I like my grandmothering in brief waves of powerful connection, separated by islands of calm. For a year or so when Colsen was a toddler, he spent every weekend in our house. Ben was living with us then; his ex-girlfriend had an apartment nearby. For the first few months, we reveled in the chance to watch our grandson grow. We applauded his mastery of the stairs; we showed him the mother raccoon who nightly led her babies down the tree outside our kitchen window. But what began as a stopgap arrangement dragged on for more than a year. Unlocking our front door on a Friday evening, I'd remember how my husband and I used to start our weekend: Ella Fitzgerald on the stereo, chilled chardonnay in the fridge, not even a phone call to disturb our hard-won serenity. With Ben and Colsen around, I'd come home to the Teletubbies theme music and the nose-crinkling odor of Kraft macaroni and cheese. Our grandson would scamper to greet us, hair mussed from rolling on the floor with his dad. Such a winsome child! Still, I couldn't wait to reclaim our house.

If I could choose my ideal grandmothering arrangement, I might pick the one that followed, in the years when Colsen shuttled between his parents' two city homes. I could cheer for his floor hockey team; I could watch the school pageant. I know women who'd never miss these landmarks in a grandchild's life, but even then I showed up only from time to time. I never offered emergency child care when Colsen had a fever, as my mother used to do when Ben was home sick. If constancy defined me as a grandmother, I would have been more present when I had the opportunity. So what, exactly, am I giving to my grandson? In the two years since Colsen moved away, I've been pondering this question.

I love the tousled reality of him, with his mystifying passion for electronic games and his unshakable belief that the Toronto Maple Leafs will win the Stanley Cup. He's not the grandchild I expected to have someday, a grave little girl whom I could enchant with my own youthful joys, like *Swan Lake* and the Brothers Grimm. So much the better: I've learned to like surprises. I've become a demon mini-golfer, although his putting will soon leave mine in the dust. I have championed, with my husband, the rules of Monopoly and the importance of spelling. A certain rigor is part of my role as Truth-telling Grandma. The other, more enjoyable part is telling him stories about his father's childhood and mine before it, so he can begin to place himself in the grand design that is his family. He has never asked for these stories, but I think of them as part of his inheritance. What's more, they show that every seemingly assured and capable grown-up was once a vulnerable child. That's something all compassionate grown-ups should know.

Between visits, I connect with Colsen online. In my latest incarnation, I'm Facebook Grandma. Oh, the discoveries I've made! Who knew there were such things as virtual food fights? Or that Facebook, like Monopoly, has rules?—not that anyone has written them down. If somebody's vampire bites you, the polite thing to do is bite back. Above all, don't drag your feet about answering messages. Colsen once chastised me for this: "You forgot to answer my Facebook!" God help me, so I did. Lesson learned. But in a way, I'm not sorry that I slipped up once. I like knowing that Colsen had logged onto the computer, looking for the message that only his grandma could send.

Sitting Here in Limbo

JILL NELSON

The summer he is five my grandson comes with me to our family home on Martha's Vineyard. In person, in letters, and by telephone we have been planning this week alone together for most of the winter and spring. We call it "Grandma's Boot Camp for Children Who Arrive Great and Leave Even Better." We have discussed how we'll walk across the park every morning and get doughnuts, scaring the geese out of our way, if necessary. We will go to the beach across the street and, if the water is not too cold or the waves too big, swim. Otherwise we'll collect jingle shells, we'll climb the jetties, and I will teach him to skip rocks. We'll walk around Oak Bluffs, the town where we live, in search of old and new friends, then stop off at the playground. We'll play the jukebox in the living room and dance to Ella Fitzgerald crooning "A-Tisket, A-Tasket" and Michael Jackson singing about Billie Jean. We'll go to the library. And we'll call his parents whenever he misses them. Our time will be joyous now that he is finally old enough to choose to spend time alone with Grandma.

These are the things my daughter did with my mother during the weeks they spent together in this house on Martha's Vineyard from the time she was a tiny girl, smaller than my grandson, through her teenage years. In the too short week my grandson and I have, the days are sunny and warm. We do everything we set out to do—and more. We chase each other through the park, play cards, and plan and execute my grandson's first cookout party, complete with Hawaiian Shirley Temples (so called because in a dusty drawer we find a package of palm-tree-shaped swizzle sticks that he insists on using). We go to the Flying Horses carousel and the store, where he tricks me into buying foods his mother won't buy, most of which he doesn't like after the curiosity of the forbidden wears off. We work in my garden—I weed; he finds worms and bugs—and at the nursery he chooses a dark purple salvia to plant that blooms all summer into October. A big boy now, he takes a shower by himself each night, and afterward I read him a book and don't say no when he pleads for another chapter, then another.

One night while I am toweling his little body dry, I ask him shyly, "Are you having a good time at Grandma's Boot Camp?" He stops squirming, turns to face me. "No," he says solemnly. His shiny face looks sad. Does he sense my heart beginning to break, then swell when he leaps into my arms, hugs me so fiercely we both fall backward onto the bed, and he shouts through laughter, "I'm having a *wonderful* time!"

My daughter has promised to let me know before she arrives on the island to take her son home. This is important to me. I have in mind a brief ceremony to mark the end of Grandma's Boot Camp—to delineate and honor our time together and look ahead toward next year. I do not get the chance. One day when we return from a drive up-island to search for the pony ride place we hear voices as we climb the steps of the back porch and open the door.

"Who's here?" my grandson asks.

"I don't know, but I'm sure they're friends," I reassure him. My daughter hears us too, because as soon as she calls my grandson's name he flies away toward the sound of her voice.

I understand that my grandson is overjoyed to see his mother after nearly a week; this does not bother me. What does bother me is that from the time she arrives I seem to disappear from his vision. There is no discussion; nothing is said or done by him or any of us; but I am abruptly, simply, seamlessly unimportant. I no longer exist for him. It's as if he cannot see how to love us both, and so he must choose.

He is five, and this transition is not subtle. He stops listening to me or coming to me for assistance. And instead of cozy chats, his few words to me are practical, perfunctory. My offers—of grilled cheese sandwiches; a walk down to the beach or into town; his ritual nightly shower, story, and rubdown—are rejected. He wants to do these things with his mother. Suddenly I am the grandma of last resort. What hurts is not that he chooses his mother; it's that he feels he has to choose at all. From the moment she arrives, she sucks up all his love—there is nothing left. To my subjective eye she revels in and encourages his attention and dependence. She is oblivious of my feelings. I simmer with hurt that, as time passes, curdles to anger. We part, not for the first time, with much unspoken.

A month later we try to talk about what happened, in fits and starts over the telephone when we are both back in our homes, in different cities, neutral territory. My daughter tells me—*confesses* would be too gentle a word—that my grandson came to me for a week under duress, pushed by her because she needed a break, to spend time with a grandmother she does not in some ways trust or like. She tells me she remembers my parenting as verbally abusive, and wonders if I've changed. I accuse her of making her son a stand-in for old issues between us, of setting me up as Mean Old Grandma so that she can sweep in as Mommy the Savior. Our past, it seems, is impossible to escape, resolve, or even discuss with civility for long. We get nowhere. After we hang up the phone I am consumed by paranoia, thinking that I have been used in terrible ways.

Until my grandson was born, unconditional love was an abstract concept, a phrase I read in self-help books or heard from the mouths of the studiously spiritual on my way somewhere more immediate and tangible than pondering the nature of love. I became a parent when I was twenty. As I was raising my daughter, for the most part alone, my love was tremendous but always freighted with the weight of responsibility, of having something to prove: that I'd made the right decision to have her; that I could simultaneously raise a wonderful child, finish school, and build a career; that growing up in a single-parent family didn't spell emotional or intellectual doom. It is, I think, difficult to love unconditionally when you're trying to navigate, survive, and thrive in the world, especially when you feel the hot breath of the naysaying hounds on your back.

But when my grandson arrived, I immediately loved him unconditionally and with abandon. Oddly, through discovering this new kind of love for him I have come to understand that the love I offered my daughter was no less profound or sincere—and may have been more so—for being thick with responsibility. But life is full of cross-purposes and flipped scripts, so why am I surprised that just as my grandson's arrival kindled my ability to love differently, for my daughter it seems to have dredged up a history of my failures and her resentments?

My mother died in 2001, just over a year before my grandson was born. During the forty-eight years I was her daughter I never thought of her love for me as unconditional. Her love was hard won, demanding, hilarious, cynical, conspiratorial, angry, mercurial, ancestral, abundant, and jealous. It wasn't until my daughter was born that I even knew my mother was capable of loving unconditionally. To her eyes her granddaughter was perfect, and she showered her with attention, opportunities, and affirmation. I was amazed by my mother's generosity and grateful for it; as a single parent I needed her help too much to be resentful or jealous. Now, years later, after doing time in a therapist's chair and spending three decades as the mother of a daughter myself, I believe that unconditional love—at least, uncomplicated unconditional love—is a special bond between grandparents and grandchildren. Realizing this, I have forgiven my mother for what I once saw as her failings. I understand that, like most parents, she did the best she could. The fact that she didn't manifest her love in the ways I wanted was my problem to come to grips with, not hers. Not until after she died did I realize that my endless fountain of lovingness had dried up. As stingy and awkward as my mother could be with the physical affection and emotional support I craved, she loved me to the best of her not-insignificant abilities. Maybe her love wasn't unconditional, but it was prodigious.

On February 4, 2002, I saw my grandson born, heard his first cry—it came without a slap—held him still bloody in my arms, and began my love affair with unconditional love. With his birth I instantly became a citizen of the state of grandparent grace, a place where, in almost all circumstances, we are able to give love without reservation, hesitation, or expectation. Why? It's not that we love our grandchildren more than we love our children, although that is not impossible. It's not because we're necessarily wiser or because, as so many people claim, "What's wonderful about grandchildren is that when they get tired (cranky, bratty, sick, obnoxious—fill in the blank), you can send them home." The secret is that when you are a grandmother there is an almost total absence of anxiety. And without anxiety, what is there to be overprotective, tense, snappish, impatient, defensive, or afraid about?

If you've raised children, by the time your grandchildren come along you know that the odds are in your favor. Your grandchild won't climb to the top of the slide, topple off, and bust his skull open. No matter what the teacher says at the dreaded parent-teacher conference, your grandchild *will* learn to read and do math. Neither television, video games, nor obnoxiously text-messaging at the dinner table will transform him into an antisocial, psychotic maniac. Babies, even colicky ones, eventually go to sleep. Knowing this lends a meditative, Zen-like aspect to holding a grandchild against your shoulder and walking the floor with him for hours. Best of all, raising a grandchild to adulthood is simply not your role or responsibility. A grandparent's job is to give worry-free, expectationless, fun-filled love. Hovering at the base of the slide, reviewing the multiplication tables, force-feeding brussels sprouts, and all the rest can be left to the parents.

For me this state of grandparent grace, which lasted four years, was almost too good to be true. I got to enjoy my grandson minus the stressful aspects associated with child rearing. My daughter and son-in-law—sleep-deprived, slightly overwhelmed, grateful to get some time for themselves but usually too tired to go out to dinner *and* have sex—actually thanked me for spending time with him. There were even signs that my daughter was beginning to grasp how difficult parenting is, how in the process of trying to do our best we make mistakes— and that in learning this she might forgive me my parental trespasses. We became closer than we already were, bonded and bound by our love for each other and her son, replicating the love between myself, my daughter, and my mother. Let the circles be unbroken.

Of course, what seems too good to be true usually is. I've searched my memory without success for a fixed moment, a portentous incident, when things changed. My daughter and her family moved to a city five hours away, so I did not see them as often, but I thought we all missed each other. Maybe I was wrong.

Now that my grandson is old enough to begin making choices of his own, it seems that my daughter holds him closer while pushing me away. Is this because she's uncomfortable that he's now capable of his own independent feelings for me? I remember how she loved my mother and insisted on spending every Friday night with her—often trying to finagle Saturday as well. Instead of feeling jealous or possessive, I was relieved to have a break, grateful that my mother was nearby and eager to help me raise my daughter. Maybe my daughter is jealous of my unconditional love for my grandson. Maybe she feels it is something to which she was entitled and which I willfully withheld. Still, maybe she lacks interest because she doesn't need me. She has a wonderful husband, and they live in another city close to friends with children my grandson's age. I am a luxury, not a necessity.

Whatever the reasons, my daughter and I are not moving forward—not even standing still—but going backward. We are stuck refighting tired battles: about whether I truly wanted her when I got pregnant—intentionally—at twenty; or my sharp tongue when she was thirteen; or why I reorganized her room so it also functioned as a sitting room after she went away to college. The list goes on and on. As much as I would like what binds me to my grandson to be simple and clear, the connection between us gets tangled up between my daughter and me. My love for my grandson roils what I thought—or wished—had been resolved, forgotten, or forgiven. It stirs up the sediment at the bottom of my relationship with my daughter and clouds the waters.

I have not seen my grandson in eight months. I used to talk to my daughter four or five times a week; now we talk every four or five weeks. Our conversations are tentative, wary, reminiscent of obligatory condolence calls in which one tries to convey sympathy without using the word *died* or *dead*. I surprise myself by yearning for yelling, tears, anything but this reserved retribution. I wish I could grab my daughter by the shoulders and remind her of the unconditional love that flowed between her and my mother, and demand to know why I'm not allowed the same with her son. Summer will be here in a few months. Last week she told me she wasn't sure if they'd come to Martha's Vineyard this year, because our relationship is "too difficult." What could I say to that? These days I mostly stay quiet and bide my time, hoping my daughter will realize, as I did, that I have done the best I knew how.

My grandson turned six recently. Now he can swim without a floatie and ride a bike. He's almost old enough to cross the street in front of the house on Martha's Vineyard and walk by himself along the winding path to town to pick up doughnuts. What he cannot do is attend Grandma's Boot Camp for Children Who Arrive Great and Leave Even Better. The battle between my daughter and me has created a chasm: I feel as though I'm stranded on one side of a raging river and my daughter and my grandson are on the other side. And though I can see them and hear them, the noise of the river gets steadily louder.

Most of all, I miss my daughter and my grandson—and myself as an involved, essential grandma. I miss living in that state of grandparent grace. More than three decades ago, when I was a nursing mother, I thought I was free if my mother kept my daughter for an afternoon or an evening. Yet always sooner than I thought fair, my breasts would fill with milk, become hard, ache to be emptied. I'd return to my daughter, my sense of responsibility and love, desire and resistance, lost freedom and found purpose inextricably mixed together. Now I am a middle-aged woman, the mother of an adult daughter, a grandmother and the proprietor, at least at this moment, of an empty camp for grandchildren. I walk around with a heart and soul engorged with unconditional love, but there are no takers. Sometimes I think the only small mercy is that this time there are no telltale milk stains beneath my breasts to reveal what I am missing.

La-Z-Nana

ABIGAIL THOMAS

Live each day as if it were your last, Nana has heard them say, but she says rubbish. Live each day any way you want. Take a nap if you feel like it.

Nana is sitting in her big chair knitting, as her grandmother did before her. What are you thinking, Nana? Nana is wondering whether if you murdered someone with a cast-iron frying pan and then made home fries in it, would all the evidence burn off? Nana wants to write a mystery. The only person she ever wanted to kill she imagined bashing over the head with her frying pan, so it is her heroine's weapon of choice. Perhaps *heroine* is the wrong word.

Nana is making a long blue scarf. She has made many scarves this winter, but given none away as yet. She has also made many blankets. She just knits; she doesn't even purl anymore. She likes to knit round and round in circles. She piles all her finished projects in a big box by the front door.

Nana thinks about time differently since she got to be sixty-six. She thinks of each moment as a big La-Z-Boy, or perhaps a hammock, and the only direction is a little back and forth, or side to side. For this Nana needs peace and quiet, and she eschews all outside stimulation. She plays music only when she is driving. Sometimes a wild random thought runs from the back of her mind to the front, and Nana can quick write it down because she almost always has a pen handy.

Nana loves her twelve grandchildren but they function (as do their parents) on linear time. When they visit, Nana mobilizes. She bakes her cookies: gingersnaps, chocolate chips, cornmeal sugar cookies, and shortbread. She bakes big chewy chocolate cookies. She gives everyone two at a time. Why not? You only live once, Nana knows. She notices that with small children everything is a beeline to the next thing. No time for lolling about, which is what she does best. She calls herself a writer, but she is stone lazy. Face it, Nana.

Nana appreciates that the advantage of getting old is not wanting to mess around anymore. In order not to want what she doesn't really want, she is careful about the movies she watches, and she plays music only in her car. (I believe we've covered that, but Nana thinks it is key.) When she watches a movie Nana doesn't want to cry or be moved or enlightened, and she doesn't want to be turned on. There are movies she cannot watch, or cannot watch more than once. She saw the one about Woodstock, and it took her almost two years to get over Viggo Mortensen. She bought the DVD because she loved it so much, but she never opened it. It has sat on her shelf for four years. Nana likes movies with good guys and bad guys and a lot of big guns. She does not want anything stirred up that she can't handle by herself.

When the twins came at Christmastime, Nana baked cookies and roasted sweet potatoes and chickens and simmered her stews. She loved it when the babies climbed into her lap. After a week of two sets of two-year-old twins having a really good time, Nana decided it was time to leave the house. "Time to flee," were her exact words to herself. She realized that her gynecologist had died fifteen years ago and thought it prudent to find a new one right now this minute and so she did. She made an appointment with a nice woman doctor. "See you later," she said to her family and drove away.

Nana lives quietly with her three dogs. She sleeps with her dogs. She does not lack for anything. Many of Nana's friends are looking for romantic companionship. Nana wants to live her life, write her stories, knit her scarves, and play with her grandchildren and then have their parents take them away. She does not want a man, and she does not want to want a man.

She thought she was safe at the gynecologist.

The nice doctor examined Nana inside and out and then called her into the office. The doctor sat behind a desk. It was a pleasant room with water trickling over stones in plug-in fountains. The doctor needed to ask a few questions. Nana sat neatly in a hard chair and she nodded.

"Have you had more than one sexual partner?" the doctor asked. Outside, sun was shining on the snow. This was not the question Nana was expecting.

"Yes," said Nana. Land sakes, yes.

"More than five?"

"Quite a few more," said Nana, as modestly as she could. She didn't want to appear to be bragging, so she added, by way of explanation, "It was the sixties."

"Have you ever had a sexually transmitted disease?" was the next question. It seemed a little nosy, but Nana answered truthfully.

"Yes," she said. But now she was remembering how she got it and who she gave it to, and it was Washington Square and she was young and slender and barefoot and it was 1968 all over again.

"Damn," thought Nana.

It turned out that Medicare will pay for certain yearly exams if you have had more than five sexual partners. (Who knew? thought Nana.)

But now, instead of being safe and sound and insulated against desire (shudder), Nana was suddenly thinking other kinds of thoughts, having other kinds of memories. She went and bought *Guitar Man* by Steve Earle instead of listening to her better self, and she even played it indoors because when she got home the kids were out. "Oh, God," thought Nana, "I shouldn't be doing this." After a bit, and despite her new relationship with time, Nana began to experience impatience. One song at a time was taking too long. She began to wonder if there weren't some way she could cram all this music in at once. Oh, hell.

"That's called fucking," Nana realized.

So we will leave her there.

Ten Straight Days

BEVERLY DONOFRIO

There are times when I'm sure I'm as inept as a grandmother as I was when I became a mother at seventeen. Take my last visit with my grandson, Zachary, age two and a half. We were off on a walk in Brooklyn, where he lives, when I had to tie my shoe. My son, Jason, had warned me that if I didn't buckle Zach in securely, he could go flying when the stroller hit a bump. And so I'd followed his instructions, even though it killed my arthritic right hand to fasten those annoying little plastic clips. Times have changed. When Jason was little I could hardly be bothered to put him in his car seat. Usually he stood next to me, and when we came to a stop, I stretched my arm against his chest to keep him upright. In 1968, this was not against the law or even uncommon. Neither was sitting your kid on your lap and letting him steer.

My son knows from having me as a mother that I am not careful, cautious, or always law-abiding. I don't resent my son's assessment, because I know that if it weren't for the grace of God, the kindness of strangers—and standing on my head to ward off postmenopausal lapses by increasing the blood flow to my brain—I could be a disaster.

In fact, I wished Jason had given me a refresher course on applying the stroller's brake, because since my last time out with Zach three months before, I'd forgotten how it works. So when I squatted down to tie my shoe, I didn't apply the brake at all. The stroller rolled a few inches into a tree bed, then tipped over as Zachary, strapped in like an astronaut, screamed.

"Oh, my God," I gasped. I couldn't see his face, which was smashed into the tree trunk. I grabbed the carriage, praying that Zach wasn't hurt, and saw an angry purpling welt forming on his forehead. "Oh, my God, sweetheart, are you okay?" I was almost crying. "You must have been terrified. Does it hurt? Oh, honey, I'm *so* sorry."

Seeing how bad I felt, Zach tried to comfort me. "It's okay," he mumbled through tears. "I'm okay."

Of course, when we returned home, I had to confess the incident to his father. Jason is a stay-at-home dad, a good one. He regarded Zach gravely, trying, I could tell, not to be too judgmental of me.

"The tree," Zach nodded, touching his welt.

It is either an act of faith or a great achievement that my son, an epic worrier, trusts his son with me at all. But it might just be a gamble he's willing to take now and then to get a break from full-time child care. For Christmas the first year of Zach's life, Jason and his wife, Jessica, gave me a gift of three trips to Brooklyn, with the understanding that I would help out. It was also understood that I would babysit for Zachary for ten whole days right after his first birthday, while Jase and Jess took her parents on an Alaskan cruise—*their* Christmas present.

It did occur to me to wonder how it happened that Jess's parents got the cruise and I got the babysitting trips. But truly, if given the choice, I would have chosen the babysitting. I lived far away in Mexico and now live far away in a monastery in Colorado, yet I'm determined to be available, to experience the joy of that exuberant kid energy, to see the world fresh through his eyes, to be a loving, dependable safe harbor for him.

If it weren't for Zach my life might be entirely different. I spent his first month with him, and then too soon it was time to leave. My last full day was a Sunday. We danced, my nose and lips brushing his rose-petal cheek as I sang in his ear, "Good Night, My Love," swaying and dipping him, gliding across the floor. I'd swooned to this song, the last dance in the gym in high school. I'd kissed men good night as it played on the radio. It was all so long ago, yet here again, in a different way, something sparked alive in me.

The new love of my life fell asleep on my chest, his legs straddling my ribs as my arms cradled him, his tiny body rising and falling with my breath. By the time we awoke it was dark outside, and Zach was hungry. When Jess lifted him off my chest, my heart ached the way it had when I was a baby myself and my mother had pulled away, handed me off, left me alone.

And so I knew that once I returned home to Mexico, I was in for a marathon weep. But I did not suspect that the weeping would continue on and off for weeks, long after I'd grown accustomed to the separation and had stopped thinking constantly of my grandson. I felt dull, foggy, flat. I had no appetite for the life I'd thought was so rich with color, interest, and fun.

After a month of this dryness, a fantasy invaded: me, as a cloistered contemplative nun. I believed I was experiencing a call to become a religious, to live outside of the world in solitude and silence. It was as though filling with love for

Zachary had cracked me open enough to hear God's call. But could God really be calling me to a monastery I would not be allowed to leave? Would God really ask me to abandon my grandson, and my son, who has no other parent but me?

I had no answer, but I did know that the longing to make God the white-hot center of a silent, spirit-focused life was like an ache shooting down the middle of me. And so I began a search for monasteries, just to see. In time I found a Carmelite hermitage that allows me to live there as a lay member, so that I can, and do, leave to see my family.

This is not only good but necessary, for there is the matter of redemption. Back when I had Jason, I cursed and whined about my fate, and never really took to my role as a mother. During his childhood, Jason was deluded and thought this was okay. "We're more like brother and sister than mother and son," we sort of used to brag.

But in his twenties, Jason saw the light—or, I should say, the dark. He became angry and depressed, and for a few years he barely spoke to me. My guilt and pain drove me into the hands of God. Not only did I ask God to forgive me; I asked my son. We had some tearful talks and therapy sessions. Eventually he fell in love with Jessica and separated from me. As he matured, he began to understand that if he didn't forgive me, he would be hurting himself most of all. This is not to say that in recent years I haven't witnessed flashes of rage, or that he's completely overcome his distrust of me. There's always more healing to do—and this is where my grandson comes in. When I heard that Jessica was pregnant, I saw the baby as a way to redeem myself. I hoped that my recurring prayer—"Please, God, open my heart; teach me to love"—would finally be answered.

Why else would a fifty-five-year-old woman who yearns for silence agree to take a one-year-old for *ten straight days?*

I decided that even though it would be an endurance feat, I'd take Zach on the road to visit family and friends. That way, at least, I wouldn't have to entertain him all on my own. Besides, by age one Zach was already a game traveler. He was renowned for passing out in his car seat, then waking as soon as we arrived at our destination, excited to be in a new place. My grandson is one of the lucky ones, a born extrovert and natural conversationalist. On my latest trip—when the debacle with the stroller took place—we visited my sister in New Jersey. On our way home, as I drove along Chambers Street in lower Manhattan, he pointed to a golden statue on top of a building. "The Statoo of Libady," he said. He's familiar with this most famous of American statues because he often takes walks on the Brooklyn promenade where one can see the lady holding up her torch. "That's not the Statue of Liberty," I explained. "It's a different statue."

"Where'd the Statoo of Libady go?"

"She's on the river. We'll see her when we cross the Brooklyn Bridge," I promised. But when we drove across, Zach was too low in his car seat to see, and the incident became the subject of repeated conversations. "We didn't see the Statoo of Libady."

"No. That was a different statue on top of the building."

"I was too low. I couldn't see."

The first stop on our road trip during the ten straight days was my parents' house in Connecticut. Both are in their eighties and failing. My mother has emphysema and sits on the same spot on the sofa day and night playing solitaire and watching television, an oxygen tube fastened to her nose. My father is less and less steady on his feet, and hasn't been the same since his quadruple bypass a few years ago. As if that weren't enough, he'd recently been stricken with a miserable case of the shingles. Our visit could kill them, I thought, but at least they'd go out happy. Their family is the light of their lives and seeing Zachary would make their summer.

Sure enough, the minute Zach walked into the house—walking was a new feat since they'd last seen him—color actually returned to my mother's face and my father began a low-register chuckle that would hardly stop during the whole visit.

Zach smiled and graciously submitted to kisses and hugs, then made a beeline for the stairs, which he insisted on climbing up and down 101 times, with me following behind as his personal bodyguard. The thing about one-year-olds, I was remembering, is that you can't leave them alone for even a second.

"That little shit," my mother kept saying, shaking her head. "That little shit."

Finally I brought a box of Jason's old toys down from the attic and dumped them in the middle of the living room floor so my parents could watch Zach play.

Here we were, my father in his reclining chair, my mother and me on the same sofa where we'd sat almost forty years ago after I'd confessed I was pregnant. I'd felt so ashamed and then, later, depressed, falling asleep for entire afternoons while my mother made dinner, did laundry, and watched my baby son.

In my early fifties I'd boycotted this house after confronting my father about the time I was thirteen and he'd caught me riding in a car with boys. On that long-ago night he slapped me over and over until my mother finally jumped on his back to stop him.

"So how do you feel about beating me up when I was just a kid?" I asked the day I finally got up the nerve to confront him.

"Fine," he replied, a snotty, aggressive tone in his voice. "You deserved it."

I called him a brute. He called me crazy. I never wanted to speak to him again. Still, because I believed in forgiveness, at least in theory, I told myself I forgave my father. I just didn't like him—and I chose not to pretend that I did.

But a year later, when Jess was pregnant, my sister called to tell me that my father had had a ministroke and lost the sight in one eye for a day. "What if Dad dies and you're still not speaking?" she asked. I wasn't sure I'd care. Then she added, "What will happen next year after the baby's born?"

That did it. I would not allow my grandson to be born into a family at war. I called my father to tell him I wanted to make peace for the sake of the family. But he didn't give me a chance. "Let it go, Bev," he said before I spoke. "Please. Just let it go."

The plea in his voice went straight to my heart. "Okay," I managed. "I will."

And so a year and a half later, we sat watching Zachary kneel before his father's old xylophone on wheels, tapping it with a wand. Ordinarily, the television is blaring, but for some reason it wasn't on. The radio was, though, and it was playing a catchy ad for Barbarino Pontiac: "Ba ba ba, ba ba barino. Ba ba ba, ba ba barino," like a cheerleading chant. My father snapped his fingers and we all sang along. Zach looked up at us, grinning. Then my father rose on legs that never straighten anymore, bent his knees, and reached for Zach, who dropped his xylophone wand and let his great-grandfather pull him up. My father is a great dancer. When I was a baby he fox-trotted me to sleep, and when I was a little older we did the cha-cha and the Lindy around the kitchen. It had been decades since I'd seen my parents dance. But now my father ticktocked his knees and pushed and pulled Zach's hands, doing the twist. Then my mother stood and joined the boys, and I did, too. The four of us danced on even after the song was over.

I was flooded with love for my dancing father, and grateful to my grandson for bringing us back together.

Dancing wasn't the only thing Zach picked up on our trip. On the car ferry across Long Island Sound to visit my friend Nancy, he developed running chops. He ran the circuit around the two massive decks every minute of the ninety-minute trip. When the boat finally docked, I strapped him into his car seat and he was asleep before the car left the boat. I drove a few miles, parked at the side of a road, and fell asleep, too. This was only day three and I was afraid I might die of exhaustion.

Zach's nap wasn't nearly long enough, because when I stood him on his feet in Nancy's driveway, he took one step and fell flat on his face. He cried and refused to walk. He was done with walking. He wanted to be held the rest of the day. I could have matched him tear for tear.

Is it possible to be snappish and still filled with unconditional love?

Was it possible for me to care for a child without pricks of guilt and waves of confusion? Had I agreed to ten straight days out of love or guilt? And why couldn't I tell right from wrong? For example, every time we sat at the table to eat, Zach got up and left. Was I supposed to make him stay? At the beach with an old friend, I took off Zach's clothes and let him play naked in the sand. Would the sand get up his bum and irritate him? When we were ready to leave, I laid him down to diaper him—an activity he was not at that moment crazy about. So I handed him a clamped-shut, barnacle-covered clam, which he immediately put in his mouth. When I was done with the diaper, Zach yelped when I tried to take away the clam. "Do you think it's okay he's sucking on that thing?" I asked my friend, a father.

He shrugged. "Probably."

"If this were your kid would you let him put it in his mouth?"

"No."

I got rid of the clam.

That night after Zach's bath, the tub was lined with sand like incriminating evidence. Then in his jammies he sat on my lap, cozy and soft against my chest, the top of his damp head under my chin, smelling so sweet. His chubby hands rested on mine as I turned the pages of his books. Finally I kissed my brave and trusting traveling companion good night and tucked him into his portable crib at the foot of my bed. The poor little guy was beginning to look worn and waiflike, with circles darkening around his eyes.

I lay down too, listening to my grandson's breathing, thinking about God and humility. I was not perfect; it was arrogant and self-centered to think I should be. I thought about how God loves me just the way I am—so maybe I should, too? It's my own self-judgments that get in the way. I remembered how as a teenager I'd condemned myself for my poor mothering, for never knowing the right thing to do. I was almost forty years older now, and I still didn't know. But I was trying, just as I'd always been trying—with one big difference. I believed in God now and could ask for help. And so I prayed, "God, I can't do this without you. Please, my dear, sweet, helpful, wonderful God, give me the energy, goodwill, love, and patience *to live through this trip*."

Perhaps it was God's hand that made Alaska cold, overcast, and dreary, driving Jess and Jase to return home two days early.

A year and a half later, at the end of my most recent, month-long visit, I forgive myself for dying to get back home to the monastery in the Sangre de Cristo mountains where it is so silent and I am so solitary that I go days without hearing or uttering a word. At my son's house the giant TV, the comfortable sofa, the huge refrigerator stocked with goodies—so appreciated when I arrived—have come to seem like gluttony. And I am so sick of playing with Zach's blocks, his train set, the erector bugs, and the plastic animals that I've begun telling the truth: "I'm sorry, honey, Nana's bored. She doesn't want to play."

I know who I am. I need both solitude and grandmother time. Living in solitude helps me stay centered when I visit my grandson, sometimes for a month at a time. I may fumble and bumble, snap and bark out the truth, but my heart is good and getting softer all the time.

The day before I leave, I lie awake in bed before the rest

of the family rises, thinking that I should dedicate my last day to Zachary.

It's Super Bowl Sunday, and Jess and Jase are having people over. I know they'd love for me to take Zach off their hands so they can straighten up the house and cook. I say, "Come on, Zach. Let's go for a walk." When he says no, I'm relieved. But then I think about how love is pushing yourself and acting *as if*—going out of your way even when you're tired. So I bribe him. "Come on. We'll walk to the Brooklyn Bridge and see the Statue of Liberty. Remember—"

"I couldn't see," he says.

"Right. But this time you'll be able to see. We'll be walking instead of riding in the car. And we'll get ice cream."

"Okay," he says.

"He doesn't even like ice cream," my son tells me.

We take his stroller, whose brake I have by this time been drilled in using correctly. But Zach wants to walk, so I hold his hand with one hand and steer the stroller with the other as we amble through Brooklyn Heights. "Hello, owl," he says to a stone owl in a patch of front yard. He stops to pick up a big dried leaf, a stick, an acorn. When he tires of holding his treasures, we place them on the stroller seat. As we pass a small flock of pigeons on the road, Zach puffs out his chest and takes tiny strutting steps like the birds, so I do, too.

We walk all the way to Montague, where I buy him a cup of soft-serve vanilla Häagen-Dazs. He puckers his lips every time he pulls the spoon out of his mouth, usually with most of the ice cream still there. It takes him half an hour, but he eats every drop.

Back on the street he still doesn't want to ride. He takes

my hand and we walk, stopping at a toy store where he plays with the trains. Then we continue, on and on.

Crossing Cadman Plaza, almost at the bridge, he begins to ask every twenty feet or so, "Where we are now?"

I feel like crying. When I return in three or four months, he'll probably say: *Are we there yet?* He'll be singing the alphabet, putting on his own shoes. I want to freeze-frame this time, this age, this moment. But life isn't like that— nothing stays the same. I am filled suddenly with the urge to pick him up and hug him, but I resist. He is on a mission. He is walking to the Brooklyn Bridge.

Two miles and nearly three hours after we began, we arrive. I hold Zach up to look at the Statue of Liberty, but he is so tired he doesn't say a word. I set him down on his feet. He takes the leaf, the stick, the acorn, places them under the stroller seat, then climbs in. I buckle the buckle and don't think of my arthritic hand. In a second he's fast asleep and I push him back home.

Angel Baby

MARITA GOLDEN

Ever since my son Michael was born thirty years ago, I've understood the spiritual power of babies. In those six hours of labor I gave birth not only to my son, but to a profoundly new, liberating sense of myself. Still, not until my grandson Vaun was born did I realize that babies are actually miniature angels assigned to break through our knee-jerk habits of resistance and to remind us that love is the real reason we're here.

Vaun was six weeks premature and painfully small. Born with weak lungs, jaundice, and low blood sugar, he was placed in an incubator in the neonatal intensive care unit soon after his birth. The tubes taped to his mouth and nose made him look like a tiny alien as they ensured life-giving breath. And though the sterile incubator protected him, it also prevented him from being held by his mother—my stepdaughter, Keesha—who hovered over the Plexiglas box, worried and afraid.

For Keesha, there had to be a good outcome. Though she had one child already, Antoinette—a spunky, precocious ten-year-old—she'd suffered two miscarriages. Another loss would devastate her in ways I did not want to imagine. I knew how it hurt to lose a child—I'd had a miscarriage myself. I wanted to comfort Keesha, but our relationship was fragile, often strained, and had been ever since I'd married her father, Joe, twelve years before. My reaction to her pregnancy hadn't improved matters.

For both Joe and me, the news sparked more concern than celebration. Not only were there serious challenges in Keesha's relationship with the baby's father, she was between jobs and looking for a new place to live. Why have another child now? How would she manage? These were just a few of the questions that bedeviled us as we struggled with our sense of foreboding. Still, we offered Keesha the moral and material support she needed. She was our daughter and we were going to be grandparents again. What else could we do?

Grandparenthood was something that Antoinette had made easy. As our first grandchild she was doted on and spoiled within reason—and she returned the favor by being studious, caring, and outgoing. Without complaint she'd run errands and help Keesha around the house. She was curious and vibrantly alive. At nine she was already on the Internet searching for college scholarships in cheerleading and gymnastics—she excelled at both. As the writer in the family I was the de facto "cultural commissar." I regularly took her to plays, museums, and art galleries. We talked about everything from the war in Iraq to problems she was having with a teacher at school. My granddaughter was opinionated, thoughtful, and open. (Remember, she wasn't a teenager yet.) I considered her as much my own grandchild as I would have if we'd been bound by blood. Besides, until recently, when Keesha's mother moved from California to Washington, I was the only local grandmother.

My son, Michael, has no children, so before Antoinette was born, I'd rarely thought about being a grandmother. I knew only that I did not want to be called *grandma*—Antoinette simply calls me Marita. Early on, however, I realized that in order to be her grandmother I had to improve my relationship with Keesha. So I eagerly helped pay for Antoinette's dance classes and uniforms, bought her books and birthday gifts, and sometimes surprised her with money "just because." Still, relations between Keesha and me remained charged. My stepdaughter and I had yet to have an authentic, honest conversation.

Vaun had been in the incubator three days when I arrived one afternoon for a visit. Keesha was in the intensive care unit, perched beside Vaun's incubator, her eyes assessing his every movement—the tiny arms and fists seeming to box the air, his legs thrusting jerkily.

I stood behind her and considered just how much was at stake. Vaun's lungs had to grow strong enough in that incubator for him to breathe easily, naturally. His future health, learning capacity, size, and strength all depended on those tiny lungs. In that moment, the memory of the many nights Joe and I had worried, groused, complained about the impact of this new child on Keesha's life—and, to be honest, on our lives—simply dissolved.

Keesha began plying one of the nurses with questions—all variations on a single theme: was Vaun getting better? The nurse smiled and gently said what we already knew. "He's hanging in there." My stepdaughter's shoulders slumped, and she looked anxious and confused. I was pretty sure she was remembering the pain of losing her other two babies.

There was nothing we could do, so finally we returned to Keesha's room, where, exhausted from keeping vigil over Vaun, she climbed into bed, curled into a ball, and promptly fell asleep. While she dozed I sat in the chair next to her, flipped through the channels on the television set hooked to the ceiling above her bed, and in one of those oddly synchronistic moments, tuned into a woman giving birth on the Discovery Channel. As I watched her pant and scream, I tried to think of what I might say or do to ease my stepdaughter's pain and help prepare her for the worst—just in case. Despite our differences, I felt intensely bound to Keesha, not only as her stepmother but as a woman, by the biological sisterhood that binds one woman to another, one mother to another.

She was eighteen when Joe and I married and we got off to a tumultuous start, despite my determination to be the world's best stepmom. Shortly after graduating from high school, Keesha left California, where she'd been living with her mother, and came to Washington to live with us. Since then I had been exposed to many varied incarnations of the young woman now dozing in the bed beside me.

The first was *Demon Keesha*. At eighteen she was jealous of my role in her father's life. This Keesha defied her curfew, was rude and disrespectful to me, and argued so ferociously with Joe that he asked her to leave our home and move in with her grandmother. Next there was *Young Mother Keesha*, to whom marriage and motherhood brought a full package of responsibilities, leading to heartbreak and, eventually, divorce. She was followed by *Back on Track Keesha*, who grew gracefully as a single mother. This Keesha was devoted to Antoinette and tried to create a real future for them both. But despite her best intentions, *Addicted to Love Keesha* had remained on the scene—her hunger for romance creating angst in her relationships with men.

There were so many echoes of my own life in my step-daughter's—including single parenthood and an uncanny talent for becoming enmeshed in unsatisfying love affairs (until I met Joe). Still, I believed that Keesha, like me, had the ability to turn her life around—if she really wanted to. I'd hoped to help guide her, for her sake as well as for the sake of Antoinette and now Vaun. But because I'd been burned so often by her jealousy of me, I had shut down. She never knew how much we had in common. I was just the interloper who had stolen her father's heart. So I learned to play my part with caution, showering Antoinette with grandmotherly attention while maintaining a pleasant but superficial relationship with Keesha.

In the year or so leading up to Vaun's birth, the arguments between Joe and Keesha escalated—intensifying, it seemed, the more support he offered. I felt helpless in the face of this turmoil. I was the wicked stepmother. I had little clout, and less influence—even when it came to Antoinette. Though most biological grandmothers discover that they have no real power, stepgrandmothers are even more disenfranchised.

Still, as I sat beside Keesha and watched another woman become a mother on television, I hoped that just as my son Michael had given me a new birth, Vaun's arrival would help me turn the page in the story of my relationship with Keesha. My grandson had enough challenges ahead of him without getting caught in the cross fire of old family dramas.

The Zen Buddhist teacher Thich Nhat Hanh writes: "When you love someone, the most precious gift you can give your loved one is your true presence. . . . With mindfulness, we can look deeply and recognize the strengths as well as the difficulties and suffering." He adds that, "with the energy of mindfulness and the capacity of looking deeply, we will find the insights to transform and heal."

Keesha opened her eyes just as the orderly was delivering dinner. After she'd finished picking at the baked chicken and rice and Jell-O, I took a chance and told her I admired her.

"Why?" she asked, eyeing me with a mixture of suspicion and surprise.

"I understand what you've been through. Miscarriages are hell. Your body has healed, but your heart and mind are still tender. You don't know this about me, but I lost a baby to a miscarriage before I had Michael."

She shifted around on the bed. I knew I was treading on sensitive territory by bringing up the babies she had lost before the one she'd given birth to a few days earlier was out of the woods, but I continued anyway.

"I know how scared you are about Vaun. When you lose a baby, most people don't realize that you've lost a whole person, a complete human being that you loved. That's how I felt about the baby boy who would've been Mike's brother."

Keesha pursed her lips, and I could see she was fighting tears. "I really do admire you," I repeated. "You're strong and loving and brave. You decided to have another baby despite your losses, despite the pain and death. I just want you to know that I've been there. You never forget, but you do heal."

I had written about my miscarriage, but until that day I hadn't spoken with anyone about the impact of losing my first child. And writing, no matter how revelatory, is still an artifact, an intellectual creation that by its very nature distances you from what you are describing. But telling Keesha in my own unscripted, halting words about one of my most painful experiences was a moment of grace. I wasn't trying to understand it; I was just remembering it, embracing it, offering it as a gift to us both. I reached for my stepdaughter's hand and, for the first time in the twelve years since I'd known her, she allowed me to hold it.

The next day Vaun started breathing on his own and was released from his Plexiglas isolation chamber into his mother's waiting arms. During evening visiting hours, he was passed around the circle of family gathered at Keesha's bed. When my mother-in-law, his great-grandmother, passed him to me, I held him close and whispered "Thank you" into his tiny ear.

Vaun is now a healthy, sharp, smart-as-a-whip three-year-old, and Antoinette has entered the first years of adolescence. Some days I feel as if I'm losing her to the rebelliousness and awkward search for identity that characterize being thirteen. But I still talk to her, and I know that behind her blank stare she's listening. I also recognize that her impatience and sullenness are both a pose and a call for attention. Recently in the car driving her home from a shopping excursion, I talked to her about how choosing a boy to date has to be determined by more than his looks, and how the poor choices your friends make can endanger you. Her response was a long bout of silence, then quiet, begrudging agreement.

Last Friday was grandparents' day at Vaun's school. I made a hand puppet with him and read him a story. Then we crawled inside a big empty cardboard box and pretended we were driving through the country in a red sports car. Because of Vaun's curiosity, innocence, and spontaneity, each time I'm with him I enter the here and now, the eternity of the moment. The sound of his voice, the touch of his hand, and the glint in his eyes seem utterly original—and make me feel as though I'm getting a glimpse of what humans can be. My grandson at three is a fresh start, the world made new—even when he is tired and irritable or asks me to read a story for the third time or hangs up the phone when I'm talking to him, because he wants to get back to playing with his toy truck.

Keesha's mother moved to the area a year ago to live with Keesha and help her with the children. She is a woman of deeply felt religious faith, a woman who shares my belief in the power of determination, optimism, and diligence in shaping a life. We liked each other from our first meeting, and there has never been a moment of jealousy between us as we have found a natural rhythm to the ways in which we love Antoinette and Vaun. Keesha is her mother's daughter, as many of her best traits show. Still, their relationship is as loving, impassioned, intense, challenging, and difficult as most mother-daughter bonds.

I now play a different role as Keesha's stepmother; the presence of her own mother has freed me. I no longer have to try to be surrogate mom, counselor, and adviser all rolled into one. I can just be Keesha's friend and sounding board, treading lightly, sometimes offering advice, which is what friends do.

On that now-distant day in her hospital room, Keesha and I became women together. I've discovered that you become a woman the way you become human—over and over again—and that both processes are rooted in surrendering to the reality of more pain than you may feel is fair, but pain woven into our earthly existence.

Something else I've come to realize: just as my son's birth was a kind of baptism, cracking me open in so many ways, giving me new speech and a new vision—a phenomenon sometimes referred to as the "double birth" of mother and child—the circumstances of Vaun's birth unexpectedly cracked me open again; but this time it was a "triple birth"—of mother, son, and grandmother.

When Things Go Tilt

CLAIRE ROBERTS

Of all the peoples whom I have studied,
from city dwellers to cliff dwellers, I always find that
at least 50 percent would prefer to have at least one jungle
between themselves and their mothers-in-law.

—MARGARET MEAD

My Gramma lobbied hard for Mom to name me something traditional, like Dagmar or Johanna. Dad vetoed that idea. Apparently Gramma forgave him, because she enjoyed a warm relationship with both my father and my mother to the end of her life. And me? Gramma loved me whole-heartedly—her love was tempered only slightly by Swedish reserve—and I adored her.

She used to ride the train halfway across the country to see us. Each time she came, we'd go out for a "grown-up lunch"— just the two of us. She loved to tell everyone that I was her favorite granddaughter. Our little joke: I was her only granddaughter, but I knew she was proud of me. Between visits, we wrote to each other. I can still picture her jagged, fountain-pen script. Unfortunately, I didn't have the sense to save her letters, and over time I've lost the sound of her voice, but never the tender tone.

Now with that background, I might seem to be a con-
tender for a Grammy Award myself. Let me just say that I'm
not holding my breath. Oh, my grandkids seem to have great
affection for me. But to my son's wife, I am the dreaded
abominable mother-in-law.

John, Rosie, and their daughters—Emma, thirteen, and
Gracie, ten—live just ten miles away from me. For the past
few years, I've gone to their house only when summoned by
Emma. She's the glue that binds me to her family. A typical
text message from her: *GmaRUOK? Howz yr day lookin' ;-)
luv em.* What she's really asking is: "Gramma, would you puh-
LEEZE come for me and take me somewhere with you?"

I used to fire back cheeky responses to Em's messages. I
gave that up once I discovered I'm under surveillance. John
monitors our text and e-mail exchanges. So these days, I
word my answers carefully: *lunch 2day? dbl chk w/parents!
luv Gma.* I'm a very cool techno-granny and a first-rate butt-
coverer.

Once our get-together has been parentally sanctioned,
I'm off to fetch Emma. Sadly, the longest leg of my journey
is her driveway. I pull up, hoping she'll see me and come
outside, but this rarely happens. I think Emma believes that
by forcing me to come to the house, she can somehow be the
catalyst for détente. Both she and Gracie understand that
there's "a situation" with Gramma and their mother—and,
therefore, with their father, too.

So, gut churning, I go to the door and ring the bell.
Through the small front-door window, I see my daughter-
in-law grab her coffee mug and sprint out of sight. Gracie
races from the television room and usually beats Emma to
the door. The moment I step into the foyer, I'm tangled in

a clutch of thin, huggy arms. The girls' freshly washed hair smells like sunshine even in the House of Usher. Promising Gracie a playdate soon, I grab Emma's hand to go. Somewhere, just out of sight, Rosie clears her throat.

It hasn't always been this way. In the beginning, Rosie was warmer, friendlier. This, despite my totally screwing up her life, as she told me once in a moment of unguarded candor. When John announced that he and Rosie wanted to marry the summer after high school graduation, I suggested that they consider holding off for a while. I'd done the too-young-married thing myself—a really bad idea. "Give yourselves some time out in the world," I advised. "Grow wings!" I said brightly. They agreed to wait, and they married the following summer. I believe Rosie has never forgiven me for that lost year.

I didn't see a lot of them before they had children. I was immersed in my career. John and Rosie had jobs, too, and John was attending college at night. When we did get together, things seemed cordial.

Over time, though, Rosie morphed from a shy, insecure young woman to an insecure young woman with harder edges and a sharper tongue. She became increasingly critical of friends, neighbors, coworkers, and, sometimes, John. He usually blew it off when she said something caustic, so I took my cue from him. I remember wondering, though, what Rosie was saying about me when I was out of range. Still, I had not yet tumbled to the fact that I was squarely in her crosshairs as she watched and waited for me to disappoint her.

I can't isolate a freeze-frame moment when things went tilt, but it happened sometime after Emma and Gracie were born. It's fair to say that my casual approach to spending time with John and Rosie spilled over to my early years as a grandparent. Though I found the girls adorable and charming, I was sidetracked by my own frenetic life. Too often, I forgot to lower my gaze to child level, and Rosie was keeping tabs. This led us from a frosty relationship into perpetual midwinter.

There's a little malt and burger joint where Emma and I like to go for lunch. Invariably, as we settle in, she lets loose a breathless *whoosh* of consciousness. "And then you know that unbe*liev*ably cute Adam guy I told you about, the one in my math class, I think he maybe *smiled* at me today, and did I tell you I *have* to get a new swimsuit, and I've been wondering if you think gay marriage is right or what, Gramma, and by the way did you watch *American Idol* last night?" Whew!

Over time I've discovered that Emma tells me things she doesn't tell her parents. She seems to trust me, and this is both scary and wonderful. Although her family closely guards its secrets, for the most part that's not Em's style. The things she reveals aren't shocking, but sometimes she steers her narrative to *the parents*. Dangerous territory. I've gotten pretty good at deflecting those side trips.

"Well, Gramma, wait till I tell you what Mother did yesterday!"

"Mmmm," I say.

"I'm living in a freaking *prison*!"

"Mmmm."

"Don't you even want to *hear*?"

"Hey, girl," I say, "you ready for dessert?"

"Gramma, you're not paying attention! Mother *grounded* me just because I didn't have my stupid *science* project totally, completely finished. She is *so* lame! I was supposed to go to Jennifer's for a sleepover! She treats me like a *baby!*"

I suck it up and give her my best let's-be-fair-to-your-mother shot. "Well, you know, Em, your mom probably just wants you to stay out of trouble with your teacher and keep up your grades."

Emma rolls her eyes and slides down in her chair, arms folded across her chest. She sighs deeply and is silent for about ten seconds. It rarely takes longer than that for her to decide it's pointless to play the blame-the-parents game with me, so she gives it up. Temporarily.

I must confess that there are times when I'm tempted to sound off. But I know it's bad karma to encourage any line of conversation that might be perceived as parent-bashing. This self-imposed boundary generally keeps me out of trouble, except when it doesn't—because in addition to monitoring my written exchanges with Emma, John and Rosie debrief her after we spend time together. And given that my granddaughter has a flair for the dramatic, the fallout from those postprandial inquisitions sometimes yields e-blasts from John.

"What were you thinking when you told Emma this war is immoral?" (*That's not what I said.*)

"Em tells me you let her be a potty-mouth, which she mistakenly believes is cool." (*Semi-guilty.*)

"Did you really tell Em that talk radio is geared to monkey-minds?" (*Um, I did.*)

I feel so weighted down by the accumulation of John's accusations that I rarely rise to his bait anymore. I would like to ask him how we got to this place where he seems to reflexively assume malicious intent on my part. But that's bound to lead us to the ultra-dangerous topic of his wife. So I do not venture there.

Emma is curious, opinionated, funny, and mercurial, and I love hearing her process life out loud. She claims I'm the only one who listens to her. Big Red Flag. It implies that her parents do *not* listen. Worse, it's an indictment of Rosie's mother, Faye.

Grandma Faye is a gentle woman, beloved by Rosie's family. I like Faye. She's been present in the lives of our shared grandchildren from the start. I've admired and sometimes envied her. But even though I lost points with Rosie for being less attentive than Faye to the girls when they were younger, I doubt I could have won Rosie over even if I'd been granny-on-the-spot. For one thing, I'm the *mother-in-law*, not the mother. But the even greater problem is that I'm *me*—which is to say, I'm not a bit like Faye.

Sometimes I'm slow to grasp the obvious. I didn't realize until the contest was well under way that Faye and I had been pitted against each other. That came into focus when John told me not long ago that his daughters adore me and would rather spend time with me than anyone else. Well, I thought, that's really something. Given my comparatively recent involvement with them, I'd have predicted Faye as the odds-on favorite. Hell, *I'd* have voted for her. But my pleasure in the girls' devotion didn't last long.

"Mother," John continued, "you have a huge responsibility. You're obliged to be a role model for the girls. They think that everything you say is gospel. So here's the deal.

You need to keep your *political* opinions, your *religious* opinions, *all* your opinions, to yourself. And you need to act your age." Whoa! Blindsided. John is essentially a kind, considerate person. I thought he'd be pleased that his children are so fond of his mother. But no. My son was channeling Rosie.

Emma sometimes channels her, too. One day we were shopping together—school clothes for her, a new backpack for me. My partner, Kenneth, and I were planning a trek in the Ozarks. As the clerk rang up my pack, Emma fixed me with her green-eyed gaze and said, "Gramma? How come you don't stay home and make cookies and knit like other grannies?"

Actually, I used to. I knit my way through my divorce, with great heart and lousy technique. I spent a lot of time unraveling my messes and starting over. Finally I gave it up. And even though I'm a better-than-average cook, it's true that I rarely bake anymore.

Grandma Faye knits. Grandma Faye bakes. Grandma Faye has been married for nearly fifty years to one man—Rosie's father. Faye believes divorce is a sin. And even though Kenneth and I have shared a home for fifteen years (sans vows), she seems to tolerate me anyway. On the other hand, when Rosie went through her brief but intense fundamentalist phase, I became her poster woman for sinners standing in need of prayer. I suspect she continues to take a dim view of my lifestyle.

Kenneth and I are a good match. We're wild about birds and other critters. We're environmental and political activists. Sometimes we stand on street corners with protest signs. My grandchildren find our behavior amusing. Rosie and John, not so much. In fact, Rosie once told me that she finds our public activism extremely offensive and that we must choose between it and the family. We choose both.

As Emma, then Gracie, moved closer to adolescence, this laissez-faire granny decided it was time to redeem herself. Thus began my *era of trying too hard*. I started showing up for everything: Emma's swim meets, Gracie's flute recitals, family fun nights. I bought lavish quantities of refrigerated cookie dough, magazine subscriptions, and enough paper and ribbon to gift wrap their school. I extended countless invitations to the girls to spend time with me—separately and together. We ate; we shopped; we played miniature golf; we saw movies and plays; we walked in the park. They talked; I listened. I began to get a really good handle on who my granddaughters are. We were having fun and everyone was happy!

Well, maybe not everyone.

During the *era*, I even attempted to thaw my relationship with Rosie. I suggested that we get together for lunch, for coffee. She pointedly sidestepped each invitation. Then, in what was to become a permanently revised tradition, John and his girls made the annual Mother's Day pilgrimage to my house without Rosie. Ditto my birthday. Rosie was boycotting me.

Even so, I showed up at one of Emma's swim meets, decked out in her school colors and carrying a little "Go Dolphins!" sign I'd made. Emma laughed and introduced me to her coach. That evening, I received another blistergram from John. He e-mailed to tell me that whatever I was trying to prove was undignified and unwanted, that I needed to back off and just be a *normal* grandmother.

How could my good intentions have been so misinterpreted? I felt shamed, hurt. I wept onto my keyboard. Surely things could not get worse.

It started with unanswered e-mails. Then text messages were ignored. I couldn't get a bead on what was happening. All I knew was that I hadn't heard from Emma for a while. It seemed as though she'd gone missing from me.

I decided that the most likely explanation, given her random study habits, was that she'd been grounded again. Still, we usually manage to connect, even when she's in home detention. I thought about phoning to check in with her, but that would have been a breach of our communication protocol. So I waited—until I couldn't wait anymore. I sent John a breezy, low-key e-mail. I mentioned that I hadn't heard from Em for a while, and hoped they weren't all down with the nasty flu bug that was going around.

John answered quickly: "Your radar must be pretty good. I was going to write. We've been waiting to see how things shake out. And FYI, we're not sharing this with anyone else. But you might as well know that Emma has been having a pretty rough time lately. And on Monday night, she swallowed some pills. We rushed her to the ER and it was touch-and-go for a while. We almost lost her, Mom. She's a little better now. But she's going to spend some time in the mental health unit."

I believe I may have vacated my body as I tried to grasp what I was reading. Emma! Suicide? Why didn't she tell me she was in such terrible trouble? Of course: John's girls have been trained to keep family secrets. But I'm family, aren't I?

"She's refusing to see Rosie," John wrote. "And she's asking for you. Dr. Harris says you're probably therapeutically appropriate, since you two seem to have a pretty strong connection. Rosie and I won't stand in the way if you want to go see her."

Won't stand in the way? Chances are, I'll never know what it cost him to extract permission from a furious Rosie to extend that olive branch. No doubt she would have been surprised to know that at some level I understood her anger. And John? I wanted to comfort him. I used to know how.

I wrote back: "I'm so sorry, John. Of course I'll go!"

He e-mailed directions to the hospital and to Emma's unit: "You have to ring the bell. They'll let you in."

Entering a lockdown ward leaves an indelible impression. I rang the bell. I was admitted through the first door by a nurse who searched my purse and asked me if I had anything in my pockets. As the second door locked behind me, Emma came running full tilt down the long hallway and dived into my waiting arms. For such moments was the word *bittersweet* created.

We were ushered into a stark little room where there was nothing sharp, nothing hard, nothing breakable; where there were no drapery cords and no access to electrical outlets. There were just a few beanbag chairs and some large, well-used floor pillows.

Emma was pale. Her pupils were hugely dilated. Prescription meds, I supposed. For the first time ever, we were awkward with each other. We plopped down on the pillows and simply held hands for a while. And then Em dragged her pillow closer to mine and curled up with her head on my lap. I stroked her hair and told her how much I love her, how much I believe in her.

She looked up at me and said, "Do you, Gramma? Do you really?"

"Oh, Emma, I do."

She sighed. Her voice was nearly inaudible. "I'm always disappointing people, Gramma. I try and try and I just can't get it right. I don't fit in anywhere. I don't. And I'm just so tired." Then she began to cry.

I wrapped my arms around her.

"I hope you're not disappointed in me, Gramma," she said softly.

There are moments in life when choice of words seems especially important. "Oh, honey," I said. "I'm not disappointed in you. I'm just sad because you're having such a hard time. They'll help you here, Emma. They know how to do that. And just so you know? I'm always, always in your corner."

"I know," she whispered. We cuddled through a long stretch of silence. When a staff member announced that visiting hours were over, Emma begged me to take her with me. I promised to come back soon.

I followed up each visit with a phone call to John. I told him in a very general way how things had gone. She seemed a little down. She seemed to have more energy. She offered to show me around the unit. She seemed angry. She showed me some of her art projects. That kind of thing. He listened attentively and thanked me for calling. I began to hope that somehow we might find our way back to each other, John and I, building on this terrible time.

Last week, John and Rosie took Emma home. I haven't heard from her since. I don't know what that means exactly. Maybe her cell phone is off limits for a while. Or maybe I'm no longer therapeutically appropriate.

I vacillate between a deep suspicion that I'm being punished because Emma asked for me and wondering if I'm being totally paranoid. I may never figure that out. The official explanation cooked up for her hospitalization is "acute mononucleosis." Is there such a thing? I don't know. What I do know is that, for now at least, my granddaughter is being held in protective custody and I don't have visitation rights.

I took a chance and e-mailed John yesterday. I said I hoped everything is OK. He wrote back to say that things are complicated but somewhat better. I guess that's good. He reminded me that I'm forbidden to share what I know about Emma's situation with anyone. And so it seems I'm sucked into the secrecy, even as I'm kept at a remove. I'm trying to be patient, but I long for Emma, for Gracie. I worry about my son and even about his wife. I've thought about trying to reach out to Rosie, but that seems futile. There's nothing for me to say or do, no way to *be* that is acceptable to her.

Emma knows where I am, though—literally, metaphorically. We have a strong bond, even when we're not together. Still, I hope she surfaces soon. I suspect she needs all the love and reassurance she can get. How long should I wait for her to get in touch? There are no rules for this. And then it comes to me. What the hell? I might as well be hanged for a sheep as a lamb. I pull out my cell phone.

"Em, RUOK? Howz yr day lookin ;-) luv, Gma."

The Road to Imperfection

JUDITH GUEST

Back when I first got pregnant, the health bible I was given began with these words: "A *married* woman knows she's pregnant when . . ." Uh-huh. And who informs the rest of us? Such myths of maternalism notwithstanding, I made up my mind early on that I would be the world's perfect mother. Of course, that idea went out the window the first day we brought the baby home and our friends came to visit, lighting cigars and blowing smoke rings toward the crib, toasting the little tyke with their beers. *Here's to the frog! Here's to George Raft!* And what of the little tyke's mom? Did she rush to his rescue, shielding him from the sins of the world? No, she stood there, smoking and drinking right along with the rest. It could only go downhill from there.

Nevertheless, when I became a grandmother I was certain I could master perfection this time around. After all, I had learned a lot in the preceding twenty-five years; and, I had *had* the perfect grandmother—my father's mother, a formidable woman, the quintessential matriarch. Married at twenty, she was five times a mother, then became a widow at twenty-nine. Left with no money and few job skills, she sold greeting cards and did telephone research until she eventually landed a position as a caseworker with the Detroit welfare department. She never remarried; she'd had the love of her life, she told us. Her sister, Jean, a PBX operator, moved in with her. By day Jean ran the switchboard at a local paper company; by night she was a second mother to her nieces and nephews. Together these two raised the five children and survived the Great Depression.

Grandma Margaret's kids, the eldest of whom was my father, worshipped her. We cousins, children of her children, grew up like brothers and sisters, spending each Sunday after church at her house. I was the oldest by four years and the pick of the litter, in my opinion—the ones who came after me were mere interlopers. Aunt Jean was the nurturer and cookie baker, but Grandma Margaret was made of sterner stuff. Still, I can remember only one time in my life when she disappointed me, taking me aside to scold me about being too "bossy" with my cousin Julie. Then she told me to quit hogging all the best costumes in the dress-up trunk. I was shocked. I was her favorite, for goodness sake! What was she up to, pointing out my flaws and telling me to shape up?

Years later, when our three sons and their wives started having babies—eventually seven in all, four girls and three boys—I knew my calling. I would best Grandma Margaret's efforts and achieve absolute perfection. I would be what she had been for me—storyteller, confidante, cheerleader—and more. Catch me dead if I ever raised my voice or criticized; that's what parents were for. My job was simply to gaze, praise, and be amazed.

For years it was a snap. They called me Hoodie, a name that has stuck, and I called them by all manner of gooey nicknames: *angel, darling, precious, sweetheart, beautyboy, pretty-girl.* I loved everything about this job: bragging, babysitting, reading to them, taking them on outings and expeditions, teaching them to cook and play cards, buying them fancy overpriced duds. Of course there were minor problems— they whined, bossed, broke things, spilled things, squabbled, scribbled, sniveled, teased, and threw tantrums. In short, *they* weren't perfect! They often resembled a tribe of unruly midgets; however, that didn't let *me* off the hook. I had sworn to be flawless, and flawless I was—until the summer I decided to take my three oldest granddaughters to a dude ranch.

The brochure painted a picture of rhapsodic adventure: we would spend one whole glorious week currying, grooming, and getting to know our horses; taking long rides into the mountains; having cookouts with the wranglers; swimming in the river that meandered through the ranch. I borrowed a friend's RV to make the trip from Minneapolis to Colorado, and it had everything—bunks, a card table, a sink with running water, a refrigerator, even a tiny bathroom with its own shower, as well as air conditioning, a television, and a DVD player. We would travel out west in our miniature *palazzo*, and when we arrived, we'd move into our own little cabin on the ranch. We would have eleven days of nonstop fun.

"Ma, don't let 'em gang up on you," was my son's parting shot. He made the gesture of a lion tamer cracking a whip at a trio of circus cats perched on stools. I laughed. The girls were twelve, eleven, and ten. I was sixty-six. I'd been around the block a few times. I wasn't worried. We left Minneapolis early on a morning in June.

The two sisters, Priya and Lollie (aka Quibley and Bickerstein), begin at once to negotiate the rules of the road.

"First leg I ride shotgun."

"How long is the first leg?"

"Let's say till I get tired."

"Let's say thirty miles."

"*Thirty miles*! How long will that take?"

"Depends on how fast Hoodie drives."

They turn to me. "Hoodie, how fast are you driving?"

"Twenty-five," I say. At this point we are still inside their subdivision, nine blocks from home.

"How many miles have we driven?"

"One."

"How many more to go?"

"Nine hundred."

Groans from the back of the van.

"We'll stop soon," I promise. "We'll find a cool spot to eat on the way." I'd brought along the makings of our first breakfast, which I planned to cook on our cunning little stovetop in a pleasant park off the main highway. When it was time to stop, however, I discovered that we had differing views on what constituted a "cool spot."

"You mean we're *making* breakfast? We aren't going to a restaurant?"

"I hate bacon and eggs. Don't we have any cereal?"

"Hoodie, there isn't room for all of us at this table!"

"Ick, there's dog poop right outside the door!"

The ensuing 900 miles progress in a similar vein:

"Hoodie, I'm *suffocating*! This air conditioning is *lame*!"

"Priya stole all the good pillows!"

"Can we stop and get some Coke? These ones in the fridge are warm!"

"Lollie, quit touching me!"

"Isn't it my turn to sit in front yet?"

"You sat there all morning!"

"What else can we watch? These videos suck!"

"Isabel, quit singing!"

"Lollie, quit farting!"

"I can't help it!"

"You can, too! You're making yourself do it!"

After five hours of this I have turned into a person I no longer recognize. I am a banshee. I am Bette Davis in *What Ever Happened to Baby Jane?* I turn around and yell:

"Shut up! Look at the scenery! Stay away from each other! Don't talk or fart or touch each other until I tell you to!"

Shocked stillness from the back. Priya and Lollie squinch away from each other, and Isabel flounces to the floor. We travel the next thirty miles in absolute silence. I put on Brubeck and hum to myself, trying to ignore the little needles of guilt. After all, they're just kids. They're restless, maybe even homesick for their families. Who wouldn't be homesick after having been bawled out by the Wicked Witch of the West? At last, beset by remorse, I say, "Okay, guys. You can talk now if you want to."

No response. I glance in the rearview mirror; all three are sound asleep. Tranquil and relaxed—the picture of trusting innocence. When they awaken they are chipper and sweet, with no complaints and no hysteria. The peaceable kingdom. I resolve to file the day's fracas under "Scenes That Never Happened."

We arrive at Sylvandale Ranch, and for a while all is well. The girls quickly learn the basics, and surpass me in both skill and natural ability. I fall off my horse and lose my glasses. I buy a temporary pair of glasses at the drugstore and soldier on. I'm glad I didn't promise myself to become the perfect horsewoman. Meanwhile, inside our cabin things start to slide. Each day we jump out of bed and scurry around, getting ready for the morning ride. It goes like this:

"Hoodie, these boots don't fit!"

"There's no hot water left in the shower!"

"Lollie, that's not your shirt!"

"Where's my clean socks?"

"Who's been in my suitcase?"

"Somebody stole all my sugar cubes!"

"Priya, you snored in your sleep!"

"You farted in yours!"

Disaster comes in the shape of a wet bath towel. It's been lying on the floor of the bathroom since morning when, on my way out the door, I ask somebody to please pick it up. It's the first thing I see when I come in after being jounced around all day on Linda, my depressed but strangely jumpy mare. I collapse on the couch.

"Somebody pick up that towel," I say.

Nobody moves. I don't know why I single out the towel, since the rest of the place is a mess: jeans, socks, shirts, boots, hats, jackets, and miscellaneous items are draped all around, and the chaos in the bathroom is even more daunting. There are shampoos, conditioners, tubes of toothpaste, toothbrushes, body lotions, creams, oils, and various types of hair equipment—bobby pins, barrettes, dryers, brushes, and ponies—thrown about. But the sodden bath towel, wadded up in the middle of the floor, is the last straw.

"Whose towel is that?" I thunder.

Three heads turn toward me: O, *Lordy, what's she on about*

now? Three pairs of shoulders shrug and three voices answer in chorus: "Not mine."

"Amazing. Somebody just sneaked in here and threw a wet towel on our bathroom floor."

Three identical smirks. "Maybe it's yours, Hoodie," says Lollie.

"No," I snarl. "Not mine."

"Are you sure?" asks Priya. Isabel laughs.

Ignition. Liftoff. I am a banshee again, shrieking about people living like slobs and what it says about class, about *character.*

"Yes! I'm sure! And I'm sure it'll be there until hell freezes over, unless I pick it up myself!" When my voice cracks and my eyes start to water, I move into the bedroom and slam the door. On the other side of it I hear sudden scurrying, the sound of shoes being picked up and pop cans emptied, suitcases being moved, beds being made. Five minutes later, timid knocking. All done, Hoodie. Everything's cool. Let's go to dinner.

They run ahead of me down the road to the dining hall, eager to escape their crazy keeper. Later, Isabel informs me, "I didn't think grandmas were allowed to yell like that."

"They are," I say. And I laugh to show it was all in fun. But the sound rings hollow. I have blown it this time. The jig is up. I am a fake. I am so far from perfect it's ridiculous. Grandma Margaret's mild rebuke pales beside my frenzied ranting. I am the bad fairy in *Sleeping Beauty*, hurling curses at all assembled. Worse, there's no way this will ever be forgotten. Humbled, I pack up the van for the drive home. The trip back to Minneapolis is hot, slow, and sticky. The air conditioning has issued the option: watch television or stay cool—you can't do both.

"Hoodie, I need a shower."

"Fine. We'll stop in the park."

"No, I mean a *good* shower. In a motel."

"Yeah, with real beds and a television that works!"

"And a nice dinner in a restaurant!"

Unfortunately for them, I am still in charge. "We're stopping at the next campground."

We drive on in silence through South Dakota. The next campground is a dump. We stumble over the rutty roads in the rain, looking for our campsite. We find it and there's no running water. We drink warm pop and eat ham and cheese sandwiches, and then we toss on the hard couches until four a.m., when I fire up the van and we take off.

The last eight hours are gray and gloomy. Priya rides shotgun and stares moodily out the side window. The two in back are whiny and worn out. I am merely sad. It could have been a perfect time, if only I weren't so stubborn. I could have sprung for a night in a motel. They'd be clean, happy, and rested, and I'd be delivering them home in a good mood. The trip had started out like gangbusters and had ended up a fiasco. I turn on some classical music, to soothe myself. Priya reaches over to turn it off.

"Hoodie," she says. "We need to talk."

Uh-oh. Worse than I thought. Now I'm about to get a lecture from a twelve-year-old.

"Listen," she says. "We have to go out there again. And we have to go *next year*."

"Please say we can, Hoodie," Lollie chimes in from the back.

"It was the best vacation *ever*," Isabel sighs. "And now it's over!"

"Everything's *over*," Lollie states gloomily. "The whole rest of the summer is just gonna *suck*."

Voltaire knew a thing or two: The perfect *is* the enemy of the good. What does it matter that my granddaughters prefer Maroon 5 to Brubeck? Or that they double-pierce their ears, iron their hair, and text-message each other non-stop? They are Valley Girls, but they're *my* Valley Girls. And I am their loony, idealistic grandma.

Not that the need for perfection doesn't still exist in the world: in packing for vacations, for instance, so that the nuts and bolts of a trip can be easily retrieved without sorting through the entire trunk of a car. In the wrapping and storage of Christmas ornaments in separate tissue-paper squares in airtight, uncrushable containers. And, of course, in the alphabetizing of spice drawers, canned goods, medicine cabinets, and bookshelves.

The Age Thing

KATE LEHRER

"Why should I be happy about being a grandmother?" screams Shirley MacLaine when she learns that her daughter is pregnant, in the movie *Terms of Endearment*. MacLaine's rant echoed in my head when Jamie, my baby, announced proudly that she was going to have a baby. No, I didn't utter the words out loud. I behaved in a more conventional way and chanted cries of delight. I regret to confess that I did not mean a word of them. To me, grandmothers signified advanced age, devotion to one's grandchildren, selflessness. Grandmothers were wrinkled, dressed demurely, thought maturely. I was too young! Nearsighted, I hardly saw the crinkles around my eyes. Actually, there weren't yet all that many to see.

With the early death of my father, I had become an old soul weighed down with an overwhelming, sometimes morbid concern for my mother. When I married at twenty, I expanded that concern to include my husband and, eventually, my three daughters. But as they began to leave home and appeared less than eager for my continued hovering, my own excessive sense of responsibility for the care and emotional feeding of others diminished. I began to spend more time on my writing, which before had been squeezed into the corners of my life. I felt feisty, vibrant with health, filled with a sense of possibility. After all, I was still in my early forties. Maybe I'd start a new career or become a travel writer or a theater critic, go back to school, or, at the very least, read more books. No matter what I decided, a whole new life lay ahead of me as it had in my teens, and I'd begun to feel almost as carefree.

But then came Jamie's announcement and, as a premier worrier, I somehow got it into my head that I'd use up a lot of valuable time and energy simply worrying about this latest addition to our family. Never mind that the new baby would be living in London; advanced-stage worriers can worry across oceans, and I didn't want to worry anymore. I wanted to feel youthful and lighthearted.

As early as when I was in grade school, being young had been my calling card. I was the youngest in my class, which resulted in lots of good-natured teasing. My classmates regarded me as something of a "pet," a bit of a class clown, not threatening but loved. This role glossed over my ambition and drive, and served to make me popular. And though the role had far outlasted its usefulness, I still in some way clung to it. It was less a matter of vanity over my looks than believing that my appeal as a woman depended on my "youthful" personality. A lot depended on the youth factor to work the magic; and that magic in turn had become the amulet against the day invisibility would strike. I wasn't quite sure when older women were shuttled offstage, but becoming a grandmother semed to me a likely time to get the hook.

Grandmotherhood represented a crossing, as had marriage, a state I also resisted. Both passages required another step into adult responsibility—and I'd had enough responsibility as a child. So when I married young, I hedged my bets, informing my new husband that I never wanted us to own possessions. (This was my feeble attempt to embrace the freewheeling, heady 1960s, even though where we lived in Texas the stifling attitudes of the 1950s still prevailed.) Motherhood soon presented that much more of a challenge, an even larger need to readjust my internal image.

Still, dismay might have resulted whatever my age when my first grandchild arrived. My own grandmothers, who would have been my natural role models, died before I was born. I have one photograph of my mother's mother, a slender, angular woman who resembled Virginia Woolf by way of the dust bowl. A stern, sad-looking woman, married to a tyrant, she'd done what she could to help her own daughters escape the confines of home. Reading between the lines of the stories her daughters told, I sensed that she'd lost the capacity for tenderness. My father's mother, a plump, fashionable-looking woman, a lawyer and president of her own oil company, revealed nothing in her picture. She had divorced my grandfather and, according to my mother, had a rather formal relationship with my father. To be honest, neither of these women struck me as grandmotherly, and I feared I wouldn't rise to the challenge, either. If I couldn't see myself in the role, how on earth would these poor unborn grandchildren of mine ever accept me?

Besides, what were the duties of a grandmother? Should I discipline the children? Should I try to be their best friend? Could I just read to them and forget about playing games? Must I go back to feeding babies and changing their diapers?

As my daughters grew up and my oldest, alarmingly, began to entertain the possibility of marriage, I had gone so far as to inform her that her children would call me Kate. No cute or corny names for me; no elderly-sounding names either—just Kate, thank you. Kate, their close friend and confidante. A new self—someone wiser, wittier, braver, and more elegant (someone not me). My attitude toward becoming a grandmother was even vaguer and more abstract than my attitude toward motherhood had been before I had children.

Someone called Kate who is a grandchild's chum didn't seem as though she would rank on anyone's scale. That's pretty much the spirit I carried with me to London to await the birth of our first grandchild; my mind refused to go beyond it. Yet, in spite of myself, there were signs that I was changing. Without having a clue as to this future baby's gender, I had, on impulse, bought a beautiful baby doll in a long white lace dress and matching bonnet. Once in London, I couldn't buy enough in the way of clothes, crib sheets, pretty blankets. I began recalling nursery rhymes and songs. Those I could do by the hour. No baby should object to nursery rhymes, I reasoned. Meantime, Jamie, whether or not she agreed, humored me as I offered advice. She made me feel needed and swept along in her and her husband John's excitement.

By the time my husband and I were sitting outside the old wooden doors of a labor room in one of London's public hospitals listening to our daughter's sharp cries in the final throes of childbirth, nothing mattered to me except the health of Jamie and her baby. When we finally heard the baby's cry, I jumped thankfully, joyfully, and—according to my husband—a true foot off the ground. To my surprise, a grandchild, not an abstract notion, now existed. To my even greater surprise, my emotions reached a depth I'd never anticipated.

A girl, Jamie and John announced when we entered the room minutes later. A baby girl named Kate, my daughter said. A jolt of happiness ran through me. Of course, this miraculous baby— already brilliant and beautiful in her first hour of life—could not possibly call me Kate. I wouldn't dream of confusing her. Thus, I became KK—a little cute, perhaps, but it was better than Grandma and so I gladly forfeited my name to this wonderful treasure. Over the next weeks I spent hours rocking her, walking her, gazing at her while she slept. I wanted to pour into this baby not my ambitions or my dreams or even my values, but whatever spirit I possess for strength, endurance, gaiety, integrity. I wanted her to learn to enjoy the trappings of the world without buying into them. Thus I willed through osmosis the essence of myself, an idea so crazy I've never before articulated it. In some mystical way, I believe grandparents and grandchildren can leap ordinary boundaries without words.

Nineteen months later, Jamie and John had Luke, their first son, our first grandson, and I found the earlier miracle repeating itself. The rush of emotion began again, yet this time I took comfort in knowing that the ties between grandparents and grandchildren do not bind with the same kinds of complicated knots and tangles as the ties between parents and children. I embraced my role as KK and walked this colicky baby for hours. I sang to him and marveled at his gender. A boy! My family had a boy! Not only did the fact of him amaze me; Luke himself did. He felt like a foreign creature. He had so many more folds than girls! Just changing his diaper was different, requiring anticipation.

Three days after he was born, however, my antipathy to grandmotherhood returned.

Jamie—earth mother extraordinaire and casualness personified (could this be my daughter?)—had the entire family, including three-day-old Luke, attend a birthday party for a friend of hers. Apparently, every woman in Britain with a grandchild is referred to as *granny*—as in, "You sure look like a proud granny!" and "What a great granny you are!" The last time I'd heard the word *granny* was as a little girl when everyone called a neighbor Granny Waddle, and she pretty much fit the description—a little old lady with gray hair, tightly curled; a shapeless dress and body; and granny glasses. Unlike more dignified *grandmothers*, grannies are born sexless with little round angelic faces that beam unless they're scolding.

Fortunately, before this birthday party no one had ever used the term to refer to me. But though I wasn't much older than some of the guests, then and there I was dubbed *Granny*. It was as if I aged decades on the spot. Standing there, I felt my vitality seeping away as I assumed insignificance. Soon I'd have to dye my hair and become stately—or worse—simply to be noticed. My grandbabies in tow, I began smiling as I imagined a granny would smile, until I could escape upstairs to the nursery.

Our hosts had thoughtfully provided a nanny for the little ones, so I, clutching Luke and squeezing Kate's hand, found the children and a couple of other nannies, in addition to the house nanny. To shake this new image of myself—as I say, far worse than that of grandmother—I remained there watching Kate play and holding steadfastly to Luke.

Fairly soon, a toddler's father appeared, slightly older than most of the other parents. Ostensibly he'd come to see about his son. As it turned out, he'd seen our group arrive and had thought I was a babysitter for his good friends Jamie and John.

"Have you been here long?" he asked.

"Not long," I said.

"Do you get a chance to get out on your own very often?"

"Not really," I replied.

"Too bad. We'll have to remedy that."

He continued to linger, paying no attention to his little boy. Although still struggling with the new post-matron version of myself, I eventually realized that he was flirting. I clung even more fiercely to Luke, who suddenly became my shield. Under other circumstances, the man's attentions might have flattered me, quite possibly encouraged me to think that maybe I looked only my age—fortyish—after all. A harmless younger man's attentions should be good for morale. But in this case, the younger man had a small child in the room and downstairs a pretty wife. His flirtatiousness began to border on the obnoxious, provoking in me the righteous sensation of wanting to strangle the jerk.

"And how did Jamie and John go about finding you?" he finally asked, not too subtly.

"Oh, I found them. It wasn't hard." I paused, hesitating, then flashed him the most cherubic, knowing smile that ever a granny did. "I'm Jamie's mother. I'm Kate and Luke's *grandmother*," I said, with great emphasis on the last word.

He had the grace to blush while backing out of the room without ever once looking at his son, who didn't seem the least bit interested in him, either.

The granny-nanny kept her mouth shut about the incident, but never again did she resist her rightful role. Maternal instincts, my need to nurture, came as naturally to me as breathing—and indeed they were fresh breath itself. Yet until that moment I couldn't go farther. Although I bragged like a grandmother, loved like a grandmother, took care of the children like a grandmother, I had not claimed the title. For the first time, I basked in it. I finally and officially had branded myself.

When Jamie had Ian—a home birth this time!—I proudly assumed my role.

Several years later, my daughter Amanda and her husband, Lew, presented us with Malcolm, then James, and then Olivia, and my response remained the same—each birth was a miracle, each child a treasure. And each time I get that stomach-flipping feeling, that glorious elixir of giddiness and promise—without worrying about my age.

When I began my journey with this younger generation, I told myself I had no role models, but that wasn't so. I had my own mother. Why couldn't I have seen that sooner? Although we grappled with mother-daughter problems, she made a splendid grandmother. She disciplined the children, scolded them, expected a high standard of behavior, and, when necessary, backed off. She also spoiled them, enjoyed them, relaxed the rules she'd applied to me, and believed in her grandchildren with all her heart. And they loved her! A career woman not given to hand-wringing, my mother certainly didn't agonize over this role; nor did she fit any grandmotherly image I'd conjured in my mind, most assuredly not that of a *granny*.

I dream myself into a new way of being a grandmother. Age stays on the periphery, having less to do with years than with my sense of self as a regenerative spirit in my grandchildren's lives, as they are in mine. Instead of limiting my discovery of a newfound sense of freedom from the everyday emotional and physical responsibility for my family, I have forged a shared purpose with my daughters, including my daughter Lucy, who does not have children herself but is deeply involved with her nieces and nephews. What's more, as a grandmother I find that my life has expanded exponentially, exposing me to younger voices and younger ways of thinking, often far removed from my own.

I have much to share with my grandchildren as well, for they have access to my acquired, often hard-earned experience, as well as the pleasure, passions, and pain that accrue over many years. At one step removed, the force of this repository of lessons isn't as overwhelming to them as the experience of their parents. I don't mean I lecture or even try to set a good example; but I do show them a life lived in abundance with its losses, mistakes, timid falterings, blatant excesses, and modest triumphs.

I confess, I am still KK to my grandchildren, and on awfully good hair days when I'm shopping with Kate and a salesperson compliments me on my beautiful young daughter, Kate and I exchange smiles and I say, "Thank you." After all, a little vanity has its place. It's too bad that when Jamie announced her first pregnancy, I hadn't recalled another scene from *Terms of Endearment*, the one where Jack Nicholson, as the playboy astronaut who is MacLaine's next-door neighbor, starts to put the moves on MacLaine, who suddenly throws her arms around his neck. He looks startled. She reminds him she's a grandmother. She knows what she's doing.

How Things Happen

SALLIE TISDALE

Two of my three children are adopted; both were born in Guatemala. Annie, my youngest, was just a toddler when she came to us. But Rafael, who is deaf, was about nine years old. He was born into a civil war, and in his short life he had lost his entire family, one by one. We brought him home, bought him the clothes and shoes and books he'd never had, and enrolled him in school for the first time. After a year, he transferred to the state school for the deaf about fifty miles from our house.

Wounds don't always heal. He was so glad to be adopted, but the gladness lasted only a few weeks. We were a disappointment: we were not permissive; we did not live in a big house or drive a fancy car. He had to share a room with his brother, and do chores and homework and go to bed on time. At Christmastime, the wonderful packages always ran out sooner or later, and when there were no more gifts to open, he would sit in a corner and weep.

I apologize for the litany of names—there are so many names in this story—but in a way, the litany *is* the story.

Here's how it goes. At twenty-one, with a high school diploma, Rafael moves out of the school for the deaf, and knocks around for a while—doing odd jobs, hanging out with friends. He has a volatile temper. He quits a few jobs in anger, and is fired from a few others. In between, he lives on SSI—disability payments—and plays basketball and watches TV.

I am relieved when he meets Corina at a party. He is twenty-three; she is twenty-one. She is living with her daughter, Jordyn, in family housing while she attends community college. Soon he moves into their two-bedroom apartment. Corina begins learning ASL, and Rafael signs up for a couple of classes. She is quiet, and I find it hard to get to know her. Jordyn, at four, is wild and undisciplined. But Rafael seems content for the first time. "My family," he likes to say. "This is my family."

A few months later, Corina gets pregnant and they both drop out of school.

I am not happy about this. It has nothing to do with becoming a grandmother, and everything to do with timing. They are so young; they barely know each other. They are not ready to take on adult commitment, let alone another child, for the long haul. They will need a lot of help. I have been rearing children for more than twenty-five years, for my entire adult life, and I am ready to be done with it.

Everyone deserves a chance. I was once a young, single mother struggling with a baby, a job, and college. My mother was so disappointed with me, so worried about me. She sent me money; I took food stamps and found good child care and subsidized housing. I stayed in school and never needed to ask her for money again.

So they get a chance, too. By the time Austin is born, they are living on cobbled-together government support: Temporary Assistance to Needy Families, the monthly check most people think of when they hear the word *welfare*, along with food stamps, Section 8 housing, and Rafael's SSI. I try to learn the intricate steps of new grandparents—the dance between helping and minding my own business.

Austin seems healthy, and Jordyn races through our house out of control, knocking over chairs. Though things settle down, Rafael and Corina sometimes fight in their small apartment. Once, he calls from a friend's house where he is sleeping on the couch for a few days. "She kicked me out," he says. "But I'm going back."

Five months after Austin is born, Rafael calls to say he has news. Corina is pregnant again.

I am angry this time. They are living on subsidies in a small apartment. Corina is not in school; Rafael is out of work.

I take Corina, Austin, and Jordyn out to lunch at the local mall. I buy Jordyn a pair of shoes and we wander for a while through the cornucopia of things that neither of us can really afford and no one really needs.

"Do you want to be pregnant?" I ask Corina. "Do you need help to end this pregnancy? Because I will help you. I will even pay for it, and you can get back into school."

"No," she says. "No, I don't believe in abortion."

I can tell that she has thought about it. She is weary and looks a lot older than she did a year before. She seems a little surprised at where life has taken her. She sighs. "I don't know, things just happen to me," she says. "I just hadn't thought it would happen like this."

I look at Austin, this unexpected child, here too soon. He is chewing thoughtfully on a crayon. His straight black hair sticks up every which way, and when I take the crayon away he stares at me in frank astonishment. Then he reaches his arms up toward me with a soft, amiable smile. I reach back, and it is like leaning into a knife. I don't want to love him, this little boy who may not be in my life a few years from now, whose mother I don't really know. But here he is.

They share a strange unworldliness. There are no books in the apartment, no magazines. They don't like to read. Corina does not know how to drive—she says that driving scares her. Rafael buys a used car. I don't ask him how he can afford it.

When our granddaughter, Taylor, is born, I sink into a dispirited silence for days, unable to celebrate this birth. It seems to be the birth of a cycle of poverty, a future of small apartments and dead-end jobs. Rafael stays home with the children. Corina finally starts school again. My husband slips them twenty-dollar bills. I bring disappointing, grand-motherly presents: pajamas, shoes, books.

I babysit Taylor for an afternoon. I hold her, sleeping, against my shoulder, and a war erupts. *No. Not this one, not this one more.* The scent of her scalp is pheromonal, irresistible. *No, not another one*: my resistance is battling something very old, something ancient, wrapping its warmth around me.

When Taylor is three months old, Rafael calls to tell us that Corina is pregnant again.

I put down the phone and pace around the kitchen for a few minutes. I don't even feel surprised. But then I start to cry, and then to shout—at the ceiling, at some distant god. At them.

Things just happen.

They ask us to lend them $500 for a deposit on a duplex for rent nearby. I call my friend Jill, who works at the housing authority. Jill often cares for her own grandchildren, to help her own troubled daughter. "You have to accept this, so you can help them," she says to me one day. "They just need so much help."

I start learning about the systems in which their lives are entangled. I call the agencies, visit the Web sites, wait on hold until I am cut off. Welfare begins to seem like a prize awarded to the worthy few who can figure out how to apply for it. They are sober. The kids are clean and fed. Is this enough? Can I really ask for more? What do I owe my unexpected, fragile grandbabies? Their parents?

I finally agree to the loan, but insist that Rafael sign a contract to pay it back at ten dollars a month.

A week after they move, Rafael calls to say they've run out of food stamps. So we drive down. The duplex is mostly clean. The kids run around our legs. But the curtains are closed, to keep the sun off the television they've just bought with the new Sears card Rafael shows me. Rather than barren, their new home is crowded, crammed with things— a new couch, a coffeemaker, crappy plastic toys, a shelf full of videos, all bought on credit they don't have.

There is plenty of food in the house—it may be all TV dinners, Pepsi, and Rice-A-Roni, but they aren't going hungry. Corina, her big belly leading her across the room, shows me her shopping list, the one that can't wait: *baby wipes, BBQ stuff, paper plates.*

I remember how tired I was when I was a young mother,

how tired I still can be—how easy it is to settle for less. Jill is right, of course—they need so much. They need everything. They need to learn.

So I take a deep breath and talk—I am patient and quiet, but I talk for a long time. I talk about budgets and bills. I talk about secondhand clothes and beans and taking the bus. I talk about how things were for us when Rafael was young, when we bought secondhand clothes and ate beans and took the bus.

I write down a recipe for a cheap casserole.

Then I talk about vasectomies and birth control. I talk about going back to school. I am talking about getting used to things, doing without, looking ahead. I am talking about acceptance and responsibility. Then we go to the store and I buy vegetables, fruit, and milk.

The world is divided into haves and have-nots. It is easy to forget that one definition of *welfare* is "good fortune, health, happiness, prosperity, well-being." The crucial line is education—knowledge and imagination, the vast safety net of opportunity. We are wholeheartedly haves in this way. They are precariously balanced on a thin wire above a tiny safety net torn in two—easy dupes for predatory creditors, victims of their own hungers. They are, I fear, forever have-nots.

An overdue bill goes to a collection agency. Their phone is restricted. One day their electricity is cut off. Their checking account is overdrawn, and the unstoppable fees begin to pile up. Rafael calls and asks for new shoes. He calls and asks for coats for the children. He sends us ten dollars toward the loan, one time, and never again. He calls and asks us to buy him a cell phone, and pay the league fee so he can play basketball. And every time we have the same conversation:

Get rid of the car and ride the bus. Make a budget. Pay us back the loan. Cook from scratch instead of ordering a pizza. Shop at Goodwill instead of Sears. Pare down. Pare down a life already pared down.

Their days go on and on, at once tedious and frightening. I feel stuffed with opinion and worry, with love and sorrow. I cut visits short or find reasons not to go at all. I refuse to send them any money, no matter what the reason may be, until they try to pay back the loan.

When she is born a month early, Kaylee has to spend a few days in the intensive care unit. In a fog of detachment, I put on a gown and mask and stand by her incubator, holding her. She is as small and quiet as a loaf of pound cake under the warming lights. She has the same silky black hair, the same olive skin as her brother and sister—as her father.

Later, I find Corina's nurse in the hallway.

"Please talk to her about birth control before she leaves," I ask. "She might listen to you."

She nods politely, but then says, "That's not our policy."

Everyone asks me about their birth control—an intrusively rude question, and yet someone has to ask. They have no real privacy. The impersonal representatives of the government ask, and everyone from my brother to the next-door neighbors asks about birth control. I am surprised that people assume they don't know about it. The central problem with birth control is that those people least equipped to be parents are also least equipped to avoid pregnancy. They know how to use birth control. They just, obviously, don't use it very well.

One day they all drive up to our house to ask for help with some "paperwork" they don't understand. Rafael hands me a long contract in very fine print. It turns out that he bought their car—a nicer, bigger, newer car than my own— after seeing a commercial for a "no-down-payment" loan. He had no idea what he was signing, and they are paying 30 percent interest to a faceless company of usurers. When I ask why he didn't ask for help first, he reminds me that everyone is always telling them to grow up and take care of themselves.

I don't mention the money he owes me.

We come up with a plan. If Rafael will get a vasectomy, we will help them trade in this car and buy a used van. No more payments. It will cost us some real money, just this once, but it looks to me like solving two problems for good. We find an old van in decent shape, we hand over a few thousand dollars, and Rafael goes to the doctor.

Six months later, he trades in the van for a newer car, on time.

I suspect this is one way conservatives are made—by meeting the sticky imperfection of people, by knowing better, by the vague threat of these unfinished lives. None of us want to be merely lucky. We want to be right.

Corina told me once that what she most wants is a house, a real house. With Kaylee, they qualify for a subsidized house—a four-bedroom house with a fenced yard in a cul-de-sac, with new carpeting, new appliances, big windows, lots of room to play. Jordyn has her own room. Austin has his own room. They ride their tricycles, our Christmas presents, around and around the driveway.

Kaylee is slow to walk and slow to talk. She sits beside me on the couch and watches me silently, her entire fist jammed into her mouth. Then she sighs and lays her head in my lap.

Rafael and Corina get into a big fight and separate. Rafael is sleeping in someone's back room; I don't know where he is most of the time. Now they no longer qualify for the house, and Corina and the four children are evicted. They find an apartment in a big complex near the freeway—a place not unlike the one where she had been living when she met Rafael.

Corina begins seeing Rafael's friend Tyson. One day Rafael calls to tell us that she is pregnant again, by Tyson.

"I will take care of this baby," he tells us. "I love this baby." This is such a brave and stupid thing to say that it breaks my heart. And I don't know what to tell him, I don't have any idea at all.

The apartment is not so clean anymore. Corina has a difficult pregnancy; she is often asleep when we visit. The baby arrives, and he is small and quiet. He lies in a car seat parked beside the couch, where Tyson folds laundry and watches television. And to my great surprise, I feel liberated. This is now so far over the top, so far beyond reasonable, that I am freed from my own persistent reasonableness. Enough.

Enough.

We visit every month, and sometimes bring the children home for the night. Taylor has secretive eyes and is good at hatching plans for games and projects. Kaylee is strong and round and mad about blowing bubbles. Austin is a sad little boy, I think—a puzzled boy, in his seventh year of chaos. But when he comes to our house, he plays basketball with great concentration, his tongue between his teeth. Jordyn is whippet thin, wary, but she always wants to come, too.

Corina is pregnant again.

I have my theories about it all, about how mistakes made often enough are simply choices, about insecurity and the way people try to bind themselves together. But I am a bit past theory now. I love the children in that same feral, painfully delicious way I loved my own children. I drive to the apartment, nod politely, take their hands, and head out the door.

The Rivals

JUDITH VIORST

So I'm at this New Year's Day party listening to my friend Ellen, who is telling me about her excursions to art museums with her barely seven-year-old granddaughter Carol. I am already feeling inadequate because none of my grandchildren has expressed much (actually, any) interest in going to an art museum, whereas Carol actively wants to. Furthermore, she walks into the Phillips Gallery and immediately asks where the Rothkos are because, as she explains to her grandmother, she likes Rothko's colors.

Carol then moves on to a Degas, noting that this painter did a lot with ballet dancers and, after careful scrutiny, she points out to her grandmother—in case she hadn't noticed—that this is a picture of ballerinas engaged in their daily practice at the barre. As Carol continues her museum tour, comparing and contrasting artists (I have repressed her brilliant insights in this matter), offering observations about perspective ("Showing that little person in the corner of the painting helps you see how huge the landscape is"), and suggesting that the name of Pollock's dripped *Collage and Oil* ought to be changed to the more appropriate "Mishmash," a couple of guards are following her around, astonished and enchanted by the running commentary of this pint-size art critic.

I, too, am astonished, and maybe even enchanted. But what I'm mostly feeling is—competitive.

This is not a nice emotion to experience on day one of my annual resolution to improve not only my body but also my character. A better person than I would surely eschew such competitive feelings. But I don't. Nor do most of the grandmothers I know.

We compete with our grandparent friends. We compete with our grandchildren's other sets of grandparents. And sometimes we compete with the very grandparent with whom we are sharing a bed—our own husband.

Even if we are known, in other matters, to be basically modest and diffident, and even if, as mothers, we refrained from shamelessly bragging about our kids, we grandmothers feel entitled to inform the immediate world that our grandsons and our granddaughters are not merely extraordinary but the most extraordinary. And if another grandmother is one-upping us in this contest, we may one-up right back.

I, for instance, wasn't able to counter Ellen's enviable report with my own Smartest in Art story, but with a deft segue I swiftly shifted the category to Most Profound Grandchild, recalling the morning that Olivia and her cousin Nathaniel were playing word games together. Nathaniel had proudly printed his version of the short form of *telephone*, FONE, on a piece of paper, and when Olivia crossed it out and wrote down PHONE, he was quite cranky, insisting that her weird spelling didn't look right, couldn't be right, had to be wrong. Olivia, four months older than Nathaniel, listened to him holler for a while and then declaimed, from her vastly superior fund of life experience, "Nathaniel, in this world things aren't always what they seem."

I rest my case.

Actually, I didn't rest my case but went on with several more stories about Olivia to nail down the categories of Sweetest, Funniest, Most Courageous, and Most Original, the last of which I sidestepped into by innocently asking Ellen if she had received any gifts from her grandchildren for Hanukkah. As a matter of fact she had, although I can't recall what they were because I was too busy preparing to tell her about mine, which I introduced by unabashedly stating, "I swear this belongs in the *Guinness Book of Records.*"

Could the gift itself live up to such a flamboyant introduction? You bet. For what Olivia had given to me, made with her own little hands, was a multicolored scarf and matching pot holders!

Perfect for those chilly days in the kitchen.

And Most Original, surely you would agree.

I could tell you 100 equally enchanting, brilliant, hilarious and most original stories about my grandchildren, but the editor of this book feels I am taking advantage of the pages allotted to me to *engage* in competitive grandmothering rather than to *discuss* competitive grandmothering. I have therefore agreed to restrain myself, and in return she is letting me tell just one more: about this Most Adorable, as well as hilarious, moment at the movie theater when my three-year-old grandson Benjamin, watching a showing of *Alvin and the Chipmunks*, loudly asked his mom, "Are chipmunks Jewish?"

(The answer is no because if chipmunks were Jewish, each and every one of them would be having orthodontia for buckteeth.)

Sometimes, I must admit, I am reduced to silence by bragging, competitive grandmas, whose claims for their grandchildren strike me as—well, I won't call them outright lies, but hard to believe. Reading at eighteen months? Give me a break! Enjoying raw oysters at two? Who is she kidding! Still, one of these grandmothers swore on everything holy that her grandson, four years old, asked her—on Martin Luther King Jr.'s last birthday—to celebrate the occasion by reciting a few lines from King's "I Have a Dream" speech.

I'm granting that kid top honors in the Most Civic-Minded category and consoling myself with the thought that you can't win them all.

I am, however, still hoping to win in the Most Adored Grandmother category, though I'm finding it hard to one-up my friend Irene, who tells me that her grandchildren, little Leo and little Mattie, stand sobbing by the door at the end of her visits, pleading with her as she heads for the airport, "Don't go. Don't go."

(I, too, could claim that tears have been shed when I've said good-bye in Denver to my Colorado grandchildren, Bryce and Miranda. But then I'd have to acknowledge that the tears that are being shed aren't theirs—they're mine.)

Competition for Most Adored Grandmother seriously heats up when the grandmothers are competing for the same grandchildren, when the mother-in-law of our daughter or son, our grandchildren's *other* granny, stakes her legitimate claim on their affections. Yes, fond though we may be of this other woman, and glad though we may be that she loves our grandchildren, and resigned though we may be to the fact that our grandchildren love her back, we are hoping that our grandchildren love us more. A whole lot more.

Now, it's embarrassing to reveal such unworthy, ungenerous feelings. It's embarrassing to be so petty, so small. It's embarrassing to find ourselves responding like teenage girls in a popularity contest. It's embarrassing to be secretly assessing the assets of our competition. And yet, we're assessing.

This granny always buys them lavish presents. That granny picks them up twice a week after school. This granny lives a short drive away from a ski slope, from a water park, from Disney World. That granny has a private swimming pool. This granny sits for hours with them doing puzzles and playing pick-up sticks and checkers. That granny has purple-streaked hair and is really cool. This granny takes them ice-skating and sledding and she brings them home-baked brownies. "So how was your weekend with your [glamorous, cool, ice-skating] grandma?" I asked Olivia. "Awesome!" was her exuberant reply. "Except when it was Sunday and she had to go back to Michigan," she added. I decided not to ask if that made her cry. I also didn't ask if she ever says that the time she spends with me is "awesome."

I'm giving some thought, however, to taking up ice-skating.

I also gave some wicked thought to competing with Nathaniel and Benjamin's "grammy," a beautiful, warmhearted woman who presents our shared grandsons, whenever they get together, with lovingly assembled "goodie bags." These gift bags, grammy's specialty, are filled with little treats guaranteed to make a boy's heart sing—chocolates, lollipops, crayons, a Matchbox car, an action figure, a movie video. The boys adore their goodie bags, put together with so much care, and, needless to say, they also adore their grammy. Hmmm.

Last year, after hearing how Benjamin and Nathaniel hugged, kissed, and thanked their beloved grammy as they checked out the treasures she'd tucked into their bags, I said to myself, "I could make goodie bags, too." Fortunately, I then chastised myself—my better nature having finally been mobilized. "Oh, no, you couldn't, Judy. Shame on you!"

Great economic disparities can make it almost impossible for a grandmother to compete in the giving of goodies, especially if the competition is able to offer the grandchildren tennis courts and sailboats, trips to Europe, Caribbean cruises, or weekends at a horse farm in Montana. "And if, in addition," one grandmother said, "they're very nice people and wonderful with the grandkids, you're really screwed."

Another great—perhaps greater—advantage for the competing grandmother is living in the same city as our grandchildren and having enough free time to be as available to them as we (and their parents) would like us to be. Taking them to the dentist, a movie, piano lessons. Taking them to the playground or the zoo. Having a sleepover date or an every Wednesday after-school date or a Saturday "adventure" from ten till two. What can a faraway grandmother possibly do, one faraway grandmother wistfully wonders, "to count, connect, make my mark on them, be remembered?"

Two qualifiers. Sometimes the out-of-town grandmother, swooping in for a weekend or a week, brings a special luster to the time she spends with the children that their everyday in-town grandma can't replicate. (See: Olivia, Michigan grandmother, and "awesome.") And sometimes the out-of-town grandmother's sense of competitive disadvantage isn't because she's living far away, but because she is the mother of her grandchildren's *father* rather than of their mother.

One such paternal grandmother notes that though Bonnie, her daughter-in-law, seems to love and respect her, she has never once turned to her for advice about child care. "I've been in Bonnie's house," she says, "when the baby had terrible diaper rash, and I know about diaper rash. But instead of asking me what to do when her baby was screaming in pain and I'm standing right there, she went to her computer and e-mailed her mother!" This mother, she adds, has no particular expertise in diaper rash, or the other matters about which Bonnie consults her. "But there's a level of safety and trust in that relationship," she says, sighing, "that I will never be able to compete with."

A mother of three grown daughters agrees, observing, "My daughters share a lot more with me than their husbands ever do with their own moms. So yes, I guess I'm competitive, but I've never questioned my status as 'first grandmother.'"

In competitions over the same grandchildren, the maternal grandmother often winds up ahead, perhaps because the relationship between mothers and their grown daughters remains more intimate and more emotionally entangled than the relationship between mothers and their grown sons. It's usually the maternal grandmother, not the paternal grandmother, who flies in, stays over, helps out when a grandchild is born, establishing early on—if all goes well, or well enough—a benevolent and welcomed grandmotherly presence. She probably also feels freer than the mother of a son to make herself at home in her daughter's household, and freer as well to ask her daughter all kinds of nosy questions and offer all kinds of pesky parental advice. Sometimes she becomes an important part of the parenting process, in touch with her daughter once, twice, three times a day. And sometimes she may get carried away and think of herself as her grandchild's only *real* grandmother.

A friend of mine complains that whenever she takes her son's children, her grandsons, on an outing, she gets a thank-you note from the other grandmother, full of appreciation for the time she has spent with the boys and the services she has rendered to the family. Though these thank-you notes are gracious, oh so gracious, they leave my friend feeling peeved and patronized. For the way this woman competes, she says, "is to treat me as if I'm some sort of helpful assistant rather than someone who's on a par with her."

But competing with other grandmothers over which of our grandchildren is the Most Extraordinary and competing with them for the title of Most Adored do not exhaust our competitive activities. For as I've already observed, we may sometimes also compete with our husband—our grandchildren's grandfather.

Readers may have noticed that grandfathers haven't been given much ink in this discussion. This is not to suggest by any means that they aren't on the scene, playing meaningful roles in their grandchildren's lives. But I'm talking about competition, and compared with their wives, far fewer of these grandfathers seem to engage in competitive conversations about their grandchildren's accomplishments. Nor, from what I've observed, are as many grandfathers taking careful, competitive note of which grandparent—the grandfather or his wife—is being regarded as Most Important by their grandchildren. But even when a grandfather is aware that his wife is considered Most Important, he seems able to acknowledge this without feeling hurt, disregarded, or left out. We grandmothers, on the other hand, should the decision go the other way, would most certainly feel hurt—and disregarded, and left out.

"If my husband and my grandchildren are in the basement and I'm hearing too much giggling," one grandmother confesses with some embarrassment, "I'll stop whatever I'm doing and go down and join them. I don't want them being *that* happy if I'm not around."

I don't think I need to say that all these grandmothers I've been talking with love their grandchildren and love being grandmothers. Of course they do. I don't think I need to say that they—that we—despite our competitiveness are usually, and in most ways, decent people. Of course we are. And I don't think I need to say that all of us wish that we were far too secure and mature to allow ourselves to indulge in competitive grandmothering. But we're not. I'm certainly not. And since there's a little space remaining, and if my competitive grandmother editor doesn't stop me, I've got one last story to tell, this Most Incredible grandchild story about the time Olivia . . .

PART III

What Counts

Our whole business in this life is to restore to health
the eye of the heart whereby God may be seen.

—SAINT AUGUSTINE

Eye of My Heart

BARBARA GRAHAM

Two o'clock on a Monday afternoon. I'm on deadline for a magazine article, but instead of focusing on the story I check my e-mail each time I manage to grind out a sentence. Then I stare at the phone for a while, as if my dirty looks will somehow shame it into ringing. But nobody's calling, and the only e-mails coming through on this sticky August day are from the VitaminShoppe and somebody called Magicklady who wants to read my tarot cards. I feel like I'm back in high school waiting to hear from The Guy—desperate, distracted, a hopeless and pathetic love slave longing for a sign.

But this time the object of my devotion, my latest heartthrob, isn't some dark-eyed bad boy; it's my baby granddaughter, Isabelle Eva. And the guy I'm dying to hear from is her father, my son and only child, Clay.

I am fifty-eight years old. I've been a grandmother for twelve days. I'm stunned by the swell of feeling: not the love part, which I expected, but the urgency, the hunger to hold Isabelle, to feel her body—her spine and ribs as delicate as twigs, her heartbeat as fluttery as a hummingbird's—next to mine. This is love beyond reason and I'm fuzzy on protocol. I don't know yet where I belong in the new order. In fact, no one seems to know how the pieces of the expanded family puzzle fit together—neither Clay nor Tamar, his wife and Isabelle's mother; not Hugh, my husband and the baby's step-grandfather; not the rest of the grandparents. We're as clueless as a bunch of earthlings who go to sleep in their own beds and wake up on the moon.

One thing is certain—we've entered a new phase. First there was the initial burst of worry over the birth (an eleventh-hour C-section) and the health of mother and baby (perfect). This quickly gave way to awe—heart-stopping breathless wonder. One moment she wasn't; then, suddenly, she *was*. Isabelle Eva. This impossibly fragile yet lusty creature who is blood of my blood and more than my blood. Her parents have been generous in sharing her: Hugh and I each got to hold her soon after she was born and often in the days that followed. My role then—which now seems like the remote past—was clear. I was backup, part of the support team of grandparents on call during the days and hours leading up to and following Isabelle's birth. And since I'm the only grandmother who lives in the same city—Washington, D.C.—as the new parents, I also took on the role of chief caterer. Ours is a food-obsessed family that prizes—no, actually demands—good cooking, even in the most extreme situations. While Tamar struggled through a difficult labor, Clay, a food photographer, *required* a pizza margherita from 2 Amys—the best in town—almost as much as his wife needed an epidural. Still, after two weeks of running between Whole Foods and the farmers' market to procure the freshest seasonal ingredients, then whipping up one culinary triumph after another and delivering them to Clay and Tamar, I need to get out of the kitchen. And since my motives haven't been entirely pure, it's time to find out how

I fit in when I'm not playing top chef in order to gain cheap access to Isabelle.

Even more important, Clay and Tamar need room to find their own way. Today is the first full day they've had to spend alone with the baby. Gale and Ken, Tamar's parents, flew home to San Francisco yesterday. A few days before they left, Clay whispered to me over the phone: "It's nice to have grandparents around, but we're ready to be on our own with our baby." Though ostensibly he was referring to Gale and Ken, I knew his comments were directed at me. *Our baby—not yours.*

It strikes me that not only was a new baby born twelve days ago, but a new family was born as well: *their* family—to which I am powerfully linked but not a member of the inner circle. No doubt I should have seen this coming. The transition from childless couple to family of three has solidified them as a separate unit in a way that marriage alone did not—at least, that's how it feels to me now. In the eight years since Clay and Tamar married—and the ten years they were together (mostly) before that, from age sixteen—my exceptionally deep bond with my son has stretched yet remained strong. I've been lucky. Tamar, unlike some daughters-in-law, has accepted me with grace. But this new chapter, though natural and appropriate, feels different. What shocks me the most is that in the midst of my joy over the birth of my granddaughter, faint traces of loss waft in and out of my consciousness like secondhand smoke.

I wonder if I would feel the same way if I were the mother of the new mother instead of the mother of the new father. Would I be granted easier access to the inner circle? As it is, Tamar seems less threatened by me than Clay does by

Tamar. During one of our bountiful suppers, he quietly confided to me his sadness that he's unable to comfort the baby the way Tamar—with her free-flowing supply of breast milk in a body that is Isabelle's home port—can. My poor darling: even he, like all new fathers, is kept by nature from entering the innermost inner circle.

So when Hugh tells me to pay attention to what Clay is saying and "dial it back," I know he's right. Besides, viewed through a wider lens, I'm incredibly fortunate: Clay and Tamar decided (with no prompting from me, I swear) to move from Paris to Washington in order to live near us when the baby was born; then they bought a house a mile from ours. One mile! I was thrilled and touched beyond imagining. Though we've traveled together for weeks at a time, the four of us haven't lived in the same city since Hugh and I left San Francisco in 1988. This is my dream come true—and with a *baby*. Hugh is right. I need to dial it back and let go—the cardinal message of the Buddhist meditation I've been practicing for decades. Let go, and give Clay and Tamar time to nest with Isabelle and reinvent themselves as a family. What do I have to be so anxious and insecure about anyhow? (Hint: plenty, but I don't know that yet.)

When four o'clock rolls around and I still haven't heard from Clay, not even a measly e-mail, instead of calling him or writing to him (or doing an undercover drive-by, which is what I would have done in high school, so there has been some progress), I distract myself by redirecting my attention to real estate—the ideal landing pad for an obsessive mind, like a heat-seeking missile, in search of an alternative target. *Hah! I'll show them*, I think. I'll rent a house by the water on Maryland's Eastern Shore for the last week of August.

Clay and Tamar, desperate to escape the pea-soupy swamp of Washington, will jump at the offer to join us—and bring Isabelle. Seven days of unrestricted access! If this is as calculating and sneaky on my part as it is generous, so be it. Before the day's end I reserve *three* large, expensive houses that we can't really afford—each with its own dock and swimming pool (and cancellation policy)—thereby guaranteeing my obsessive mind fodder for days to come.

I wonder if my besotted state is normal. Do other women feel this way about their grandchildren? I'm not sure, since I'm the first among my boomer friends to become a grandmother. I know my Nana adored me, but was she positively blotto? My own mother wasn't exactly a role model in the grandmotherly love department, especially when Clay was a baby. When I called her in New York from the hospital in Vancouver to tell her the news of his birth, all she said was: "Clay? What kind of a name is Clay?" And the look on her face, preserved in photographs, when she visited my common-law husband and me in our run-down farmhouse in British Columbia, was one of undisguised horror. (Okay, so there was a dead cow lying outside in the barnyard, and a multigenerational family of mice sharing our kitchen.) Still, there was a baby. *My* baby. Irene, who didn't seem all that eager to hold her new grandson, certainly didn't restrain herself on the subject of my holding him. *Too much* was the verdict. This became her battle cry throughout Clay's childhood: "You spoil him. He's a mama's boy." So if I was guilty of being a mother who loved too much, did that mean that now, as a grandmother, I was doomed to repeat the same terrible crime?

By late Tuesday morning, I start to panic. It's been more

than thirty-six hours since I've had any contact with Clay or Tamar, by far the longest we've gone since the night Isabelle was born. Did something awful happen to her? Did she stop breathing and turn blue? (One thing I have inherited from my mother—and her mother before her—is a tendency to catastrophize. This is not exactly what it appears to be, however, because beneath this hysterical, worst-case-scenario habit of thinking—but never stated, because then it wouldn't work—is the notion that if you worry hard enough, you can stop bad things, say cancer and death, from happening. A hypothesis that, unfortunately, never holds up in the end.) I'm almost certain I'm being irrational, though. If something bad had happened to Isabelle, surely I would have heard about it by now. Then I have another alarming thought: maybe it's me. Maybe I've done something truly unforgivable—beyond being in a swoony state over the baby—and they're royally pissed. Even more troubling than my offensive-behavior theory is the possibility that they're plotting to leave Washington and move back to Europe.

That's really demented, I tell myself. They bought a house a mile away. They live here now. Get a grip.

Not so fast, sister, I muse. Ever since they landed in Washington there have been steady rumblings of discontent, like distant thunder: *The weather is disgusting. You have to drive to the suburbs to buy anything.* And perhaps the most damning of all: *Everybody's a lawyer.* These are all valid objections—about which I can do nothing.

Luckily, I'm enough in touch with reality to talk myself down. They're probably just exhausted. And I'm the grandparent, not the parent. I'm not supposed to see Isabelle every single day. I have my own life—something I'm prone to forget. My friend Susan, an amateur astrologer, says it's because I have no earth; there are only water signs in my chart, which, metaphorically speaking, cause me—like some free-floating sea—to pool in the nearest empty riverbeds and basins instead of defining my own landmass. Still, whether it's due to my watery nature or to garden-variety neurosis, I am unsettled. Everything is so new: Clay and Tamar being here, the baby. Clay feels it, too. One day shortly after moving into their house, he joked, "Now that I practically live around the corner from you, are we supposed to hug every time we see each other or what?"

After all the useless mental spinning, I launch a verbal weather balloon. "Hi, just checking in," I say breezily when I get the recorded message on Clay's cell phone. "I'm going to Farmer Jim's today to pick up some lettuce. Do you want anything?"

Food prevails again, and within minutes Clay e-mails me back. Yes, he'd love some baby romaine, baby arugula, and zucchini blossoms. He doesn't mention fleeing the country or banning me from seeing my granddaughter.

Tamar is napping when I deliver the baby vegetables, and Clay asks if I'd mind holding Isabelle while he prepares dinner. Oh no, I say, I don't mind. So while he slices and dices, I swaddle her in the bright blue-and-orange blanket made by Amanda, her step-grandmother, and rock her in my arms. As soon as I start to sing "All the Pretty Little Horses," she drops right off—bolstering my reputation as Narcolepsy Nonna. (I'm already famous for inducing narcolepsy in her; Nonna is the name I've chosen to be called—the Italian word for grandmother, which sounds hipper and younger to my ear than *grandma*.) As we rock I sniff her sweet-salty baby essence and study her changing facial expressions. She appears to be dreaming. I wonder if she's traveling back in time to the dark watery underworld from which she so recently emerged.

I am completely happy. I am getting my fix—for a physical craving I never expected to feel. It is a moment of complete presence, the kind I strive for in meditation. I don't want to be anywhere else or do anything else. Just right here, right now.

So this is how it works. I think I'm finally starting to grasp the rhythm of being a grandmother, which is a lot like being a relief pitcher. I'm on the bench until Isabelle's parents decide they need a break.

Which is how it goes during the week we spend together on the Eastern Shore. Everything flows smoothly, except when I *ask* to take care of Isabelle. This lesson is drilled into me after dinner on our first night, when I volunteer to hold her. (There's no question in my mind that this little girl is held more than any baby outside Bali, where babies are famously cradled twenty-four hours a day. No one ever considers actually putting Isabelle down—at least not yet.)

"I always feel like I'm depriving you," Clay says, clasping his daughter firmly in his arms.

"I'm the mother and *I'll* hold her." Tamar snatches Isabelle from Clay and disappears upstairs. He follows her.

"Sorry," I say after them. I don't make the same blunder again.

But twenty minutes later when they want to go outside to have a glass of wine on the dock, they're more than happy to turn the baby over to me.

This becomes our pattern. Clay and Tamar are with

her until they want to do something else, and then she's mine. At which point I turn into a character in some kind of wacky operetta. I immediately burst into song. I can't help myself, even though I'm more or less tone-deaf. I've worked up a whole repertoire in addition to "All the Pretty Little Horses." There's "A, You're Adorable," which has one verse for every letter of the alphabet—but since the only verses I know are the first two, it's different each time I sing it. I also sing "Michael, Row the Boat Ashore," another classic; and "Yes, Sir, That's My Baby," Isabelle's favorite. I know this because whenever I launch into it, her eyes roll back in her head like an epileptic or a Pentecostal catching a whiff of the Holy Spirit.

One of the best things about being a grandparent, I decide, is getting a free pass to act like an imbecile whenever you're with the baby. And, as it turns out, I get to act this way a lot during our week at the shore. Clay and Tamar take frequent long walks and spend most evenings sitting out on the dock, talking. In fact, there's quite a bit of talking going on—talking and e-mailing. At one point I overhear them whispering about someone named Julie.

As far as I know, the only Julie they're in touch with is the realtor who sold them their house, the charming 1915 Craftsman Bungalow Clay and I stumbled across one day on our way to lunch (at the best sushi place in town)—right after they decided they'd be better off renting. Still, they seemed jazzed about the prospect of having a real home, and made an offer on the house the following morning—winning the bidding war that afternoon. Lately, though, they've been complaining about the pressures—financial, practical—of maintaining an old house. What's more—though nothing of the sort has been said to me directly—I've heard through the family grapevine that Tamar blames hormones for making her crazy in the early stages of pregnancy—crazy enough to want to leave Paris and return to the U.S., a move she now regrets. And so I'm uneasy. Even though both Tamar, a life coach, and Clay, a photographer, have found work here, as freelancers they can live anywhere. I worry that our presence won't be enough to hold them. They aren't exactly saying this, but the airwaves crackle with static. Like a secret agent, I'm trying to unscramble the signals so that if and when my heart is broken, I am prepared.

I don't have to wait very long. And I am not prepared at all.

A few days after we return from the Eastern Shore, Clay invites me to go for a walk. It is a blistering afternoon in early September. He seems nervous as we snake our way through the neighborhood, keeping under the cover of trees. I'm nervous too.

"For the first time in my life, I feel responsible for your feelings," he confesses after opening pleasantries. "I used to feel this way about my dad, but never about you."

"I'm so sorry, sweetheart." I know how hard it must be for him to say this to me. "Please believe me when I tell you I'm sturdy and resilient. You are in no way responsible for my happiness."

"That's not how it feels."

I try my best to reassure him. "You don't have to take care of me," I say, experiencing a wrench of the old grief—over the nasty divorce when Clay was two; over the endless tug-of-war that kept him shuttling back and forth between his father's house and mine; over the succession of bad boy-friends who hijacked my attention when he was young. "I'm fine. Honestly. You have your own family now, I get that."

"It's just that, well, you have a strong personality." He pauses. "Plus, I never expected the grandmothers to be so involved."

At any other time, no doubt, I'd appreciate the irony. Me, a former rebel wild child of the sixties recast as a med-dling grandma, like some awful stock character on a tele-vision sitcom. But now I feel like crying. Hollering, too. *If you didn't want me to be so involved, why did you move here? Why did you buy a house a mile away?* Instead, I say, as neutrally as I can, "If I've intruded or overstepped my welcome, then I'm truly sorry. I'm just trying to find my way."

With Isabelle everything is so simple: there's nothing to do except love her. With her father and mother, however, I feel as if I'm crawling blindfolded up a steep ravine studded with land mines. Is *this* normal?

Clay and I walk along in silence for a while. He still seems anxious, so I know there's more. Then: "I thought that owning a house would give us a sense of stability, but it's done just the opposite," he says, his voice cracking. "I've never felt so stressed out or insecure."

My first impulse is to take my darling boy in my arms and comfort him the way I did when he was small. So many pressures—new baby, new city, the awful uncertainty of freelance work. But he's a grown man of thirty-four, so I just nod my head, and listen.

And then: "We're putting our house on the market and going back to Paris."

My body contracts as if a blow delivered by a fist, not words, has just landed squarely in my chest.

My mind spins. I miss Isabelle when I don't see her for a few days. How will I manage when months go by? Who will I be to her? I'm afraid I already know the answer: an occasional treat, a confection, not daily sustenance; important theoretically, but in practice, nonessential personnel. There will be other caretakers besides Clay and Tamar whom she will come to rely on, others she will know better than she knows me—and who will know her better than I.

And then it hits me: in a sense I *am* nonessential personnel. If I were to die tomorrow, Isabelle would grow up fine without me. The early death of a parent may leave track marks on the soul; but unless a strong bond has formed, the absence of a grandmother is a loss more abstract than palpable. Which, in fact, is how nature—unsentimental in its practicality—seems to have designed it. Grandmothers and grandfathers are links in the chain that bring their grandchildren into being, but not direct links. And except in families where grandparents are caretakers—or when they play a part in a child's daily life because of geographical proximity—we are, more or less, expendable. We may be loving and helpful when we're around—but our presence is optional.

I am learning this lesson early, harshly. *Now you see Isabelle, now you don't.*

At first I don't think I'll be able to speak. But after a few minutes I manage to mumble something about wishing Clay well, wanting nothing more than his happiness—platitudes that are true enough, but not the whole story. Still, I don't want to add to the burden of guilt he already feels for disappointing me. *For the first time in my life, I feel responsible for your feelings.*

The other reason I don't say much is that I'm the grandmother and, in point of fact, I have no say at all.

Five days after our walk, Clay and Tamar put their house up for sale on Craigslist. Twenty-four hours later they have a buyer who offers to meet their price—in cash. Six weeks after that—with ten-week-old Isabelle strapped securely to Clay's chest in a baby carrier—they board a plane bound for Paris.

The Buddha taught that human suffering is caused by the desire for life to be different from the way it actually is. When Clay breaks the news about leaving Washington, after the initial shock I know there's nothing for me to do but let go—of my longing to live near my beloved son and his family, to see them often, casually, in the way that's possible only when every meeting doesn't involve juggling busy schedules and crossing an ocean. Hardest of all will be letting go of my yearning to know my granddaughter intimately, to see her often enough to be able to detect the subtle changes in her as she grows from a baby into a toddler and then into a young girl. This yearning is so strong, so forceful, that it feels cellular—like an undertow in my blood drawing me toward her.

Letting go.

The Buddha in his wisdom also taught that you can't get from point A (intense longing) to point B (letting go or, at least, loosening the bonds of desire) without walking through fire. And so I do not let go—or even begin the work of letting go—without first giving in to raw emotion. Fury whips through me like a rogue tornado, followed by sorrow and an overwhelming sense of betrayal—as if Isabelle Eva is being ripped from my body. Grief unlike any I have ever known.

At times I wonder if this is my karmic comeuppance: I, who never for a second considered raising Clay within three thousand miles of my own parents. I, who when Clay was six months old moved him from the farm in British Columbia (which had heat and indoor plumbing despite the dead barnyard animals) to a plywood shack in the Trinity Alps of northern California, where we had no running water, no electricity, no phone, and our nearest neighbors—sometimes way too close for comfort—were bears. Compared with me, Clay and Tamar have made a mature, responsible decision. And in choosing to live where they feel most at home in the world, they're being true to themselves—without putting Isabelle in danger of being attacked by wild animals. The irony is not lost on me—Clay even noted it in one of our many conversations after the Big Talk—that *being true to yourself* was my mantra when he was young.

"We came to Washington to be near you and we're not leaving because of you," he tells me in the days leading up to their departure. "This is about us, not about you." In my heart I believe him, but I'm unable to take comfort in this knowledge—not yet.

The day after Clay, Tamar, and Isabelle take off for Paris, I call my friend Carmelita in Oregon. "How do I do this?" I wail into the phone. Carmelita is in her early seventies and the grandmother of five—two of whom live in the Czech Republic. She sees them maybe once a year, twice if she's lucky.

"It hurts like hell," she says, "like an ache that gets better over time but never really goes away. The thing I try to remember each time I say good-bye to the kids is that if one of them got sick or hurt, this grief would look like happiness."

I flash back to the August afternoon when Isabelle was two weeks old and I had a near meltdown because I hadn't heard from Clay in a couple of days. From this vantage point, that fleeting blip looks like bliss. I feel foolish when I think of it. And at some point, even this moment of grief will look like a passing thundercloud. After all, there are fates worse than spending time in Paris.

Letting go.

Clay was simply telling the truth when he let me know shortly after Isabelle's birth that she was *their* baby, not mine. He and Tamar are writing their own story—and though I'm certain to show up in the unfolding plot, I am not a central character. My wishes, no matter how deeply felt, will never drive the action. There's nothing wrong with this. It's just that I got a different idea in my head when they moved here. For a time, anyhow, it seemed as though I were being offered a bigger, juicier part in the story.

One day when I'm at my gloomiest, I give up trying to write and take to my bed like the tragic heroine in some Victorian novel. Just as I'm settling in for a spell, the doorbell rings. It is my next-door neighbor, Katharine, stopping by to check up on me. Bedraggled and in no mood for company, I nevertheless invite her in for tea. I light the fire under the kettle, and while we wait for the water to boil, she tells me about a theory she once heard that has helped her to take her own family struggles less personally. The idea, she explains, is that our relationships form a series of concentric circles, like the rings of a tree, with each of us stationed at the center of our own innermost ring. Next to us in that first circle are the people dearest to us—our mate; our children; our siblings or other family members and possibly a best friend. The pattern continues through each succeeding ring of the circle: Those closest to your center are—literally—the people closest to you. And though parents normally belong in their child's innermost circle when the child is young, they don't necessarily remain there.

"There's the rub," says Katharine, "because even though we may drop back a ring or two in our children's lives, especially when they start their own families, they stay forever in our innermost circle."

"Grandchildren, too." When I say this, I know it's true— no matter where Isabelle lives.

Letting go.

Even Clay, who came wise into this world, already seems to grasp that, in the end, there is nothing to do but let go. I know he knows this because the night his daughter is born, with her cradled in his arms and the full moon shining in on both of them, I watch him bend down and whisper into her perfect, tiny ear:

"Someday you'll break my heart."

Gained in Translation

BHARATI MUKHERJEE

On an unseasonably hot April morning in 2004, we gathered on the roof deck of an apartment building on the Upper West Side of Manhattan to hold a naming ceremony for a fourteen-month-old girl. "We" were her family and her parents' friends. Relatives had flown in from California, Oregon, Wyoming, Minnesota, and Michigan; one had come from India. There were Catholics, Protestants, Jews, Hindus, Buddhists, and atheists among us—the usual modern American mélange. Each of us had memories of christenings or naming ceremonies as practiced during our childhood by our own culturally homogeneous families.

We inherited those rites (and all their proscriptions) from our ancestors. I come from an unbroken line of caste-observant Hindu Bengalis who have followed unvarying rules for choosing names. Women were named after goddesses of wisdom, prosperity, and righteous ferocity; queens from the epics, known for wifely devotion and self-sacrifice; sacred musical instruments; sin-dissolving rivers and waterfalls. My name, assigned to me at my formal *namkaran* (naming) ceremony at an auspicious hour on an auspicious date, is a variant of Sarswati, the goddess of learning.

But on that April day in 2004, an American baby girl born in China—adopted by an Iowa-born father who is half Bengali, a quarter Anglo-Dutch, and a quarter French-Canadian; and a Chicago-born mother who is part German and Irish—was formally named Quinn Xi Anand Blaise (in her Chinese orphanage, she'd been named Qin) without any direction from priests, pastors, swamis, or monks. We were celebrating mixture, not purity; improvisation, not uncompromised ritual.

The new parents—our son Bart Anand and his wife, Kimberley Ann—shuttled between their ground-floor apartment and the roof deck, soothing overexcited children, seating heat-exhausted senior citizens in the only sliver of shade, setting up a "station" for the naming rites and games at one end of the deck and buffet tables for a potluck lunch (designed to please carnivores, herbivores, and vegans) at the other. The day's festivities ended with my hosting a dinner in Bart's favorite neighborhood Indian Bengali restaurant, owned (of course) by a Bangladeshi Muslim.

In my mother's girlhood, a Brahmin eating food cooked by a Muslim would have been punished with permanent caste-expulsion. The Sunday brunch following the naming ceremony featured (of course) lox and bagels.

The ceremony couldn't start until Quinn woke up from her mid-morning nap. Meanwhile we handed out fans, sun hats, visors, sunblock, bottled water, and other chilled beverages. It was hotter than India. Balding men pulled caps over their melanoma-prone heads; a great-aunt in her late sixties whipped an ice-cooled washcloth out of a ziplock bag and mopped her face and neck. A videographer caught moments of informal bonding between the two sets of grandparents.

Finally Quinn, glamorous if a little sweaty in a pink silk suit bought in Shanghai for this special celebration, was ready to claim her name and receive our homage. From the security of her mother's arms, she eyed the objects laid out on a small table: a toy medical kit, a pen, a ten-dollar bill; a ceramic Buddha, and three small vials of holy water and oils. The presence of the statue of Buddha at the naming ceremony was to ensure a lifetime of peace for Quinn. (I kept to myself the Hindu superstition that bringing a statue of Buddha into one's home results in asceticism and exile in a forest.) The three objects on the tray were said to be part of a traditional Chinese game. If a baby chooses the paper money, she will be a prosperous businesswoman; if the pen, she will be a scholar or a poet; if the doctor's tools, she will be a physician.

What do I want for my granddaughter? Almost eight years earlier, at a public discourse on race in America organized by Senator Bill Bradley at the Field Museum in Chicago, I had been asked the same question. My prayer, I'd announced then, was that my recently married son and daughter-in-law would be blessed with a daughter who would run for the presidency of the United States. Barring a constitutional intervention, however, Quinn Blaise's inauguration will not take place. But in any case baby Quinn had other plans for her future: she shot out a fist and grabbed the medical kit.

Kim invited our benedictions. Say it, sing it, dance it, perform it, or write it on a slip of paper.

Grandma Ruth, raised Catholic, anointed the baby with holy liquids from the vials she had brought from the Midwest. As I watched, I understood the potency of personal ritual. This was a hot Manhattan rooftop, not a church; there were no priests and no prayers; there was no basin of holy water. Like all of us that morning, she was improvising.

We couldn't give up the shells of ritual as we cut away hundreds—even thousands—of years of pomp and ceremony. We both wanted to protect this grandchild: we just had to figure out the new words and music.

The line of celebrants was long. My niece-in-law from Mumbai, who was a doctoral student at the University of Pennsylvania, sang a Sanskrit hymn. My older sister, a retired child psychologist who has lived in suburban Detroit since the early 1960s, performed a Bengali folk song and dance despite arthritic knees. When my turn came, I chanted the only verse I remembered from my late father's full-throated recitation of the Sanskrit hymn in which the mother goddess, Durga, slays the Buffalo-Demon and saves the world. A Delhi-born friend, who broke through ceilings in the U.S. corporate world in the decades when few Indo-Americans received corner offices or country-club membership, delivered a brief, moving speech and said that the future belonged to Quinn's generation of American pioneers. Quinn is, after all, an inheritor of three of the most vibrant cultural traditions in the world.

Truly, as Conrad once wrote of another time and a very different character, the whole world has gone into her making.

That weekend we had no idea that in a little over a year, we'd be blessed with one more adopted granddaughter, Priya Xue Agnes Blaise. What I did know (courtesy of a California-born Chinese-American writer friend) is that in some Chinese dialects, grandmothers are called Popo and grandfathers Gong Gong. "Call me Popo," I whispered to the infant already asleep in Kim's arms.

Four years later, in their Noo Yawk accents, the girls call my husband, Clark, and me Po and Gongie.

A traditional Bengali upbringing is the worst possible preparation for American grandmothering. Bengali grandmothers, especially those from the father's side, call all the shots. Their sons are submissive; their daughters-in-law are terrified. If I grew up with a promise to myself, even before I left India, it was this: never become a typical mother-in-law.

Until I was eight years old, my parents, my two sisters, and I lived in a multigenerational household ruled by Thakuma, my autocratic, long-widowed paternal grandmother. The family lived on the first floor of a two-story stucco house on a tree-shaded block on a noisy avenue in Kolkata, India. Rooms opened on an inner courtyard that served as a stage for family melodramas, as a children's playground, and as an additional cooking and washing-up area. Nothing except schooling happened outside that house. Patriarchal joint-family living was the norm as well as the ideal in our homogeneous neighborhood.

"Family" included paternal grandparents, parents, siblings, paternal uncles, and their wives and children. When I was a child, the only "nuclear" family I encountered was a fictional one in my kindergarten textbook, imported from Britain and used to teach English in the Protestant missionary school I attended. Mastering the book's alien vocabulary was easy for me, but visualizing a micro-family of four relatives (a husband and his wife, and their son and daughter) occupying a house so large that it had separate rooms for sleeping, lounging, eating, and cooking required a dizzying imaginative leap. I felt sorry for the girl child, who appeared to be my age in the illustrations, because she had to sleep in a lonely bedroom of her own. How could you be a happy child if you didn't have scores of live-in cousins to play with? How could you drift off into exciting dreams if you had no grandmotherly capacious lap to curl up in every evening and listen to stories of gods, demons, kings, and queens?

Our Mukherjee household was made up of forty-five relatives, swelling to sixty or more in monsoon season when great-uncles and their large families moved in with us to escape floods and epidemics in our ancestral village in river-laced East Bengal (now Bangladesh).

My maternal grandparents, the progressive and tolerant Dadoo and Didima, along with my maternal uncles, aunt-in-law, and cousins, lived half an hour's rickshaw ride away. My mother took us for informal visits to them—rest and recreation breaks from Thakuma's imperious rule—during weekday siesta hours as often as she could sneak away from household chores. About once a month, we also visited Didima's widowed mother, who lived with Didima's older brother and his family. She looked very much like Didima, except that she walked bent double because of osteoporosis. Since I, too, closely resembled Didima in appearance, I assumed that one day my face would become jowly like theirs, and that my spine would shrink. Being surrounded by grandmothers and a great-grandmother, I saw aging as a natural and inevitable process, not as a humiliating physical degeneration to be retarded or disguised with cosmetics.

My two grandmothers demonstrated their affection in very different ways. Thakuma, though she had been taught to read and write as a child by her childless older sister and progressive brother-in-law, embraced reactionary Hindu traditions as her form of resistance to British colonial rule.

She was vociferously against the education of women, and especially against English missionary schools. In Hindu tradition (although many modern families have overcome millennial prejudices) sons are prized (they will look after their parents in old age), but dowry-sucking daughters are devalued. Educating them is a waste of money.

Having borne eight sons herself, Thakuma taunted my mother daily for burdening the Mukherjee family with three daughters and no sons. She was the proud guardian of a long scroll that depicted the Mukherjee family tree, and she reminded me frequently that because daughters cannot appear in genealogical charts, even though my father was the main financial support of the household, the branch that should have recorded his offspring had been hacked off.

On the other hand, Didima, my maternal grandmother, whose father had placed his faith in social reform and equality of education for all classes and both sexes, and whose daughters and daughters-in-law had made her a grandmother of fourteen girls and no boys, defied traditional attitudes. She instilled in each granddaughter a solid sense of self-worth.

Both grandmothers agreed, however, that the individual's absolute duty was to increase the health, wealth, strength, and fertility of the family to which he or she was related by blood. In selecting brides, Thakuma screened for caste purity and size of dowry; Didima insisted on a family history of outstanding respectability.

What I didn't realize during my girlhood was that I was growing up in a newly independent nation in an era of unprecedented social change and legislated reform. Though Thakuma continued to hold fast to her traditional ideas, the Indian constitution granted women the right to inherit property and to sue for divorce. And the times eventually empowered my mother to insist that my father move our nuclear family of five out of the joint-family household under reactionary Thakuma's autocratic rule while still continuing to financially support it. My two sisters and I were the first in my parents' families to study in the United States, and the first of the Mukherjee women permitted to leave the protective confines of the patriarchal home before marriage. Still, I expected to return home to Kolkata when I received my master of fine arts degree; marry the Bengali Brahmin bridegroom selected for me by my parents; settle in a comfortable neighborhood not far from theirs; and raise two brilliant, beautiful children, who in their turn would reward me with the experience of grandmothering.

How could my parents have guessed that desire would sabotage family destiny? In the fall of 1963, a riptide of love pulled me into marriage after a two-week courtship. My husband, a Fargo-born American of French- and English-Canadian parents, had no intention of making his life in India; and I had no intention of making my life without him.

Both my granddaughters came into our family through international adoption. As soon as it became clear to Bart and Kimberley that their only option for raising a healthy family was to adopt, they made preliminary inquiries of agencies specializing in finding homes for abandoned South Asian children. A South Asian adoptee, they reasoned, would bear my ethnic likeness, and so would feel a special sense of belonging. But they worried that I, having grown up in a reactionary household, might have a visceral resistance to adoption. The easiest country in South Asia for American parents to adopt from was Bangladesh—my putative homeland, but now a predominantly Muslim nation. They wanted to know specifically how I would feel if they were to adopt a Muslim-born infant. Their query involved a gut check for me. For my entire adult life I had prided myself on being a taboo-breaker, but had I truly transcended the biases I absorbed in girlhood?

I confronted my prejudices without confessing them to anyone. I was ashamed that I was even engaged in an internal debate about my capacity to love a grandchild of unspecific (but regional) origin. A surge of flashbacks saved me: a smiling Didima, greeting Clark, Bart, and Bernard, our younger son, the very first time she met them, with a practiced phrase: "Hullo, I am International Great-Granny"; my father, in Kalamazoo on business the night that Bart was born in Iowa City, riding a Greyhound bus all night and splurging the money he'd saved on filling my hospital room with baskets of fruits and bouquets of flowers. If he, a practicing Hindu, had had any misgivings about my having broken caste taboos, he did not show it. Instead, to the hundred-strong community of Indian students and faculty members who kept sneaking into the university hospital nursery in order to view his famous "mongrel" offspring (we're talking about forty-five years ago), he had announced his pride in his grandson. And my mother-in-law, whose marriage to a French-Canadian Catholic had been unacceptable to her family (and the subsequent divorce, inevitable), had embraced me, a brown, Hindu Caucasian, as the bride of her only child. So had my French-Canadian father-in-law, from a far more restrictive community. How could I have done anything less? I was undergoing the same test my father and mother had undergone, and I trust—after the same internal anguish—that I would have come out on the same side.

But I never got the chance to find out. Kim's brother's experience clinched it. He and his wife had adopted from China, with total satisfaction. Bart and Kim were inspired to follow suit. And so first came Quinn, then Priya.

We celebrate their birthdays with home-baked cakes, and their adoption days with "lucky noodles." The sisters switch effortlessly from New Yorkese to Mandarin, which they've learned in Chinese classes in Manhattan. The little girls are also learning the intricacies of Americana just as I learned them, as a sheltered Bengali bride in the Midwest during the early 1960s. But they're learning from the inside, not as note-taking observers—sports and politics, triking and biking, building bird feeders and naming the visitors, identifying insects and flowers in the backyard, going on nature hikes, pulling dandelions, and decorating the Christmas tree.

Because Clark and I live in California, it is only now, forty-five years after the births of our two sons, that I understand the pain my parents suffered as long-distance Bengali grandparents in a time before e-mail, before Skype, when even international phone connections between us were iffy and exorbitant. My parents got to know my sons through my letters and a few black-and-white photographs. We made as many summer visits to India as we could afford, and when we did visit, Bart and Bernard drew pictures with crayons on the walls of my parents' home. Lonely grandparents, they instructed the servants never to clean off the boys' drawings.

Thanks to modern technology, I am up-to-date on my granddaughters' adventures and their meltdowns. On Skype, I see two-year-old Priya hold out a three-legged toy frog and exclaim, "The leg came off my *ching wa*. What a bummer!" I am a virtual witness to their picnics in the park, nature walks in the Hamptons, and playdates with friends from preschool and the Mandarin Treehouse school. I hide my anxiety at their eagerness to upgrade from three-wheeled micro-scooters to two-wheeled Razors. I savor Quinn's current obsession with numbers, and Priya's discovery of reading. We thought that Quinn, with her elaborate storytelling and furious painting, was destined to extend the family's commitment to the arts—until she discovered numbers. Can the medical profession be far behind?

Because we don't get to visit each other often enough, each hour together is precious. Last month while Clark and I were in New York for a conference that coincided with the pope's visit, we squeezed in an afternoon and evening of family adventures in spite of the snarled traffic. The girls chose to take me to MoMA, where Quinn loves her art classes. Priya raced around the outdoor sculpture, pointing out her favorites; Quinn contemplated the mechanism that made the fountains gush to different heights. Inside the building, we rode the escalator all the way up to the top floor and took in an exhibit on color. In the museum cafeteria, over chocolate milk and brownies, Quinn gazed intently into my eyes, then asked, "Popo, is your eye shadow a pinkish lavender?" Afterward, we sat before a row of impressionist paintings while Quinn counted flowers, hats, trees, and umbrellas.

We took the subway instead of a cab back to their home because Quinn loves to read off the names and numbers of the stations. At home, Priya improvised a game she named "Hop-on-Letters," which involved spreading out the plush-covered magnetized alphabet I had bought her at the museum gift store and jumping on each letter I called out. After that, they sat Clark and me down in the living room and took turns performing Chinese ribbon dances, which nearly led to a meltdown, as there were two eager performers and only one baton-hilted ribbon. The evening ended with dinner in a neighborhood Italian restaurant owned by the parents of a couple whose adopted daughter is Quinn's friend from the Mandarin Treehouse.

At the end of the visit, as we—grandparents, parents, and granddaughters—waited with our luggage outside their apartment building, a cabdriver pulled up, asking, "All you one family?" On the drive to the airport, he added, "You look happy." He explained that he had felt marginalized growing up half-Chinese, half-Vietnamese in Vietnam.

The week after Clark and I got back home, we received a postcard from Priya of Van Gogh's *Self-Portrait with a Straw Hat*: "Dear Popo and Gong Gong," she had dictated to Kim. "I love you so much. When you go, it makes us cry. I went to the Met and we saw this picture. I love you so much and wish we could go to your house but we have to go to ballet. Love, Priya."

Priya means "beloved" in my mother tongue. When I read the postcard, I am so happy I start to cry. In the imaginary scroll of the Blaise family tree, Quinn Xi Anand and Priya Xue Agnes straddle the sturdiest branch.

Déjà Vu

MARCIE FITZGERALD

"Mom, how did the first people figure out how to talk?" Porter asks me. "And how did they get the other people to know what they were talking about?"

Two more questions I don't have answers to. But I love the way my son thinks, this six-year-old who knows more about negative numbers and square roots than I did at twice his age. I love the way when we played "Twenty Questions" last night, Porter dreamed up "a flying peanut wearing underpants."

"Is it something I could touch?" my husband, Carl, asked.

"In your imagination," Porter replied.

I love my son's dimpled cheeks, his shining dark eyes, his curly black hair. I love how he runs for third base like nobody's business. He's fun to play ball with, even though last spring I cracked a rib when we crashed into each other shooting hoops in the driveway—just one of the hazards of motherhood postmenopause.

I'm afraid for Porter, too. He can be volatile and insensitive to the feelings of others. More days than not, he gets into trouble at school for what the professionals call "impulse control issues"—hitting, pushing, and kicking when he feels threatened or disrespected, which is often. At our conference at the end of the school year, Porter's team (his teacher, a behavior specialist, a psychologist, the principal, and a mentor for the highly gifted) noted that his aggressive behavior was diminishing—at times. Mrs. Watchhorn, his teacher, even reported that although Porter is bossy, "the other kids often love playing with him because his ideas are so interesting." Still, I would have been more heartened had the principal not added, "But he'll probably never be easy or age-appropriate."

The sinking feeling I get when I hear such things is all too familiar. So are the behavior forms I'm filling out this week. I've initiated a psychological assessment for Porter, and I'm half sick imagining the results. How can I bear to watch another beloved child fall to ruin? I try to tell myself that I'm worrying prematurely. But I've been through this before, and I'm steeling myself for the diagnosis. *Asperger's syndrome? Bipolar disorder? Incipient schizophrenia?*

There's also the looming worry about my son's future. Who will care for him after Carl and I are gone? He'll be orphaned earlier than many children—and there won't be any siblings or family members left to take him in.

That's because in addition to being Porter's adoptive parents, Carl and I are his grandparents.

Rewind seven years.

"The baby is okay," my seventeen-year-old daughter Nicole was telling me from her bed in the emergency room. She handed me an ultrasound of a twelve-week-old fetus.

I didn't want to look. Since Nicole had announced her pregnancy, I'd been determined to avoid growing attached to her unborn baby. My daughter was unfit to be a parent, and I quailed at the thought of taking on another child. Still,

I couldn't help peering at the shiny gray piece of paper. Oh! That bright dot would be his fiercely beating heart.

The suicide attempt (hundreds of aspirin) came after Nicole stole a wad of cash from my safe, took my first new car, and disappeared for several days. It turned out that she treated a bunch of people she wished were friends to a big party in a motel in a nearby city. This was not the first time she'd tried to kill herself, but it was the most serious attempt.

She began to weep as I struggled to summon sympathy from the other emotions—anger, fear, despair—slamming into me like killer waves. "Nicole, I don't get it. If you won't have an abortion, why try to kill yourself *and* the baby?"

"Because," she said almost inaudibly, tears falling faster. "If I wasn't there to know about it, it wouldn't matter."

Over the years Nicole had become increasingly difficult and out of control. By her sophomore year of high school, I'd begun to understand (though Carl disagreed) that our daughter's problems went beyond simple rebelliousness. Even her latest diagnosis, bipolar disorder, seemed inadequate to explain her behavior.

Nicole seemed to be losing touch with reality. Earlier that year, several parents of the girls on her basketball team asked how they could help during my chemotherapy—only I didn't have cancer. Another time I overheard her talking on the phone about her famous dad, who played guitar with Los Lobos. At school she'd punched a girl in the face, then screamed obscenities at the principal. She was expelled and soon, I discovered, was missing whole days of the expelled students' program. Where did she go? What did she do? The baby was one answer.

Until Nicole became pregnant, it had been easy to fool ourselves, especially during months of apparent normalcy. She would work hard with her therapist, attend classes, do her chores, practice the violin, and beat us at gin rummy as we sat and played—and laughed—around the kitchen table. Desperate to believe our daughter was getting well, Carl and I would convince ourselves that this time the changes were real. But when Nicole's behavior deteriorated again, as it did, invariably, we'd wonder if we'd been in denial all along.

Now, thanks to three previous psychiatric hospitalizations, the current one would max out her lifetime insurance benefit for mental health, and put us more than $30,000 in the hole. We had no choice but to make Nicole a ward of the state.

Although Carl believed that a baby might force her to become a responsible adult, in my heart I knew this wasn't possible—no matter what our beloved daughter said or what we wanted to believe. The question was: who would step in when she failed?

The summer Porter is six, I'm sitting in a coffee shop nursing a granita with friends after dropping him off for his first day at Explorers Club, a summer child care program. On the way there he'd worried aloud that he might not know anybody—a remarkably transparent statement for my close-to-the-vest little guy.

I responded with a line from my own mom's repertoire: "You'll have lots of friends by the time I pick you up this afternoon," silently praying it would be true.

At the coffee shop, we're talking about exercise: Eleanor's fiftieth birthday has inspired her to walk fifty miles a week. She and Marie plan a walk after supper—and I notice they don't invite me. Melancholy descends briefly, but I'm not hurt. My friends are sensitive. They know that in order for me to join them, I'd have to organize—find a sitter or get Carl to rearrange his hours at the photography studio. In any case the point is academic: since Porter's in child care all day, I'd feel guilty going out in the evening.

Next there's talk of a writers' conference in Chicago. Wouldn't it be fun to get a few rooms together, take in the readings, hit some great restaurants? I hate the jealousy that creeps in when my friends start making plans. No way I can go—Carl's work schedule is simply too unreliable.

With their nests now empty, Eleanor and Marie are eagerly exploring new interests. Like them, I'd once imagined a time when I'd be free to indulge the delicious solitary pursuits I'd sidelined to raise Nicole: music, writing, gardening, art. But now I feel as though my friends are moving forward while I'm stuck at home playing Monopoly Junior with a boy who often calls me "the meanest mom in the whole entire universe."

Carl and I had the legal right to force Nicole to have an abortion, but in reality no doctor would perform one against her will—and her child would be old enough to testify before the Supreme Court by the time the matter was settled. So I lobbied for adoption, but Nicole wouldn't budge on that, either. *Her baby.* And though soon after the latest suicide attempt Nicole became a ward of the state—placed in our home—legal decisions regarding the baby were hers.

I didn't need the *I Ching* or a deck of tarot cards to read the future. Nicole would parent her baby enthusiastically at first, just long enough for us to bond with him. Then sooner or later she'd lose interest or find herself in over her head.

By that time, I'd feel responsible for the child, who would need us—me—desperately. And well into my sixties, I'd be dealing with whining, poop, strained peas stuck to the walls, setting limits, and supervising homework. My only hope for a child-free future was for Nicole and the baby to live someplace else.

That's why I'd started scrambling as soon as I learned that she was pregnant, jumping through hoops trying to land her a coveted spot in the Young Mothers' Home. In truth, I hoped that under the watchful eyes of professionals, my daughter would screw up early enough to give her baby a chance at a nice life with a loving (not old, not discouraged) adoptive family. Finally, with her due date just two months away, we received word that she and the baby had been accepted.

But Carl said, "No way."

"I've been trying to get her into this place since we found out she's pregnant," I pleaded through my tears. "If you can't let her go, then the three of you are going to have to move somewhere else."

When eventually Carl gave in, it didn't feel like much of a victory. Like him, I understood that sending Nicole to the Young Mothers' Home would mark the end of our hope for a "normal" family life—even though hope had been flying on fumes for years. It was the hardest decision of my life. I loved my daughter. I wanted desperately for her to succeed, but I was terrified not only that she would fail at motherhood—even with our support—but that she'd take us down with her.

I felt I was coming apart at the center.

When I pick Porter up at Explorers Club, his teacher reports that he got along with the other children all morning and didn't hit anybody. (I decide to ignore the slight dampness in his pants.) This is a triumph for a boy who has been described as more aggressive than 90 percent of his peers, a boy who carries the genetic blueprint for mental illness in his DNA.

To celebrate his success I drive through Pedro's, the fast-food joint whose current contest features an Xbox as the grand prize. Porter is so sure he's going to win that he immediately starts to negotiate with me about its deployment.

"At least an hour a day!" he insists, scratching the waxy black coating off the card that came with his strawberry malt.

He looks so much like Nicole, I think, catching sight of his grin in the rearview mirror. And how like Nicole to be so fired up over a goofy contest. I flash back to the time when she was a little girl, how captivated I was by her joie de vivre, how awed by her intelligence and musical gifts. A quotation from her first book, written when she was four: "Uirs past bie and she becam bag." ("Years passed by and she became big.") Back then Nicole's rough edges, her lying and fiery independence, seemed like typical disciplinary issues. My heart aches for the optimism I once felt toward that lively little girl's future. I ache for Porter too, saddened by how quickly my fearful, jaded heart is losing the optimism it once held for him.

It is a fine line we walk, desperate to head off problems before they grow insurmountable, but also wary of courting self-fulfilling negative prophecies. Can Carl and I parent perfectly enough—setting those damn limits, following through, avoiding the stressful situations that seem to set Porter off—to avert disaster this time around?

Nicole's psychiatrists have told me that her genetic predisposition for mental illness is so strong that even Ward and June Cleaver couldn't have prevented it. And though this knowledge has allowed me to begin to forgive myself, to stop second-guessing every parental move I ever made, it also carries the implication that Porter might succumb, too, no matter what we do.

In my darkest moments, I tell myself to look on the bright side: I'll be dead by the time Porter falls off the deep end. When I'm feeling more balanced, I tell myself that at least I'll be able to say I did my best.

I wasn't thinking so much as feeling sad and guilty when I agreed to be Nicole's birthing coach. Having moved her to the home, I thought that this small gesture was the least I could do. Besides, with her living across town, I'd finally let my guard down and begun to imagine myself a real grandma, with all the attendant joys: coaxing smiles, babysitting, and someday cheering at soccer games. And like other regular grandmothers I'd have the luxury of going home when I felt like it.

Still, nothing could have prepared me for the instant Porter's pinched face emerged into this world.

It had been a long day. Although Nicole wasn't due for another month, her blood pressure was dangerously high from toxemia, and the midwife had decided to induce labor early that morning. Nicole was frightened and in pain; her cervix was slow to dilate. But, finally, at nine-thirty in the evening, there he was: Porter Carl, all six pounds of him. For a small baby, he wasn't scrawny—just a compact, hairless creature who screamed with vigor.

My reaction was immediate, visceral, and infinitely more powerful than anything I had imagined. Bonding, hell—however much I loved Nicole, at that moment she could have been a distant acquaintance. But the baby? Gravity seemed insignificant by comparison.

The nurse whisked Porter to a brightly lit table and I followed, hypnotized. I touched his skinny arm, stroked his enchanting face. *Hello, beautiful.* After he was deemed healthy and Nicole had fallen into exhausted sleep, I rocked him in the dim light of the nursery, then gave him his first bottle. I sang to him for a long time before straggling home. That night, in a dream, I told Nicole, *Let go. He's mine.*

Get a grip, I told myself when I awoke the next morning.

But later, while I was holding Porter's tidily swaddled body, the vow arose unbidden inside me. "I'm here, Porter," I whispered, before I even knew what I was saying. "I promise to keep you safe. No matter what."

Adoption by strangers? Nicole wouldn't consider it. Now, neither could I.

Mother and son stayed with us for two weeks. Then, with the same sense of heartbreak we'd felt when she first moved to the Young Mothers' Home, Nicole returned there with Porter, promising to spend weekends with us. Though by this point I was less certain that this was the right course, the trajectory had been set. What's more, I was not Porter's mother—a point Nicole made daily. Clearly, she loved her son. I hoped she might surprise me and succeed at mothering him.

She did—to some extent. With supervision, she mostly kept him clean and well fed. Some days I'd hear good news: Nicole was better than other young moms at interacting with her baby. But soon afterward, I'd learn that she'd been disciplined for leaving Porter wailing in his room, while she was out partying on the deck. As had become her pattern, nearly every triumph was followed by failure. I was especially dismayed to discover that Nicole allowed Porter to spend most of his waking hours in the home's day care center, so I picked him up often and kept him with us for days at a time. I wanted to inoculate this baby with blasts of grandmotherly love.

Still, as smitten as I was, those visits were hardly idyllic. I'd forgotten just how boring baby care can be, how hard it is to get anything done with a little one around. And Porter's fussy crying got to me as much as Nicole's had. My vow notwithstanding, I realized during those long days that at this stage in my life I was better prepared to be a grandmother than a mother. I felt relief when I dropped Porter off at the Young Mothers' Home—relief, too, not to be dealing directly with Nicole's crazy behavior. Motherhood hadn't stopped her from skipping school, hiding beer in her room, and lying extravagantly.

When Porter was eleven months old and Nicole's eligibility for staying at the home was about to run out, Wendy, Nicole's caseworker, arranged to move mother and son to a charity-funded apartment where there would be less supervision. My daughter was overcome with joy at not being scrutinized "every single minute." She hung hippie bead curtains and, defying the rules, invited boys over within hours of her newfound freedom. On day two, just a week before Porter's first birthday, Wendy made an unannounced visit and found Porter crawling on a floor littered with cigarette butts, beer cans, and filthy diapers.

The call came a few days later. Nicole had left Porter in

the care of a visitor, an action she'd been warned would constitute neglect.

"If you want him," Wendy said, "you'd better come get him."

Nicole hadn't lasted a week.

During Porter's second week at Explorers Club, I use my free time to gather more data for his psychological tests. I also make calls to help Nicole, who's in jail after having assaulted someone. I learn that she's been evicted from yet another publicly funded apartment.

Nicole—or whoever inhabits the body that once was Nicole—is not safe. Earlier this year she accidentally set fire to her apartment. Recently she told me that she'd accepted a three AM ride from Jesus, and was thrilled when he invited her back to his place. "He's really sweet," she said.

Her ultimate diagnosis came when Porter was five years old: schizoaffective disorder, a cruel combination of bipolar disorder and schizophrenia. My daughter claims to be an immortal god who has appeared on earth just in time to save civilization.

In my opinion—and in the opinions of the legions of social workers who try to help her—Nicole should be placed in our regional mental health center, where she would be protected and made to take antipsychotic meds. But despite the fire and numerous assaults, she doesn't meet the standard that would allow her a therapeutic stay: "imminent danger to self or others." Frankly, I think our state system is even more deranged than my daughter.

The phone rings. It's Nicole, just out of jail with no place to go. Can she stay with us?

No. She can't. Even if I set aside the danger of her burning down our house, I can't allow Porter to hear the woman he knows to be his biological mother shout, "Don't cross me or I'll send you to hell. Haven't you read Revelations?"

It's impossible to parent both my daughter and her son—and probably crazy even to try. Doing well by one often comes at the expense of the other—and Porter must come first, a call that's clear but excruciating to make.

Most days I think I'm getting used to this life I never could have imagined for myself—even though often the best I can muster is a sort of grim resolve. But then when something truly scary happens with Porter or Nicole, I feel as though I'm being swallowed up by quicksand. Again. That's when I realize I'm *not* getting used to it, not really—though family, friends, a kindhearted psychologist, and antidepressants help, as do music, meditation, and writing. And without Carl's support I'd be a puddle on the floor.

One foot, then the other.

Bit by bit, I am getting better at allowing myself the genuine laugh, the gasp of awe—to take in joy as well as pain, knowing they're both as real and as transitory as the clouds streaming outside my window.

Take today. Following a screaming, door-slamming scene with my son after I asked him to put his socks away, after telling my daughter that she cannot take refuge in the home that once was hers, I hear Porter singing in the bathtub. So what if we're a musical family and this kid can't carry a tune? He's singing now, chirping away in the soprano range. "You want a piece of *this?*" he warbles over and over. Then as

I pass by the bathroom door he switches to a little-kid bass voice and bellows, "You talkin' to me?"

Suddenly he stops. "Mom," he shouts. I brace myself for what might come next.

"Mom!"

"Yes, Porter, what is it?"

"Mom, I've been wondering. Do you think I could use math to solve God? Could I, Mom?"

Okay, so this may not be how I planned to spend my life. Still, it *is* my life—and at moments like this I am blessed cell-deep by its surpassing perfection.

The Owie Tree

SANDRA BENITEZ

My four-year-old grandson Harper and I enjoy taking walks. In good weather, we stroll hand in hand around the neighborhood, our frequent destination an ancient gnarled oak a few blocks from his house. We've named the oak the "Owie Tree" because of the burly knots rising all over its thick trunk. About a year and a half ago, when we first came on it, Harp held up his arm. "Look, Tata," he said, "that tree has owies too." On the inside of Harp's left wrist rose a small ball of flesh. I loved to ask him about it.

"What do you have there, Harp?"

"It's my synovial cyst," he'd say, peering earnestly down on it. There is something quite charming about a two-and-a-half-year-old speaking like a physician. Of course, I had Googled his condition and knew all about it. So, in fact, did he. Also called a ganglion, the saclike swelling is a collection of thick jelly-like fluid normally contained within a joint or tendon sheath. It's one of those conditions that can arise quite suddenly, and just as abruptly disappear. Sometimes you can get rid of ganglions by giving them a good whack. In the old days, the Bible, usually the heaviest book in the house, was used to smash them. My grandson's ganglion had been growing for about a year. After consulting the pediatrician and being assured that his owie was benign, my son and daughter-in-law had decided against such curative violence and were allowing nature to take its course.

Strangers observing this scene between Harper and me—a grandmother and her young grandson taking a walk through the neighborhood—would no doubt view it as normal, commonplace, not worthy of a second glance. As Harp and I wrapped our arms around the trunk and gave the tree a squeeze to make it feel better, the strangers would have no way of knowing that they were witnessing a sacred act of redemption.

I was sixty-three before Harper came along. Now there is Dashiell, his brother. Harp and Dash live near me in Minneapolis. A few months ago the boys got a cousin, my granddaughter, who lives in Los Angeles. The distance between us is an owie of sorts—but a small one.

There have been other owies, passed down along bloodlines by the women in my family. The ones centered on my grandmothers and my mother are tender, and at times flare up. To this day, these women live inside me. Like those wooden Russian dolls, they nestle, one tucked inside the other, in the center of my heart.

Because I had a Puerto Rican mother and a Missourian father, my grandmothers live in my memory as polar opposites: Marina and Hazel. The former, august and dignified. The latter, noble and down-to-earth. Their presence in my life brought two worlds to me: Abuelita's Latino elegance, Grandma's midwestern hardscrabble ruggedness. You had only to study their hands to know how different their lives had been. Abuelita's hands gave off a scent of lavender lotion; her fingers were long and slender; her manicured nails looked like the interior of seashells. Grandma

Hazel had plump hands, sun-speckled by never-ending farmwork. Her fingers were stubby; her nails were clipped short. The only ring she wore was her wedding ring, a thin circle of gold, which I wear now. When I look down at my own hands, it's Grandma Hazel's hands I see.

I was fortunate to have spent part of my life with both of them. Abuelita and Abuelito resided with Mami, Daddy, me, and my younger sister, Anita, when we lived in El Salvador in the 1950s. While my parents worked, Abuelita helped run the household. After half a day of management duties, she'd retire to her chair—one with a high back and hand-carved arms that sat on the verandah—and take up her daily needlework and embroidery. From her throne, if prompted, she recounted stories: stories about *su isla*—Puerto Rico—about its deep blue waters, about the colorful hummingbirds that punctuated the air, about the singing frogs that filled the night with music.

Years later, when I was grown up and Abuelita, now a widow, was living with my uncle Rafael's family in Miami, I made a trip from the Midwest to see her. A semi-invalid in her mid-nineties, she was in bed, propped up by big pillows. Ever *la coqueta*, she wore a pretty silk bed jacket; and on her cheeks were spots of pink rouge, *colorete*. I spent one unforgettable afternoon at her bedside while she told me the truth about her mother, Alejandrina.

When Abuelita was eight years old, my great-grandmother committed suicide.

She did it in a slow and methodical manner after discovering my great-grandfather Dario's infidelity through a folded love letter left in the pocket of his white linen shirt. When he returned home after work, she confronted him with the evidence and made a terrifying pronouncement: "From this time forward, you will never set eyes on me again. When I die, you will not be allowed to see my corpse." She then banished him from their bedroom and from her sight. Starting then and there, she stopped eating. It took her almost one year to die. When she did succumb, one of her devoted servants carried out her wishes. The undertaker delivered the wooden casket into the house through the back patio. My great-grandmother was placed inside and the top was nailed down before Dario was informed of her demise.

That afternoon, at Abuelita's bedside, I learned of her buried grief over her mother's abandonment. I didn't know it then, but this deep wound was to have repercussions in my own life.

Way up north, in Missouri, Grandma Hazel and Grandpa Orion lived on the family's dairy farm. Grandma's mother, my great-grandmother Myrtle, resided with them. Like Abuelita, Grandma Myrt had suffered an abandonment. For the first few years of her life, she was raised in an orphanage; she never knew who her parents were. Myrtle and Hazel were devoted to each other and were rarely apart. Their longest separation came in 1941, after I was born in Washington, D.C., one of a pair of identical twins. My sister Susana died thirty-seven days later. Grandma Myrt left the farm by train and moved into my parents' little cottage to look after me. The loss of my twin sister was a blow from which my mother never fully recovered. She told me once that when I was a baby, she sometimes was afraid of holding me, lest I too be taken from her. So it was Grandma Myrt who became my second mother.

When I was fourteen and living in El Salvador, my father decided to Americanize me. He sent me to Missouri to attend high school and live on the farm with my grandparents and Grandma Myrt. But this·time, there was little coddling. I was a teenager, and my relatives spent their time laboring at their chores: cows to milk, cream to separate, fences to mend, hay to be lifted into the mow, wood to chop, the garden to keep, the canning to put up for the pantry. Day in, day out, they struggled with the perfidious weather.

Living in Missouri, I imagined myself as a comic-book heroine, like Veronica. Freed from chaperones and strict cultural dictums, I was a bilingual teenage American girl with circular skirts, crinolines, bobby socks, and penny loafers. It was only late at night, in bed under Grandma's feather blanket, high up in a room beneath the pitched roof of the old house, that I allowed myself to mist up and mourn what I'd left behind: my parents, my sister, my friends, and what had been, until then, my country. At times, after school, I'd walk down the long empty hallway. I'd sing under my breath: "Sometimes I feel like a motherless child. So far away from home."

Betrayal. Suicide. Abandonment—physical and emotional. Loss and dislocation. These were the ancestral owies that marked my family tree and that were rooted inside me when I become the mother of two sons, Chris and Jon, in the early 1960s in St. Louis.

I was young and inexperienced. Having been raised by nursemaids, I'd never even babysat. When my boys were born and placed in my arms, I was instantly in love with them, but completely overwhelmed. I learned by trial and error how to hold, nurse, diaper, and bathe my babies. We grew up together. I hardly ever played freely with them, the way I do now with my grandchildren.

I was too busy coping with the realities of my own life. I was preoccupied with the past, the old, familial owies that sometimes plagued me. But more than anything else, I worried about the future of my family. My marriage was in trouble, but as I had been raised to do, I kept my fear and anxiety to myself. I took solace in sitting on the back deck of our house, late at night, and looking out at the dark woods and the little creek that meandered among the trees. Some nights, I remembered a Salvadoran myth I'd heard as a child, of La Ziguanaba, a woman who had abandoned her children for the love of a man. Regretful soon after, she haunted the riverbanks, tearing at her hair and wailing forever in search of her loved ones. *Ay ay ay*, she keened.

Like La Ziguanaba, I experienced my biggest owie in relation to my children. When Chris and Jon were eleven and thirteen, their father and I finally realized the time had come to call it quits. We were living on the shore of one of the city's loveliest lakes. Our neighborhood wound around a long cul-de-sac road, and it was jumping with children. Because I could not afford the big old house we lived in; because we didn't want to uproot the boys, who attended the local school; because my husband worked from home, we decided together that I would be the one to move out.

Still, there was no escaping the fact that I was leaving my boys behind.

If I were a tree with multiple owies, this event would cause my trunk the biggest knot of all. In fact, my own trunk— that is, my torso—did have a huge owie then. Six months before I left the family home, I'd suffered a grievous accident: I was leaning against a balcony railing, about fifteen feet from the ground. In a moment that would later mark my life's *before* and *after*, the balcony railing broke and I plummeted to earth. My spine was shattered at three places. I spent three months in the hospital, lying ramrod-straight on a Stryker frame to keep the shards of spine from severing my spinal cord. When I finally left the hospital, I was wearing a full body cast. I would wear it for almost six months, after which I still had to undergo a difficult six-hour back surgery.

I moved into an apartment close to my work and did my job in the body cast. And though perhaps in some karmic record book, my shattered spine might be atonement enough for the decision I made to leave my children—despite seeing them regularly—the truth is that when my boys were vulnerable, I wasn't there.

Unlike the story of La Ziguanaba, who was destined to wail eternally for her children; unlike Abuelita, who pined until her death for the mother who abandoned her; unlike my mother, who never recovered from the loss of my twin sister, my story has a happy ending. Perhaps this will spare my own grandchildren the burden of carrying my pain and the pain of my ancestors. Time, patience, and love mended the rift between my sons and me. As they grew older, they began to see why I had decided to leave. Over the years, I've been favored by their understanding and forgiveness. Four years ago, when I held Harper in my arms right after he was born, it was as if I were seeing my baby Christopher again. My redemption story started then, with the birth of my first grandson.

Then one day a few years ago, when Karen, Harper's mom, was pregnant with Dashiell, Harper and I took one of our walks. It was late May and the weather was exactly what we Minnesotans pray for each winter day. After visiting the Owie Tree, we lay on the grass and looked up, scanning the sky for airplanes. We made grass angels, moving our arms up and down by our sides. Inadvertently, my hand bumped into Harp's, the one with the cyst. I sat up and held his hand. "Did I hurt you, sweetie?"

He sat up too and shook his head gravely, then gave his owie a little poke. "There's a baby in there, Tata." He said this so matter-of-factly that it took me aback.

"A baby?"

Harp nodded again. "Like Mama's belly. I have a baby, too."

"Well, can you feature that?" I replied.

A month later, when Dashiell was born, Harp went to the hospital to meet his new brother. I was waiting at the lobby entrance when Harp came bounding toward me. "Look," he said, holding up his arm. "I still have my baby." He wore a quizzical expression, as if trying to puzzle out why his mama had had her baby, but his was as yet floating in the thick liquid of his cyst. He didn't have to wait long. A few weeks later, Harp's owie disappeared. He was not at all surprised.

Last year, I traveled to Los Angeles to attend the birth of my first granddaughter. Jon and Nancy had told us the baby's gender ahead of time, but they were keeping her name a secret until after she was born. Nancy invited me into the birthing room, where I sat on a little couch, a few feet from the end of the delivery bed. I held my breath and quietly grunted hard each time the doctor commanded Nancy to *push*! I saw my granddaughter's head emerge, then her whole body. She was slick and shiny, rosy and wet when she surged into the light.

As if that miracle weren't enough, when the doctor was ready to cut the baby's cord, my son Jon said, "Ma, we want you to do it." And so, teary-eyed, I took the scissors from the doctor and snipped the ropy cord that tethered my granddaughter to her mother. In that moment, I felt showered by grace. Just as Harper's ganglion had suddenly disappeared after the birth of his brother, cutting my granddaughter's cord somehow freed me from lifelong guilt and shame, from my history of brokenness. With a firm snip, I was finally forgiven by the one who had never been capable of granting me forgiveness.

I forgave myself.

After the baby was cleaned, swaddled, and brought to her parents, Jon looked at me, his eyes glistening, and spoke his daughter's secret name.

Lila Susana. *Susana*, my lost twin sister's name.

The trunk of the Owie Tree is still marred by knots and bumps, but now when Harp, Dash, and I hug it, we look beyond its rough trunk, high up to where its branches spread out into a leafy crown like bright green hope.

Grandmothers Should Be Seen and Not Heard

ANNE ROIPHE

When my daughter's first baby had colic and woke every twenty minutes, I suggested that she be left to cry a little while before being picked up. My daughter glared at me, a thousand daggers. "You would suggest that," she said, and burst into tears herself. Was I a monster mother? Was I known round the globe for my callous indifference to crying children? I could see that my daughter was at her wit's end and could tolerate no suggestions at this tender, early stage of motherhood. She needed me to say, "You're doing everything right," as she was, essentially—or would be soon enough. I regretted my remark for the entire hour-long subway ride from her home back to my apartment.

Some days it seemed fine to say, "I think the baby might need an extra blanket," but every once in a while even such a mild comment, meant to be helpful, would cause my daughter to get tears in her eyes. Those tears would make me want to cry, and there we were: two tearful grown women and one slightly chilled infant.

Open lines of communication are fine in theory, and frankness and honesty are virtues most of the time. But if you happen to be a grandparent who hopes to be invited to the school play, the piano recital, or the birthday party, you had better seal your lips. Not speaking your mind is the number one commandment for would-be beloved grandparents. Silence on certain issues is not just golden; it's essential. No one is as sensitive as a young parent or more apt to snap your head off if you criticize; if you offer help when not asked; or if you comment, even ever so gently, on anything—from food choices to bedtimes, from discipline to reading habits. I am tempted to break this commandment all the time. I see clearly what is not so obvious to my children. I am calm when they are rattled. I am clear when they change their minds, muddle, weaken, spoil their offspring. Ah, my poor tongue is sore from being bitten.

I've managed *not* to say, "Why is your daughter wearing that dress to her birthday party when I have given her a far more beautiful one?" or, "It's time to get that child to give up her really revolting blanket. It smells so bad that I have to open all the windows after each visit." In time the blanket will go, and it doesn't matter what dress is worn to the party. I don't want to risk hurting my children, who hear my voice in a special way. A friend or neighbor can say almost anything without raising hackles. I can say almost nothing without causing pain. When I say, "I think the bath is too hot," I simply mean that the water may be too warm for the baby. But my daughters might hear me say, "You can't get the bath temperature right. What's the matter with you?" Their distress is an expression of their fear that they might be doing something wrong when they want so urgently to do everything right. From me, my daughters want support, admiration, encouragement—and that is all they want. They have books, the Internet, and friends for everything else.

Did I do a perfect job of raising them? No one is in jail. They're reasonably happy and productive. They are capable of love. Most of the time they're neither lazy nor wicked. They share my politics. They share my love of books. They like animals, they cook, they clean, they make a living. But every once in a while I hear a whine, a resentment, a deeply felt reproach, and usually, I have to admit, there is justice in the complaint. And though I don't think this disqualifies me from all advice on child rearing, I see a certain look in my children's eyes even if I begin a very mild, "You might want to . . ." I have learned to change the subject, drop the sentence midway—just as I've learned not to jump into a flaming lake or cross against the light if I see an oil truck bearing down.

My own mother died when my first child was barely two. I have no model for how I should be in this wonderful but sometimes strange role. I often think of my mother and how much she would have enjoyed being a grandmother. I resolve to do it right, as best I can, in her memory.

One day my daughter snatched a packet of raisins out of my hand just as I was offering some to her child. "That is a choking hazard," she snapped. Raisins were once a staple snack, and none of my children ever choked. I said so. My daughter turned away from me and her disapproval swept me out into a sea of despond. Things have changed since my grown children were babies; the dos and don'ts have altered. I am tempted to leave the child seat in the car empty and hold the wriggling baby on my lap. After all, my children never saw a car seat and still made it to Freshman Week. But when I mentioned this, I was greeted with such deep disapproval that you might have thought I'd suggested throwing the baby out the sixth-floor window. So now I buckle the protesting toddler into the seat and say nothing about what a peaceful drive we might have if car seats had never been invented.

Then there's *discipline*—a word with a very nineteenth-century ring to it and a kissing cousin of the word *no*. Although necessary once in a while, *no* is not a way to win hearts and minds. Nevertheless, as a grandparent I am willing, able, and eager to say *no* to my grandchildren. My children, their parents, sometimes can't. It's simple enough, I think. Just say, "No, I am not going to buy you that toy. No, you may not spill the sugar. No, you may not kick your sister under the table." Sometimes my children rise to the occasion and utter the word, but at other times they waffle and offer a weak "Maybe," "Maybe later," or "I'll think about it." But if I were to remark on what I see as an excess of yeses, my daughters would roar and rage at me. "Not your business," they would say. "What do you know?" And they would have a point. So I don't say anything. I smile. I nod. I hug. I bring a little present. I sit and watch a DVD with a child on my lap. This is all good, but it wouldn't be so good if I were a nagging, critical presence, a voice of law and order.

There are generational differences in how we respond to our offspring. My friends and I were hardly Victorian parents—invisible, authoritarian, dictators of the nursery—but this generation of parents seems especially sensitive to the horrors of stunting a child's developing joy and confidence. I believe the reluctance to take on the role of the naysaying parent is due, at least in part, to the fact that so many mothers today work away from home. Perhaps the pervasive guilt that all parents feel affects working mothers in insidious ways that make it particularly hard for them to say no—but easy for me. I go home from a visit, guilt-free, aware that more order, more *no*, would be a blessing for everyone.

Still, I don't think it's simply a change in manners, style, or work habits that makes it easy for me but difficult for my daughter to resist her daughter's imperious demands. Although the love of a grandparent is not weak or humble or without its own obsessions, it is not the same as parental love. The difference, I believe, comes from the degree of identification with the child. As the grandmother I do not feel every twitch, disappointment, or restraint on freedom as a rip in my soul, but I notice that my daughters respond as if they themselves are the ones who want a third helping of ice cream or who desperately need to stay up another half hour past a frequently unenforced bedtime. It's easy enough to be stern when the baby is not your baby, so close to your heart, a baby whose every breath is your breath. Love my grandchildren as I may, I still love my own children more, and I can't sleep when they get mad at me.

My concern is always split between my child and her child. "Your mother is tired," I want to say to a grandchild. "She doesn't want to play that game again. Let her sit in peace." Out of my love for my grandchild, I want to say to my daughter, "Enough television and video. That child's brain cells are about to turn into bird feed. If she's watching that model show at age ten, what is she going to be doing at fifteen?" But then I can't help thinking about what's best for my daughter, who needs a rest from the constant requests, needs, questions. "You should go away for a few days," I want to say. "*Buy* the cupcakes for the class party; go *out* to a movie." On the other hand, I can see the child's view, too:

My mother was too busy to make my cupcakes. My mother went away for four whole days and I wasn't sure she would return. I haven't seen her all day and now she is going out again. The two views knock against each other in my heart and create a certain acid burning that is not relieved by over-the-counter medication. I have learned that it is best to smile at both parent and child, to offer to make the cupcakes myself, but never to judge or come out on one side or the other.

Diplomacy is a skill honed through years of parenting. It comes in very handy when, as a grandparent, you are permitted into your children's days. I could say, "I think that lion is too big for the stroller and will fall on the ground and get dirty," as we head out the door to the park. But this would upset the child and challenge my daughter's judgment, since she has already agreed to bring the creature along. And though it's possible that my intervention might prevent tears later on when the oversize lion gets his tail ripped off by a passing bike, I've learned that it's better to keep quiet and offer to carry the lion in my arms until it's time to send him down the slide.

You could argue that as a grandparent I have a responsibility to say what I think, and my children should feel free to disregard my comments—but it isn't so simple. The pride, hope, and vulnerability of a young parent are so enormous, and her confidence is so easily shaken (I remember), that critical words can be heard as an attack on her very soul. Challenge her competence and you strike at her heart.

Grown children don't welcome criticism of their offspring any more than they appreciate advice about their parenting style. So there's no point in suggesting, "Why don't you get his hair cut?" Or, "I don't think you want to give that child piano lessons, he's tone-deaf." Or, "Don't bother sending her to gymnastics class, she's too large-boned." It makes no difference if criticism is mild or serious; it will be especially painful coming from you. Far better to let the outside world provide the corrective: the gymnastics teacher will suggest another afternoon activity; the cello will be dropped before the semester is over; the pigeon-toed child will give up ballet long before she can sit through *The Nutcracker.* Despite our clearer, colder eyes, grandparents should avoid making any remark that diminishes the absolute perfection of the grandchild. Maybe later, maybe if that child's parent notices a problem and comes to you for advice or help (or, more likely, money), then the two of you can have an honest discussion. But, unsolicited, any comment that chips away your child's vision of her perfect child won't change anything. Worse, it will leave in its wake some very hard feelings.

When a child is sick or damaged in some way, our role as grandparents is to support our children in finding the best care for that child and to help them survive their pain. It's not in anyone's interest to let our fears and worries be a further burden. This requires care and sensitivity: too much cheeriness will be perceived—correctly—as fakery; too much empathy will be unwelcome. Mostly, we need to be aware of how sensitive our children are about their children, and how deep the wound is when something goes wrong— even something minor and fixable. And when something happens to our own children, such as a divorce, it doesn't help to say, "You shouldn't; it's bad for the kids." They know that. They need our support, not our emotional response. It isn't helpful to weep with them—they have their own grief and anxiety. Best to say little and think what we think in private. I have silently removed a wedding photo from my table, and spoken aloud only of the future and good things to come.

When they become parents, most children try to outdo their parents. *My mother never let me have a dog, so my child will have a dog before she can say bowwow. My mother and father took long vacations every year without me, so I will never leave my children even for a weekend. My parents were lunatics about saving money, so I will buy anything that is shiny and plastic and lights up.* This natural response is hard on grandparents. By seeing what choices they make for their children, we suddenly see what our children objected to in their own childhood. *You never let me play football, so I am going to enter my son in the junior football league at age four. You were a vegetarian and a health nut; we go to McDonald's every Sunday.* There's no point in arguing about these choices or commenting on them. If we interfere, we will surely get an earful of complaints about what we did wrong. No parent is perfect. Almost all children wish that something were different about their childhood. *It was boring in the suburbs. It was terrible in the city.* As grandparents, we can only watch and hope that our children's choices will prove in the end to be like ours—a mixed bag of good and bad.

I look at my grown children pushing their strollers, picking up their children at school, arranging lessons, buying clothes—and I remember doing all those things myself. I know that this is their time; mine is over. That makes me sad sometimes. I wouldn't mind if a baby were delivered to my apartment door with a note, "Take care of me," pinned to a diaper. I wouldn't mind starting all over again. But that isn't going to happen. I remind myself that just as I had to step back when my children became teenagers and whispered things into the phone they didn't want me to hear, now I have to step back, admire from a distance, carry a photo or two in my wallet, listen to a report on the telephone—but not be at the center, not express every thought that comes to mind, not play a significant role in the important decisions, such as which school, what doctor, which camp? Wonderful as it is, being a grandparent doesn't provide you a second chance to do everything over again. It does allow you to play in the fields of the next generation—to enjoy the laughter, the games, the physical contact, the accomplishments of children you love beyond reason. Being a grandparent allows you to appreciate your own children in a new way: *Look what they do, look what they've produced.* It gives us, as we age, a glimpse of the future and promises us a presence—if only through our DNA—in years to come.

Making Memories

LETTY COTTIN POGREBIN

I've been in love with my husband for forty-five years, but when I look at him I don't see the pure wonder of life or think about keeping him safe from nuclear proliferation as I do when I look at Ethan or Benjamin.

I love my twin daughters fiercely, but I don't work my butt off trying to find creative ways to amuse and entertain them or make them eager to spend time with me as I do when I'm with Maya or Molly.

I have a son I adore, but when I watch him reading a book or riding a bike I don't feel I'm witnessing a miracle and my heart doesn't get all squishy in my chest as it does when I look at Zev or Arlo.

As you've undoubtedly guessed, Ethan, Benjamin, Maya, Molly, Zev, and Arlo are my grandchildren, and, speaking of miracles, all six of them live within forty blocks of me. Their schools, too, are within walking distance of our house. In Grandma Land, this is an embarrassment of riches. When I meet a contemporary of mine for the first time, I almost dread the moment when she tells me her children live in California or Houston or Rome, but luckily she gets to see her grandkids four or five times a year. Then she asks me how I often I see mine, and I have to tell her, "Usually once a week."

Each of our three children has produced two of our

grandchildren, the eldest of whom is eleven, the youngest six. Before they came into my life, I didn't miss them. Now, if I haven't seen one for a longer stretch than usual, I feel grumpy and incomplete. When I'm scheduled to pick up one of them at school, I'm as excited as a teenager looking forward to a date. Seeing their faces light up when I enter their classroom or watching them run across the yard to fly into my arms, you would think I was a rock star. Which is how they make me feel. They are the only human beings on the planet who can send me over the moon with the words "When can you come over, Grammy?"

Millions of grandparents are equally enamored and millions enjoy similarly heartwarming experiences with their grandchildren. But from conversations with my friends, I don't sense that others share my intense yearning to leave an imprint, or harbor the same need as I do to connect with their grandchildren at a deep level and create the kind of fun that leaves lifelong memories.

If you know my history, my obsession won't surprise you. I lost my mother when she was fifty-three and I was fifteen. Subtract the period when her mothering was compromised by her illness and cancer treatments, and for all intents and purposes I had thirteen years of my mother's best self. Then take away the first three years of my life, which are a complete blur, and that leaves ten years during which I consciously experienced her influence and love. Yet in that brief time this extraordinary woman managed to leave an imprint that has nourished and sustained me my whole life. The trouble is, she didn't leave enough memories.

Or rather, I wasn't paying close enough attention. Had I known she was going to die so soon, I would have spent more time with her, asked her questions about her past, learned what she had to teach me and who she was as a woman beyond being my mom. Had *she* known she would be gone so soon, she might have done things differently, too, shared more of herself while she was clearheaded enough to assess her life and pass along her wisdom.

Since she never lived to see them, the only way my children know their Grandma Ceil is through my recollections of her. I've plumbed my memory for images that might make my mother real to them, but all I can come up with are generic homemaker scenes—Mommy in her flowered housedress spooning blueberries into the hollow of a half cantaloupe, stuffing celery with cream cheese, beating a rug in the yard—and maternal images, such as Mommy brushing my hair "one hundred strokes to make it shine" or sitting patiently in a dressing room at S. Klein's on the Square while I tried on dresses for my bat mitzvah; Mommy reading to me—not ordinary children's fare but Charles and Mary Lamb's *Tales from Shakespeare*, the poems of Robert Louis Stevenson, the novels of Louisa May Alcott.

The one image for which I have concrete evidence is that of my mother as an enthusiastic amateur painter. Today her landscapes and still lifes fill one wall in my home. Because I was present at their creation, all the canvases take me back to the objects and places that were her subjects, and to the look on her face when she set up her easel on our back porch or in the field behind my grandparents' house—a look that said, *This I can control.*

Besides the time I spent observing her at her easel, my most vivid memories of the years I spent as my mother's daughter involve her superstitions. Born in a shtetl in Hungary—think

Fiddler on the Roof, the "little village of Anatevka"—she was raised with a mystical, primitive, folkloric Judaism in which old wives' tales were more authoritative than Bible text and the evil eye was more intimidating than God. In that society, girls were not considered important enough to educate and women were denied access to the Torah and the teachings of the sages; not surprisingly, women found succor and refuge in magical thinking. And just as Jewish knowledge was passed from father to son, every mother passed to her daughter the body of folk knowledge with which she made sense of her world.

When my mother came to America at the beginning of the twentieth century in tattered clothes and cardboard shoes, along with her battered suitcase she carried the beliefs and incantations of the Old Country. If they were good enough to protect her parents and siblings from the Cossacks and pogroms, they were good enough to protect Ceil Cottin and her new family from whatever hazards might lurk in the streets of suburban Queens.

What my mother learned from her mother, I learned from her and passed on to my children, though not because I believed tying a red string to a baby's bassinet would scare away the devil. My rational mind knew that was nonsense, just as it knew that half saying, half spitting "Thpu, thpu, thpu" wasn't going stop bad things from happening. Still, I tied the string and made those ridiculous sounds anyway. I closed the window blinds in my children's rooms so the moon wouldn't shine on them while they slept, not because I really thought the evil eye would swoop down and take them (the moon should shine only on one's grave), but because that was what my mother did for me; that was how she showed that she loved me and wanted to keep me safe. I have preserved and honored those superstitions as symbols of my mother's impact on my life, and because I want her grandchildren, who never knew her, to have something to remember her by.

Another reason I'm so motivated to create enduring memories for my grandchildren is that I have no sense at all of my paternal grandparents, who died before I was born, and few specific images of my maternal grandparents, though they were intermittently present in my childhood. My father's mother, for whom I was named, emigrated with my paternal grandfather to Palestine in the early 1930s. Though my father, who lived to be eighty-two, had plenty of time to harvest his memories, all he ever said about his mother was that she was "a sweet, kind woman."

I can personally attest that my mother's mother, Grandma Jenny, was a sweet, kind woman because my first seven or eight summers were spent with her and my grandfather in their farmhouse in Shrub Oak, New York (the inspiration for several of my mother's paintings), and they subsequently lived with us in Queens for a couple of years. I knew my Grandma Jenny as a quiet, loving presence, but not as a person. Though she outlived my mother by several years, I don't recall ever having had a real conversation with her, or having done anything or gone anywhere with her. I remember she once took out a cardboard box and showed me her ratty old *shaytl*—the wig many Orthodox Jewish women wear after marriage—that she'd put away as soon as she arrived in America. However, my dominant image of her is of an old woman (she must have been only in her sixties) with an ample bosom who spoke mostly Yiddish, stayed in the kitchen, and never seemed too happy with my grandfather;

an old woman who cooked on a cast-iron stove, ate stewed prunes with softened white bread, and put her false teeth in a glass of water before she went to bed.

I want my grandchildren to remember more about me than my quirks, which is why I work so hard to make our time together worthy of permanent storage on their hard drives. When they're grown, I want them to be able to say something I could never say about my grandmothers, and my children could never say about my mother: "Grandma and I always used to . . ."

In my grandchildren's infancies and toddlerhoods, I spent countless hours on the floor with them playing blocks, trains, Legos, and Mr. Potato Head, and reading Dr. Seuss. Hanging out at home was fun, though when all six were there— especially when they played dress-up and everyone needed help with their costumes and the living room was ankle deep in accessories for Spider-Man, Dorothy, the Tin Man, two cops, and a firefighter—the chaos was sometimes overwhelming. During the last few years, I've preferred going out and about with them, either individually or in pairs.

I plan our outings, which I call "adventures," with considerable forethought and little trust in serendipity. An adventure might be a museum visit, especially when there's a child-friendly special exhibit. Central Park is a constant kid festival, what with the zoo, merry-go-round, rowboats, playgrounds, and grassy meadows for picnics. Ethan and I have gone Rollerblading in the park two or three times, but he's gotten too good for me. I found a pet shop in Greenwich Village that lets kids play with the puppies "to socialize them." FAO Schwarz is an adventure if you avoid the expensive toys and go directly to the giant electrified piano keyboard where kids can stamp out tunes with their feet, just as Tom Hanks did in the movie *Big*.

Then there are birthdays. For the last few years, rather than give them wrapped and beribboned birthday presents, I—sometimes with my husband—take the grandchildren birthday shopping individually and let them choose their own gifts. Not only is this a celebratory way to spend time with them, it lets me keep up with their changing tastes and reassure myself that they're not the sort of kids who say "Gimme" the minute they hit a store. (Ben always wins my heart when he holds up his pick and says, "I'd like this, Grandma. Unless it's too expensive." And the others are so well trained in grandchild etiquette that I sometimes have to call a halt to the thank-yous.)

Since our adventures often take place after school, we usually share a snack or an early dinner. As adventures go, eating with a child can top them all because the experience isn't really about the food; it's about the conversation—and with my grandchildren, that's as likely to be about family, love, God, homeless people, war, divorce, or death as it is about Harry Potter, *American Idol*, or dinosaurs.

Our most ambitious and satisfying enterprise is Grandparents Weekend. When Ben and Ethan, the two oldest boys, turned seven (they are cousins, born seven weeks apart, the sons of our twin daughters), my husband and I took them away for a weekend in Washington, D.C. Since that time, we've replicated the experience in different venues with all the grandchildren, two at a time—a tradition we have thankfully (though who knows for how much longer) been able to afford.

Ben and Ethan get an autumn weekend—the year after

Washington, we took them to Boston, and the year after that to "the only authentic dude ranch in New York." Molly and Maya (also cousins, seven months apart, and the daughters of our daughters) get a spring weekend. Thus far, they've been to a mountain lodge, to Philadelphia, and to Hershey, Pennsylvania. Last February, we took our son's sons, Zev and Arlo, for their first Grandparents Weekend, a two-day ice-skating event, and from now on they'll get a winter weekend each year. (Lest you think we would let a season go by without a healthy dose of grandchildren, in the summer the two youngest spend a great deal of time at our beach house, where the four eldest stay for a week in August *without* their parents.)

Planning three separate Grandparents Weekends a year presents a major challenge to my research skills and puts a large dent in our finances. At times, I get pretty stressed. This year was great—will next year measure up? Will one pair of grandchildren think the other pairs' destinations were better? Will I run out of ideas? Will we run out of money? When they're teenagers, will they still want to go with us? What will happen to the tradition when my husband and I are too old to do anything physical or after one of us dies? We've decided not to worry about the last few questions until we have to.

Although we strive to entertain the grandchildren, what makes our weekends so precious and meaningful is not any particular activity but the intimacy of our time together. We always book one hotel room with two double beds for reasons of economy, but also because sharing a room and a bath allows us to see each child's habits and routines close-up—and them to see ours. They know Grandma will insist they put away their clothes in the bureau the minute we arrive instead of letting them dress out of their suitcases, and they know it's futile to talk to Grandpa in the morning until he puts in his hearing aids. Our snoring has become a running joke with them. But they also know they will have our undivided attention from Friday to Sunday, and that we relish our breakfast, lunch, and dinner chats even more than the things we do between meals.

By the same token, concentrated weekend exposure has allowed us to know them not just as "the grandchildren" but as remarkable and unique individuals. We know that the minute we hit the hotel room, Molly will start pretending she's the concierge or room service or she'll set up a spa; Ben will charm the waitstaff with his politeness and in no time be worrying about whether they enjoy their work; Maya will want a room key of her own, flash her incandescent smile at everyone, and refuse to wear shoes to the pool; Ethan will memorize the hotel floor plan and immediately suggest he and Ben go off on their own; Zev will want onions on his salad and be fine with either bed as long as he gets to read before lights-out; and Arlo will have strong feelings about which bed he gets and will bounce on it until we tell him to stop.

A friend of mine recently returned from abroad after a ten-day visit with her daughter, son-in-law, and granddaughter. "Were ten days enough?" I asked. "Not enough with my grandchild," she said. "More than enough with my kid."

That's the weird thing about this stage of life. Because we and our kids have a long backstory, we may have issues with them, tender spots, flash points that set us off. But our grandchildren see us afresh and we see them as a living, breathing opportunity to correct the mistakes we made the first time around. We reach over the heads of our children and hold hands with our future. My mother never lived long enough to do that, or to plan adventures, or to teach her grandchildren to paint. My kids never got to hear her stories about me, what I was like when I was their age, how I gave up sucking my thumb, the time I ran away from home. I never heard these stories myself. My mother's death obliterated not just her life, but my history.

That's probably the biggest reason I value memories so much, why I want to make new ones with my grandchildren but also to bequeath to them—and to their parents—the old ones. My husband and I are the repositories of our son's and daughters' pasts. Our memory is our children's biography and our grandchildren's legacy.

In June of this year, I turned sixty-nine. The "nine" of each decade has always been harder for me than the round number because it means I have to get ready to exit the ten-year cycle it took me nine years to get used to. Being a time-obsessed person, I have already begun preparing myself to leave my sixties behind and enter this bizarre-sounding new place, my seventies. The next birthday will be traumatic, no question about it. But as I lurch toward that previously unimaginable number, I hope to console myself with the following thoughts:

First, if I make it to seventy, I will have lived seventeen years longer than my mother. I need to focus on that fact so that when the day comes, I will feel grateful to be alive rather than pissed off at my age. Second, at seventy, if my health holds out, I could be looking at ten more years of adventures with the grandchildren and, assuming three per year, thirty more Grandparents Weekends. That's worth seventy birthday candles, if you ask me. Finally, here's the clincher: Only by growing old can we witness our grandchildren growing older. It's an existential trade-off. We lose years, they gain them. Someday I will be addled or decrepit and unable to organize adventures. But at that point it won't matter. If all goes well, my grandchildren will be too busy making memories of their own. And every now and then, in the midst of some perfect pleasure, maybe they will smile at their kids and say, "You know, this reminds me of something I used to do with my grandma."

On Becoming an Ancestor

ELLEN GILCHRIST

The day my first grandchild was born I looked at him and knew that I would never die. All my life I had searched for first causes, tried to reconcile mortality with the goodness of life, tried to comprehend infinity, to understand how I fit into such incomprehensible vastness. I had studied philosophy, read thousands of books, contemplated particle physics, meditated, done yoga, sat zazen.

And here was the answer: a little boy carrying my DNA, looking up at me with huge dark eyes. My lifelong dread of death fell from my shoulders like a worn-out cloak. My DNA was safe in this little boy and he would care for it when I was gone. To hell with infinity. My lifetime and his seemed like all the time anyone could ask for.

Twenty-one years later his wife gave birth to their first son. I looked at that small baby and said to my grandson, "Well, I'm in the gene pool for another hundred years. Thanks for that."

"Thank Courtney," he answered. "She did the heavy lifting."

Now I have fourteen grandchildren and two great-grandchildren. I think of them as a flock of blessings, a vast treasure that has been bestowed on me by a benevolent universe of cause and effect and great good luck. That all of them are healthy and beautiful and smart makes my breath go soft.

I am only one of many people who love them. My great-grandchildren have a great-grandmother on their mother's side who lives 200 miles away. Her name is Tellie. We have never met, Tellie and I, but there is a deep understanding and love that moves between us. We send each other messages. The children tell me stories about her and they tell her stories about me. She sends me homemade caramel cakes when the children visit her on their way to see me. These cakes are fit for the gods. There are probably only a handful of people left in the world who can caramelize sugar to exactly the right temperature so that the caramel icing is half an inch thick and does not crumble or fall off, even after days on the road. My granddaughter-in-law tells me Tellie will only make the cakes on days when the temperature and humidity are within a certain range.

So how do I pay these children back for being born? I worship them and they know it. I think they're smarter than I am and I tell them. Occasionally, I let them watch me take out my partial plate and clean it, but you have to be careful with that sort of scientific information. My oldest grandchild screamed when his baby teeth fell out because his grandfather on his mother's side had shown him his full set of false teeth so many times. That grandfather was a NASA scientist and had been trying to explain lightweight plastics to the child.

Some of my grandchildren live far away on other continents and it is becoming increasingly difficult for me to fly to where they are, so I keep up with them by mail and e-mail. For the ones who are near enough to visit, I have a home on the Mississippi coast. It is a small townhouse on the beach full of beds and toys and drawing materials. I am not a perfect grandmother, but I am the best one I can figure out how to be.

I wish I never let them watch television, but they overpower me. I wish I were better at making them brush their teeth. I wish I would cook organic vegetables and never take them to McDonald's, but I would have to get a brain transplant and have had a different childhood to be that grandmother.

I am essentially the same sort of grandmother as I was a mother. Though I am a very self-disciplined person, a hardworking writer and college professor when I'm with other adults in Fayetteville, Arkansas, I don't like to discipline small children. They live in the present. They know how to have fun. As the Cat in the Hat said, "It's fun to have fun but you have to know how." I know how.

Whenever I get a break, I get into my car and drive like a bat out of hell down some bad highways to my little house on the beach and wait for the children. They climb out of their parents' automobiles and come running in the door to hug me and give me viral colds they picked up at their schools and ask me in conspiratorial voices if we can go to the Wal-Mart to buy plastic toys made in China. My house on the beach, which was rebuilt after hurricane Katrina, contains all the Barbie furniture recently featured in the television warnings. I even have a real sofa and chair and ottoman almost identical to the light green ones that are supposed to contain the most lead. We keep the doll furniture on a high shelf so the two-year-old redheaded boy won't chew on it.

He loves the girls' dollhouses. He likes to put plastic turkeys in the plastic oven. After he puts one in, he sits and watches the oven with a serious expression on his face.

My joy at the children's arrival rises to euphoria when they run into the kitchen and check the refrigerator to make sure there is plenty of chocolate pudding for us to eat as soon as we get rid of their parents. They also make sure there's plenty of Quaker Oatmeal Squares cereal and high-fat milk and Chicken Lean Cuisine. We don't like complicated meals at my grandmother house. They take too much time away from playing with the plastic toys we already have and plotting to get more without raising their parents' hackles, then going to the beach to try out the new post-Katrina pier and daring our bodies against the jellyfish in the Mississippi Sound and later, God forbid, God forgive me, watching videos. There's a new one the preteen girls and I love. It's called *The Pacifier*, and I highly recommend it if you like to see bad little boys get put in their place by little girls who have been trained in the martial arts. My great-grandsons just keep on liking *Scooby-Doo*. Their parents are so sick of *Scooby-Doo* we have to keep the volume low until they leave the premises.

I worry about the children spending so much time watching videos and I limit the amount of time they spend watching them at my house. I'm also very careful about what they watch. If there is anything that by any stretch of the imagination could be scary, I watch it with them and pretend to be terrified when the scary part comes on. "Turn it off," I yell, and pull the covers over my head. They tell me not to worry, "it's only an actor in a costume like on Halloween."

My paternal grandmother used to pretend to be little

people locked up inside the radio talking to us. "Let me out," she would scream. "I'm tired of being stuck in the radio." I was always in bed when she did this. It was a ploy to keep me from being afraid of the dark.

"It's all right, Granny," I would tell her. "It's just electricity. No people are in there. The people are in Memphis or Nashville."

My mother was the same sort of grandmother I am, only she was better at getting people to brush their teeth. She was also better at making pound cake and chocolate sundaes and macaroni and cheese and carrots and green peas. Anything she cooked seemed like health food because she loved the children so much while she was making it. Like me, she had plenty of toys. She had swings in her yard and whirligigs and seesaws and waterslides. In her house there were dolls, crayons and coloring books, and books to read. There were photograph albums, too, that went back to the early 1900s so little children could look at their ancestors' pictures and find out who they were and where they came from.

I am as good as my mother was at taking people shopping, although she bought shoes and haircuts instead of plastic toys. Part of my luck since I became a grandmother is that I have enough money to help the children and indulge them. An unending thrill for me is taking my granddaughters shopping for clothes, since I never had a daughter. The oldest one is six feet tall. She is slender and gorgeous with wild red hair. The second one is five foot ten and has darker hair and dark brown eyes. They both have exquisite taste and look wonderful in clothes. When my oldest grandson, who is six feet six inches tall, had to have a tuxedo and there were not any long enough to rent, I took him to the Beau Rivage Casino and bought him an Armani. His mother just shook her head. He was going to the senior prom with an older girl. That was nine years ago. The older girl is now his wife and the mother of my great-grandchildren. My grandson still wears the tuxedo.

It's natural that I am childlike when I am with children. It's my natural bent, coming to me from all sides of my family. We are mostly Scots and English, but there is enough Welsh and Irish blood to explain all this. We come from people who believed in fairies and elves and gremlins and four-leaf clovers. My mother could find four-leaf clovers anywhere. She was renowned in the Mississippi delta for her luck in finding four-leaf clovers. I could never find them and thought my lucky life was because I was her daughter. She had found so many four-leaf clovers I figured she had luck to spare.

There is so much going on that we don't understand. When I looked at my first grandchild and knew, in a blinding illumination, that I would never die, maybe that was a glimpse behind the veil of all we do not know about chemistry and biology and connections.

I don't think you have to have children to share in this wonder. We are all part of the great gene pool of our species. If I were a Zen master I might be able to see even deeper than that. I might see connections that are vastly wider and infinite.

For now, for this life, I'll just go on being grateful for this smaller knowledge. And for the luck that has put me here and has kept me here this long.

Everything That Goes Up
Must Come Down

SUSAN GRIFFIN

There they are in my memory, my grandmother and my great-grandmother, two very different women, both formidable. When I think of Nanny, my father's grandmother, she is either in her kitchen or in her garden, the small plot of land behind her modest home that, with its rows of corn and its free-range chickens, seemed like a little farm to me. I rarely saw her outside this realm. Yet she was not at all diminished by domesticity. Anyone who entered her house or her garden could feel the considerable force that emanated from her thin, aging presence, the force of her being.

My grandmother on my mother's side had gravitas of her own. She inspired a certain fear, not of whips or branches but of her disapproval—expressed through exaggerated sighs or a drawn, disappointed expression. One did not want to disappoint her. After all, she was in charge. She was like a cornucopia, producing celebrations, decorations, candies, jams, and jellies; reading poems and stories; making red velvet dresses; planting flowers that bloomed in the night.

To my young eyes both women possessed a large measure of magic. There was so much they could do; they had skills I do not have, like canning, sewing, raising chickens, and gathering eggs. Yet as I think of all that my ancestors knew, I find myself reaching for still another meaning. I am a grandmother myself now, and it seems to me that starting with the birth of my first grandchild I have entered a new stage in my life.

One is accustomed to observing such changes earlier. The transitions from infancy to childhood, from childhood to adolescence, crowned by the stage of maturation, when we reach full and legal adulthood, are marked and celebrated. But though the inevitable transitions into middle age and then old age are certainly noticed, they have become nearly unmentionable, a necessary but unfortunate decline, an embarrassing challenge to the illusion of immortality, as twenty-first-century America pedals along with youth culture, Viagra, and Botox.

Who among us is not happy to be thought younger than she really is? Certainly I want to remain vital, resilient, and enthusiastic, if not beautiful, forever. And yet there was a strong sense I had—unmistakable, with its own beauty, its own undeniable spark—as I began to consider that I was going to be a grandmother. With the birth of one and then two grandchildren this feeling only got stronger. Not just the circumstances of my life and my family were changing; I was, too. I was moving into a new stage of my life, experiencing not simply the erosion of age, but something new, a different awareness, a different way of being.

When I reflect on this stage, what arises are images of my grandmother and great-grandmother. I am not very much like either of them. My life is so different. And though at times I do cook for my grandchildren, I am a working woman. Often tired at the end the day, I take them out to dinner. And my attitudes, especially toward women or child rearing, are so much more modern. Yet as I look more closely at those images of my elders in my mind's eye, they are stretched out, as if in an unbroken line, from one generation to the next. And if once as the grandchild, I was standing at one end as the future, now I stand at the other end, as the past, a grandmother.

The image, unpremeditated, arising from some less articulate part of my imagination, seems to hold the essence for me of the passage into a new stage of my life, with a new awareness of the passage of time. It is difficult as a grandmother to escape that simple feature of life.

I was in the room at the hospital holding a movie camera when my granddaughter, Sophie, was born. Since I gave birth to my daughter using natural childbirth, I had seen her come into the world, too. To see the birth of a child is an astonishing, even transformative experience. I remember days of wonder and awe, feeling close to the line between being and not being, with all the mysteries that this boundary holds.

To see the birth of your grandchild is just as moving, in the same way. But there is another dimension. You are seeing your child give birth to her child. If you did not fully take in the raw miracle of existence when your own child was born, or if you forgot, now you will be given a stronger dose of the same medicine, as you see her open wider than you thought a woman's body could open, and then, covered with blood and afterbirth, a little head emerges, a body, a child who on hitting the air, amazing as it seems at that moment, starts to cry.

I could not be there when, almost five years later, my grandson, Jasper, was born; but I joined the family in the hospital room soon afterward. Sophie was there too, peering at her brother with curiosity. My son-in-law and my ex-husband and his partner, La Le, both of them my friends now, were all in a jubilant mood, especially since both mother and child had survived a difficult pregnancy. We passed little Jasper back and forth, all of us aware to the point of tears that this was the first day of his life.

Gravitas. As the word springs to mind, I remember an evening a few years back when Sophie and Jasper were taking a bath together. They were throwing various bath toys up in the air, and responding with great glee and excitement when each object would splash back down in the water.

At some point in the middle of all this hilarity I said, almost by habit, "Everything that goes up must come down." Of course I should have predicted that neither Sophie nor Jasper had heard this before. Jasper did not have enough words yet to question me about it, but Sophie sat up, and speaking with all the fierce ability that seven-year-olds have to disagree, told me, "No, it doesn't!" She described all the exceptions to the rule she could think of, including what happened when she threw a toy designed to stick to a surface on the wall. Oh, no, I thought to myself, how will I ever explain *this* to her? But somehow I managed to her satisfaction, and watched her indignation fade into curiosity.

Gravity is also apparent in the faces of people past a certain age. What once was firm now sags. The motion of maturation is upward until midway it all starts to turn down. If you fail to observe the passage of time in yourself, you will always be able to see it in your grandchildren. Now I am coming to understand that tone of surprise, even shock, in the voices of elders who say to a young child, "My, how you've grown!"

I grasped the subtext of that expression even before Jasper was born, while my daughter was still carrying him. Because of the trouble with her pregnancy, I used to try to imagine him as a twenty-year-old. Tall, lanky, of course handsome, with light hair. This was the Pascal-like wager I carried on with the new age: think positively, I told myself. Whenever I was overwhelmed with anxiety, I would sink into a fantasy. Jasper aged twenty and Sophie aged twenty-five would come to visit me and I would give them lunch. Being fond of realistic details in stories, when I pictured myself at these future meals, I had become considerably less robust and more wrinkled. After all, according to my own math, I had turned eighty.

Before Jasper was born, when Sophie was four, she began to ask questions about aging and death. One morning she asked my daughter, "Mommy, are you almost dead?"

"No, Sophie, no. Why do you ask?" my daughter said.

"Because you are soooo old," my granddaughter replied.

She was trying to wrap her mind around the concept of chronology, especially as it plays out in a human life. Her sense of age had nothing to do with appearance. Nearing forty now, my daughter still looks youthful. It was just the numbers that had confounded Sophie. She was not good yet at reading the more subtle signs of age. I know this because despite the fact that my hair is nearly white, in the same period she told me she thought I was younger than her mother. Soon I realized that she thought this because whenever I wasn't sure of the rules, I told her I would have to ask her mother. Clearly she must have thought that whoever has the most authority must be the oldest.

As she grew up, she began to understand age better. We used to play a game in which she would ask how old I was and I would tell her—sixty or sixty-two or however old I was at the time—and she would laugh as she considered such an incomprehensible number.

When you become a grandparent, you cannot escape the fact that you are older, soooo much older, and if not "almost dead," much closer to death. As you watch, thrilled by each inch your grandchild grows, each new skill and concept she masters, your own time you begin to realize is limited.

Does this bring you to instant enlightenment, wisdom, or perfection? Not at all. You may grow inwardly, to be sure. Faults and foibles may lose their disguises along with any vestige of youthful charm that mitigated them. At the very least, at this age most us of begin to drop any pretense of perfection or even perfectibility, along with moral superiority and a host of other similar illusions.

But this is all gratis, an extra donation, not the defining edge of this late territory. With or without all our faults and sins, the role we play as grandparents, the real wisdom we pass on, is just in being. We *are* age. We have come to embody what has passed and is passing. And in the eyes of our grandchildren, we are the past come to meet them, a living link ready to connect them to a larger lineage—their own history, ours, the history of the planet. We are the doorway to the vast continents of time that existed before they were born, and that will exist after they too die.

This knowledge has always been available intellectually. The passage of time is taught by clocks, calendars, and stories from history. But like sunrise, sunset, and the passing of the seasons, the presence of grandparents provides lessons in the passage of time that are not only more vivid but integrated. The roots of the past live in you. I am thinking again of my grandmother, the way she would set up the kitchen to can fruit on a Saturday in late summer, her face flushed with the steam from the boiling water she used to sterilize the glass containers. She kept jars of canned peaches, figs, nectarines, and strawberry jam on shelves in the cellar. The cellar was like a small museum—a visit back in time. Where, for instance, the wooden hand-cranked Victrola, with a speaker shaped like a trumpet, was kept. But there were drawers upstairs that held treasures, too, not just the family photographs, some themselves reminders of another time, framed with filigreed gold on embossed red velvet—another style, another sensibility. In the back of Nanny's house there was a small cottage that had intriguing contents, too, including bridles for horses, which spoke of a way of life that had long since passed.

My grandmother and great-aunt occasionally told us stories about their lives, but what gave me an even greater glimpse into the past was how these sisters were in the present. Even their names bore the scent of history: Emily Ivalou and Nelle. Every year the family would gather in northern California, in Davis, to celebrate Thanksgiving at my great-aunt Nelle's house. The night before our turkey dinner, all the women would sit around the table to pluck the feathers from the bird. It was on a Thanksgiving night, after we had all eaten, and the adults were warm with whiskey, that my grandmother and great-aunt began to reminisce about their mother and father. Try as I might, I can never recall much of what they said. But the moment is still with me, as if tinted sepia, with the lovely glow that comes from the soft, bleeding earth tones of that tint. My great-aunt's face seems transfigured as she thinks of her father and how he was in his last year, his hair so long and so white. "So white, and he liked to have it brushed," she said, her eyes suddenly misty, her voice sweetly reverent.

It was a new view into the mysterious past, giving me the palpable knowledge that indeed my grandmother had a father and a mother; that despite everything a long line of love ran back in time, far beyond my own memory; and that once, these two formidable women were not a grandmother and a great-aunt, but both daughters, vulnerable, small, lively, and eager to embrace the future.

And there is this, too. What a thrill as I grew older to realize that this shadowy man they spoke of, whom I never knew, was probably born just before or just after the Emancipation Proclamation, when Abraham Lincoln was still president and Walt Whitman was still writing his poetry. Through the breath of life in my great-aunt's voice, I was able to take in this history and make it mine.

Like many grandmothers today, I still feel hip and modern (though at least one of those words may already seem antiquated). But I know I have the past inside me. In Los Angeles during the 1940s and early 1950s, my grandmother and I used to take the trolley down Pico Boulevard to shop for my school clothes. I remember crowding with my family around the radio at night while George Burns and Gracie Allen made us laugh. I remember a time before computers, when telephones were still hooked to the wall and cords were short, and you made long-distance calls only on holidays. I was close to my father, the great-grandfather my grandkids will never know, except perhaps through some of his manners that live in me. I tell them that sometimes he took me to the firehouse, where he would stay overnight and slide down a brass pole whenever the alarm sounded. And— well, I never saw a battlefield, but images from World War II surrounded me, and I grew up seeing uniformed soldiers returning home. Our favorite game, when I was a kid, was to pretend we were landing on the beach at Normandy. And, yes, I remember a time when even my strict grandmother would let me play kickball in the streets with my friends, and I'd walk a mile to school by myself when I was only seven years old. It was a different world, and in many subtle ways I know I pass something of it on to my grandchildren.

But the most important legacy I have to give them is simply my age. I am an older person. The mother of their mother, a concept it took each of them a while to grasp, and grasping it was a sign of maturity. Folded into my age are invisible signs. I have seen a life span, witnessed birth and death; I grasp the fragile bliss of being incarnate from the slightly higher vantage point of all the time I've spent on earth.

And I know this, too: that the more I accept my age— not as a form of condemnation or a license to be brittle and boring, but as part of a natural process that has its own profundities—the better and happier I feel. It is true what people say: knowing that it all will end makes you appreciate every moment more.

My grandkids help me on this path. They make me laugh all the time and wonder at the world, too. When he was very little, Jasper laughed a lot, and all of us loved to try to get him to do this. One day when her father was having great success with him, Sophie pleaded, "Stop trying to make him laugh!"

Perceptively, my son-in-law answered, "Are you afraid you won't be able to make him laugh? Do you think he'll run out of laughs?"

"Yes," she told him.

"Children never run out of laughs," he said.

To which Sophie replied, "But grown-ups do." Intrigued, my son-in-law asked her if she knew why that was. She thought for a while before she finally said, "Maybe because they are closer to death."

When he told this story to the family, we were all impressed by the sagacity of her answer. But I hope that through the presence of her grandparents she learns something else, too. As you get closer to the realm beyond the veil, especially with the help of your grandchildren, you may laugh more as you begin to experience what I think of now as a certain lightness of being.

Highway Helen

LYNN LAUBER

In bed in Missouri, a female sandwich—on the left, a white woman in her fifties, blond and crumpled; on the right, a long-legged bronze woman in her thirties; in the middle, squeezed and happy, the latest distillation, nine years old, with gilded ringlets and a long velvet neck. The bronze woman, my daughter, is reading aloud the jacket copy to *The Secret of the Old Clock*, a Nancy Drew book that I once shivered over myself.

Nancy begins searching for the clock, but it seems that some-one doesn't want her to find it. Will Nancy be able to overcome the challenges of her investigation and outwit those who are trying to stop her? And will the clock's contents turn out to be what she's expecting?

Why do these questions sound so personal, as if someone is asking them about my own odd life, about my search for this daughter, whom I relinquished years ago to adoption?

I'd given her up as a newborn, without a peek or a hug, the method of choice of both the home for unwed mothers where I'd spent seven sodden months, and the Methodist children's home, which had placed her promptly and with a sniff of righteousness. I had been advised that this was the way to proceed, without sight or sound. Several girls from the home who had resisted and viewed their babies or even nursed them once became troublesome about signing relinquishment papers and developed pesky separation problems. But it had been borne in on me what a heartache and trouble I was. So I signed the release forms. I had my breasts bound. I did not speak of what I felt or thought. But I couldn't do anything about my face, which had developed, during my months of pregnancy, the grave, melancholy cast of the victim of some terrible tragedy.

But the victim of whom or what? There were plenty of culprits. Wasn't it a calamity to be a teenager on the dull side of my segregated town, a flat plate of earth without hills or vales, only the far-off scent of processed soybeans, a perpetual vegetable fog?

Hadn't I been left to hog roasts and mother/daughter banquets, tulle dresses that made me break out in hives? Hadn't I been allowed to stew in Methodist pews, to be served up on toast to boys who would have just as soon slugged as kissed me? Hadn't I been caught in the wind of the civil rights movement, as it blew north through Ohio toward Canada?

Still I knew the truth: there was no one to blame but myself. Who else had walked up the steps of a clapboard house to lie next to an African-American boy merely to make another boy jealous? That I lingered awhile, snagged by the seasonal allure of Christmas, by salt pork on the stove, by Smokey Robinson on the hi-fi, was immaterial. Left on its own, our love affair would have lasted only a few months.

But my pregnancy memorialized it, sharpened it, gave it heft. This boy would now stay with me forever, reemerging in the faces of my daughter and—impossible to imagine then—my granddaughter, beside me now.

When you lose people and then find them again, you become aware of the complex circuitry, the convergence of luck and fate that threads beneath life. This scene of the three of us in a Missouri bed is the result of the most improbable of intersections: the tardiness of abortion laws; hormonal levels in an attic bedroom on Rosedale Avenue; a female predisposition to rebellion and discontent.

Even as a girl I had a taste for estrangement, and it seemed as if I might just bring it about myself. By sixteen, I was intent on something that appeared to be simple trouble, crossing not only the railroad tracks but all local prohibitions to reach an inner-city world where some distant bell seemed to be summoning me.

For these girls to emerge from the torn page of the future, I had to swim like a salmon, eight miles to the east. Up Market Street, then right on Main, past the Dairy Dip Drive-In and Bindles Bargain City, where my father, perpetual salesman, once expounded on the virtues of Frigidaires. Left on Pine, then right on Reece—no locomotive could have stopped me.

And it's only now, watching my granddaughter absorb Bess, George, Nancy, and Hannah, that I realize that she was that distant bell.

Here's a favorite game I play with my granddaughter: she arrays her herd of long-haired plastic ponies—pink, blue, and magenta, daisies embossed in their polyurethane flesh. All are named and linked by a system that only she can keep track of—the little yellow one aligned inexplicably with the tinier blue one with wings.

She murmurs to them as she brushes their manes, lines them up, and enacts her own private dramas: the ponies bestow jewels on the poor, divide themselves into duchesses and queens, fight over territory and alliances.

Then out gallops the wild one, the renegade, named Highway Helen. Highway is the headstrong, sassy pony who rejects rules and urges others to break from the herd.

"Be wild, girls!" Highway urges. "Don't wait in line! Don't listen to what anyone tells you!"

My granddaughter squeals, shocked and pleased by my misbehavior, which prompts her own pony alter ego to intervene, mediate, and calm.

If I go too far, she becomes more shocked and says "Grandma!" Some women don't like to be called that, but I've loved it from the start.

I'm Highway Helen, grandma, unwed mother, freelance writer, the formerly depressed and disassociated, all rolled into one.

Of all the things I imagined I might be one day, a grandmother wasn't one of them. I hadn't even been a mother, except in the most anatomical sense.

I had been encouraged to view my pregnancy as a transport job, a cart-and-dump operation, a detour in what might otherwise be an unblemished teenage life. But in order to do this, certain inner rooms needed to be walled off, the heat turned low, as if for eventual renovation. I had to build up a stone wall that could be pierced only by occasional bolts of deep feeling.

My pregnancy was crammed into the overflowing dustbin

of the sixties, stuffed with never revisited rusted feelings and scalds. My family never spoke of *it*, let alone *her*—my personal fantasy. I wasn't even sure I'd had a girl, just a hunch that what I'd been covertly producing was of a strong, female stripe.

I blundered out of high school, then college, cool, tough, and impervious. It was unclear what could ever push the rock aside.

Reuniting with my daughter, when she was twenty-five and I was forty-two, was the beginning. As she walked across the airport terminal, something long nonaligned in me began to shift.

There she was, a mobile compendium of all those years, the confluence of so many people I'd loved. My mother's arch, my great-aunt's brow, a laugh that harked back to her father—my former boyfriend.

Relief is too small a word for it. Something cracked in my chest—a china plate; old, worn armor.

One thing I could never recapture was her childhood, those years she wandered through South Dakota, Missouri, states I could barely locate on a map, with parts of me plastered across her face. I had been assured that she would be adopted by "professionals"—a doctor or lawyer, in contrast with my middling status. But it turned out that my daughter's adoptive life was far more unstable than I could have imagined. When I reunited with her, she'd never had a mother who'd remained with her family; I'd never had another child.

But with my granddaughter, I could be there at the inception. I could view the beginning I'd missed: the lavender lids, the down at the back of her neck. I could buy her buntings and bonnets. I could see the alphabet form in the roof of her mouth.

It wasn't until I saw my daughter nurse my granddaughter that I finally believed the facts of my own labor—those long hours tussling under hot lights.

I'd always avoided babies, maneuvering adroitly around them as dogs do puddles. They had nothing to do with me. But this one did.

When she peered up at me the first time, I feared she'd see my past of relinquishment; my bumbling lack of maternal expertise. Even late in my forties, I had remained a perpetual adolescent. But my daughter handed her over to my clumsy arms and gave me a second chance.

There is a slice of time, just past now but already golden when I was a grandmother and still had one, named Detoh, sitting in a nursing home in northwestern Ohio. After everyone she had nursed, loved, iced cakes for; after all the pharmacy assistants, restaurant managers, and X-ray technicians she had indirectly spawned, it was sadly ironic that she should end up here, alone in a corner room with a view of the highway.

When she encountered my daughter and granddaughter for the first time, my grandmother rounded them to her with the wing of her arm, the same way dogs bring near their puppies or cats the kittens from whom they've been separated. My grandmother had nature in her still—she sniffed and saw that they were ours.

She was more at ease than my mother, who had worked

long shifts in a fertilizer company to send me to college, to help me escape my past. Why dig it up? She had a point, but there was a child hidden under the rubble, the only one I would ever have.

By the time I found my daughter I still hadn't a clue about being a mother, but being a grandmother was another story. I'd had four grandmothers while I was growing up—two grands and two greats—so that for a brief time during the 1950s in northwestern Ohio, I was the apple of a number of fading female eyes.

But the anchor was my Detoh, my maternal grandmother, who'd beamed her personal pilot light especially on me. I'd spent fifty years pressed against her fragrant flanks—fattened early on her pork roasts and homemade butterscotch pie. She had been my pants hitcher, ribbon tier, fever breaker, blister lancer, afghan knitter.

So when my daughter produced her own daughter not long after our reunion, I was in territory of which I had long knowledge, though from the other side.

Probably only someone like me, with such a fractured history and so many grandmothers behind her, could so appreciate being a grandmother now.

My granddaughter's memories of me will be nothing like mine of Detoh. No floral aprons or deft hems; just a complex rubble.

I watch her pick through old photos of me, miniskirted and blank-faced; of my daughter's birth father with his afro and dashiki, frozen in amber, circa 1969.

"Were you ever married to him?" she asks me.

"No."

"How about to John?"—my daughter's adoptive father.

"No."

My daughter steps in, to try to save me. "Grandma was too little to get married when I was born."

"But if she did, would he have been my grandfather-in-law?"

"There's no such thing, honey," my daughter says, then gives me a rueful look.

Poor thing—so much to sort out and understand. It requires complex cognitive skills, or maybe just a strong imagination, and that she has.

Even at five, she lay awake, brooding about stray dogs, war, death.

"Can I take my body when I die?" she asks my daughter.

"Don't worry about such things."

"How about just my neck?"

I hear about these conversations with equal parts thrill and guilt. That I have passed on anything is still a shocking pleasure, though it's dismaying to note that my more troubling traits seem to have dominated any slim positives: that anxiety, teeth grinding, and restlessness have rushed across bloodlines, to live on another day.

Even though I never laid eyes on my daughter until she was in her twenties, the two of us grew up remarkably similar—rebellious and moody, wild and heedless, one eye in the mirror, the other out the door.

If we are a movable experiment of the power of genes versus environment, then what of this newest vintage?

Is there a gene for trouble?

I watch my granddaughter as you would an approaching

storm—waiting for the hormones to begin their golden, glandular drip.

How can I be a grandmother when I've never been a mother?

I do my best. From my perch near the Hudson I've introduced her to pad thai, corned beef, coneflowers, *All About Eve*, and the score of *South Pacific*. (She seems to know about everything else.)

And she's had the dubious pleasure of having a grandmother drive her in fifth gear over the George Washington Bridge into the Emerald City.

As she's grown older, I've tried a subtle retooling of Highway Helen's message: "Don't let any boy ever use you. You're beautiful just as you are!"

This advice sounds off, not in Highway's character. Still, my granddaughter humors my pathetic attempts, a small smile on her face. She is far worldlier than I ever was at six, eight, nine—she can work computer keys swiftly with one hand while text-messaging with the other. She will trudge through the morass of girlhood on her own with whatever tools she has already gathered. Whatever wild path she chooses, she knows I'll be waiting at the end of the line.

Back in Missouri, I've lost track of the plot of *The Secret of the Old Clock*—Nancy Drew is too slow for me now. I am snagged as I often am by the profile of my bighearted granddaughter, with her black belt in tae kwon do, ready to kick the world into shape—the distillation of two families who never dreamed they'd be mixed together. If our dead rose up, the dust reconfigured, there they'd be—housekeepers and forgotten wives, numbers runners and electricians, "The Blue Danube" and Fats Waller, all there in the white square of light in her eyes.

With this child I've reentered my long-vacant body; the foreclosure signs are down. I've finally located the soft, wet heart thudding behind the rock wall.

In her flesh is my trail, faint and glittering as a snail's. Along with a few books and a leaning house near the Hudson, this, unaccountably, is who I will leave behind.

Epilogue

Before the hardcover edition of *Eye of My Heart* was published, I had a hunch that the book's twenty-seven essays might strike a previously untapped chord in women who, like me, were grappling with the role of grandmother. I'm delighted to report that my hunch was confirmed—and more. The book hit the *New York Times* bestseller list a few weeks after publication, and dozens of e-mails from grateful readers started landing in my queue. Clearly, this was a book waiting to happen. The fact that seven essays were excerpted in major national magazines, including *O, The Oprah Magazine, More, AARP The Magazine,* and *Good Housekeeping* was another telling sign.

To my mind, there are several reasons why the book has been stirring up dust in the collective psyche about how we think and talk about grandmotherhood. For starters, look who's talking. Most of the contributors to *Eye of My Heart* are either baby boomers or slightly older, a generation of women famous for teasing apart experience in order to make emotional sense of it. (Interestingly, more than half of the grandparents in the United States are now boomers too.) We're the *In Treatment* crowd, the first generation to engage in therapy not because we perceive ourselves as psychologically troubled but because we hope to lead richer, more fulfilling lives. So we talk.

But the conversation has not been limited to our personal lives. The writers in *Eye of My Heart* are part of the wave of women who have spent the last forty or so years reconfiguring the landscape of marriage, motherhood, and career. It's only natural that, when the time came, we would turn our attention to grandmotherhood—the first role we may not be able to alter to fit our desired specifications. Still, we're trying to sort out which aspects of this often demeaned, sometimes romanticized archetype jibe with our demanding lives and our evolving sense of who we are.

Today's grandparent is living longer, working longer, and pursuing passions we had little time for while we were raising kids. What's more, many of us live at great distances from our grandchildren in the ever-shrinking global village. (Alas, the actual distances we must travel don't shrink.) As a result, our grandmothering must be more intentional than it was back when Bubbe lived around the corner and didn't pursue a career. Add to this the fact that many grandparents today find ourselves feeling like the chopped liver in the club-sandwich generation, taking care of aging parents while doing everything possible to establish strong bonds with our grandchildren. Some of us are even raising those grandchildren.

Yet despite the seismic social and cultural shifts of the

last decades, most grandparents discover that some things about the role never change. Most obvious, of course, is our love for our grandchildren. For so many, the bonds with this younger generation are the most joyful and least complicated we have ever known. The second-most obvious—but somehow continually surprising—discovery is just how sensitive relations can be with our own children and their partners. One reader wrote, "I picked up *Eye of My Heart* thinking it was another gooey book about grandmothers. Boy was I wrong! I have four grandchildren and the descriptions of the tribulations and heartache involved in communicating with adult children really hit home."

This seems especially true for grandparents on the paternal side. Here's one grandfather's account, sent to me by e-mail: "We have two sons who have given us three grandchildren. With the firstborn of each son, it felt as though we had to wade through a china shop with fat suits on trying not to break something. Being the parents of the father adds a different dimension. Mom defers to her mom for advice, and seems obsessed with earning her approval for her parenting ways. In the meantime, we sit there with open hearts and arms, waiting our turn."

Since publication of the book, I've been traveling around the country speaking to thousands of grandparents, and I've heard this refrain repeatedly. It's also been echoed in comments to my columns on Grandparents.com. But grandparents on the paternal side aren't the only ones tiptoeing on eggshells. Any grandparent may at times feel excluded, hurt, or vulnerable to tangled family dynamics over which they have no control: grandparents on either side, stepgrandparents, long-distance grandparents, local grandparents whose grandkids live two blocks away, custodial grandparents, and, especially, ex-mothers- and fathers-in-law whose adult child is a noncustodial divorced parent. What's more, it's not always the grandparents who long for a more satisfying connection. I've heard from mothers of young children who despair because none of the grandparents in their family has displayed more than fleeting interest in their kids. Everyone has a story, and *Eye of My Heart* is helping to ignite a long overdue conversation.

The response to the book has underscored what Mary Pipher, who wrote the introduction, told me the first time we spoke. At the time, I was a relatively new grandmother walloped by love for my then-baby granddaughter, Isabelle Eva, and the staggering awareness that she was mine but *not* mine. "So many core issues that we thought we'd resolved get stirred up all over again when we become grandparents," Mary said. "Competitive feelings, all sorts of old fears and insecurities. We're no longer in charge and that can be very unsettling. Getting clear about our role as grandparents is essential."

Mary's words that afternoon, the generous humor and wisdom of all the contributors to this collection, and the shared experiences of readers and audiences wherever I go continue to help me clarify my role as a grandmother, and for this I am profoundly grateful.

Still, in the three years since Isabelle's birth, I have discovered that roles and relationships in families shift over time. Along the way, of course, old issues and insecurities come and go—and come again. For me, this was driven home the summer Isabelle turned three, the summer her baby sister, Azalia Luce, was born in Italy.

"You're my *best* friend," Isabelle tells me after lunch—a "flat egg" just like I used to cook for her father.

"That's the nicest thing anybody ever said to me," I reply. "You're my best friend too."

We are having a very good day in what has been a week of very hard days for Isabelle. Her mother and father have been at the hospital where Azalia Luce, Isabelle's baby sister, was born two days ago.

Even though she's excited about being a big sister and carts her gigantic Dora the Explorer doll—"*my* baby"—with her wherever she goes, Isabelle is worried. Last night she pointed to her green plastic frog and said, "He's really sad. He doesn't know where his family is."

I have tried my best to comfort and reassure my granddaughter, but let's face it, as far as Isabelle is concerned, I am a lousy substitute for Mama and Papa. Two days before—the morning the baby was delivered—she woke up distraught. It was as if she sensed the presence of the interloper even before we got news of her arrival. *No! Go away! I want Mama!* It took a long time for me to console her.

So it's nothing short of a triumph to be told I am her best friend—this, on the heels of a peaceful morning and a successful playdate at her friend Amelia's house.

It was also a bit of a triumph that the morning went off without a hitch. My son and daughter-in-law live in a house up a bumpy unpaved road in a rural outpost in northwestern Italy; this was the first time I'd ventured out onto the winding country byways without getting hopelessly lost or into some sort of vehicular predicament. The day before, I had nearly driven us off a precipice. (It was a smallish precipice. Still.)

I knew I would be out of my comfort zone when I agreed to fly over to stay with Isabelle while her parents were at the hospital—but I was game. I was thrilled to be asked, thrilled by the prospect of helping out when I was most needed, even though my knowledge of Italian is pretty much limited to *grazie, pronto,* and *prosecco*—and the driving terrifies me.

I am even thrilled to be with Isabelle when she is upset. There is an ineffable bond between this granddaughter and me. I felt it the first moment I held her, minutes after she was born. I love her spirit and her stubborn brilliance. The kid is a character, a big personality with a crackly voice and an accent that makes her sound like a miniature Brooklyn dock worker. She is simply irresistible to me. When she was two days old, an astrologer told me that the position of the planets and stars at the moment of her birth ensured that she'd be a spitfire. Some people who know us both say she reminds them of me.

I would dive into a burning building for this girl.

As a parent I've never felt insecure about my place in my son's life. But as Isabelle's Nonna—one of a clutch of grand-parents—I am embarrassed to admit that sometimes I feel as anxious as a seventh-grader comparing herself to the rest of the girls. Which is why, on the long transatlantic flight to Italy, I found myself worrying, *How can I possibly love another grandchild as much as I love Isabelle?*

My fears are dispelled the instant I meet Azalia Luce. There is simply no way *not* to love this shiny new girl.

"*Benvenuto*, little one," I say when Clay carries her inside in her portable car seat. He lifts her out and hands her over to me. This baby is not only plump and beautiful, she is perfectly content. I can tell right away that she's going to be an easy one.

Her big sister, however, is not so content. Or easy. "Go away!" she screams at me. "That's my baby!"

Things go downhill from there. "You *can't* look at me! You *don't* love me!" And the clincher: "*I am not your best friend!*"

In the two minutes since Clay and Tamar came home with the baby, I have been demoted. The very sight of me seems to set Isabelle off, and I spend the remaining three days of my visit trying to charm my way back into her good graces, with uneven success.

She loves me. She loves me not.

Now I am a (reasonably) mature adult. I am aware of the tumultuous effect of a new sibling on the life of an acutely bright and sensitive child. I know that Isabelle's reactions are about her, not about me. Moreover, as someone who is present only intermittently, I am a safe target for her unease. In other words, her rejection ain't personal. And yet I cannot claim that I am sufficiently mature *not* to take it personally—at least a tiny bit.

Isabelle is still asleep when it's time to leave for the airport, so I don't get a chance to tell her good-bye. As Clay starts the car in the early morning half-light, I feel unsettled—pangs of loss and yearning mixed with the sense of time whooshing by. I don't want to leave, but I don't exactly want to stay, either. Which is the basic conundrum for those of us whose grandchildren live far away. No matter where we are, there are always traces of longing. For home. For our children and grandchildren. In any event, it's time for me to go. My daughter-in-law's parents will be flying in tomorrow from San Francisco. I imagine that Gale, Tamar's mother, who is also my friend, will be Isabelle's next new best friend.

The heart is a generous muscle capable of loving many people at once, I remind myself as we bump our way down the pockmarked road. And though it saddens me that my son and his family live so far away, secretly I'm relieved (and ashamed of myself for having such pathetic junior-high-school thoughts) that they're equal-opportunity heartbreakers. As things stand, none of the six grandparents is around very much. If anything, my husband, Hugh—a.k.a. G-Daddy—and I visit most often. In fact, we'll be back in a month to celebrate Isabelle's third birthday. Which is why, when I kiss Clay goodbye at the Torino airport, it seems like no big deal.

To physicists—and mystics—all matter in the universe is composed of energy, and energy is perpetually in motion. That solid slab of wood we call a table is really just a bunch of molecules colliding in space, endlessly rearranging themselves. The same is true of families.

It happens like this:

Hugh and I are in the lounge at Dulles Airport waiting to board the plane that will take us to Italy when I get an e-mail message from Clay.

"Are you still reachable?"

"Yes," I write back. I wonder what's up, why he's still awake at 2:30 a.m., Italian time.

If the plane hadn't been late coming in, if we'd already been on board, my BlackBerry turned off, I wouldn't have gotten Clay's message. We would have been on that plane when it took off, which, God knows, would have been inconvenient, but it wouldn't have changed the big thing that happened. Or everything that has happened since.

My cell phone rings. Clay is on the line sounding shaky. "There's no good way to tell you this."

Because what he says next is still so fresh, so raw, even now, several months later, there's no good way for me to tell it either.

Ken—Gale's husband of forty-one years, Tamar's father, Isabelle's and Azalia's grandfather, Clay's champion and benefactor in so many ways, our friend of twenty-plus years, himself a licensed, experienced pilot—died that morning when the single-engine plane he was flying fell to earth.

Just like that, a person you love vanishes.

Just. Like. That.

When terrible things happen, bits of luck sometimes follow—kindhearted strangers, small mercies. The airline people scramble and manage to get our luggage off the plane moments before it pulls away from the gate.

Hugh and I fly to San Francisco the next afternoon and stay for two weeks—the time we would have spent in Italy. Most days we take care of Isabelle, who is happy and adjusting well to being a big sister. We go around and around on the vintage carousel in Golden Gate Park. We don giant bumblebee wings and chase one another through the halls of the Discovery Museum in Sausalito. G-Daddy and I take turns pushing Isabelle on swings all over town until our arms give out and it's time for us to return home to Washington.

A few weeks later, the night before Clay, Tamar, and the children are due to fly back to Europe, the molecules of the family suddenly rearrange themselves once more, and they decide to make San Francisco their base. After years abroad—except for the six months they lived in D.C.—they are home.

When Clay breaks the news to me over the phone, I applaud the wisdom of their decision. "Good for everybody," I say, and I really mean it.

But as soon as I hang up, I panic. In a flash I have gone from being the grandparent who sees these two little girls the most—once the designated local grandmother—to the one who will see them the least. Now they'll be blessed with three other grandparents—Tamar's mother and Clay's father and stepmother—living mere minutes away. I wish I could report that my better nature instinctively took over and that I was thrilled for everyone, especially in light of the tragedy that has rocked this family. I'd like to tell you that I did not feel jealous or threatened. I'd love to say that my old insecurities did not shoot up like weeds at the first faint sign of spring. I would like to say all these things, but then I would be lying.

Still, when I stop and parse my anxiety over my role in the lives of Isabelle and Azalia—*Will they know me? Love me? Love me as much as their other grandparents? Will I matter to them?* and the scariest, *How will I be remembered?*—I know that my fears are about much more than these two little girls. When I recognize this, thankfully, the fear loosens its grip and I glimpse a more spacious picture in which there is room for everybody and plenty of love to go around. Besides, I'm in Washington, not jail; I'll be able to visit often and more easily than if they were in Europe. Nonetheless, I am getting another crash course in the art of letting go.

This seems to be my karma as a grandmother, as it was as a mother, and, existentially speaking, I suppose, the karma of anyone who loves with abandon.

But in moments when fear and envy still get the best of me, I think back to Isabelle's third birthday.

Four days after Ken passed away, the shards of the broken, scattered family are gathered on a playground in San Francisco. In the midst of grief—and, really, more so because of it—we all know that this is an occasion that must be celebrated. Amanda, Clay's stepmother, and Jessica, his half-sister, have organized everything. The pile of presents doesn't much interest Isabelle, but the same cannot be said for the killer chocolate cake or the brightly burning candles.

"It's my boitday," she announces in poifect Brooklynese. "I want to blow them out again!"

Isabelle has been told by her parents that they have come to San Francisco so that the whole family can celebrate her birthday. There will be plenty of time later on, when she is older, for her to grasp the bigger story that has altered the geography of her childhood.

After she polishes off her second piece of cake and hits the swings, a sleeping Azalia is passed around and held by everyone, including Brian, Clay's father (from whom I separated when our son was two); his wife, Amanda; and Dylan, Clay's half-brother and Jessica's twin. Mike and Ari, Tamar's brother and his husband, also take turns holding the baby. So does Gale, for whom the presence of Azalia cradled next to her beating heart seems to provide the only trace of solace. Ken held this grandchild, too—just a few weeks before, when he and Gale were in Italy.

The sunny, pleasant afternoon—rare for typically windy,

fog-bound San Francisco in August—is matched by the quiet mood of the partygoers. We don't forget for a second why we're here; this is one surprise party in which everyone, not just the guest of honor, is startled to be present. Still, there are moments of lightness. In one of the day's more—ironic? poignant? sweetly ridiculous?—episodes, directed by Isabelle, my current husband pushes my ex-husband in one of those swings that looks like a giant car seat, and both grandfathers and grandchild seem to be having a very good time.

This is a party where nobody feels left out or insecure, where everybody's old stories simply get dropped.

I think this may be what people mean by grace.

BARBARA GRAHAM
January 2010

About the Contributors

SANDRA BENITEZ is Puerto Rican and midwestern by heritage. She is the author of four novels, including *A Place Where the Sea Remembers* and *Bitter Grounds*. Her most recent book, *Bag Lady: A Memoir*, is her first work of nonfiction. She was the recipient of an award in 2004 from the National Hispanic Heritage Foundation for Literature, a Gund Fellow, and one of the winners of the first United States Artists Awards. She resides in Minnesota.

ELIZABETH BERG is an award-winning author of twenty best-selling books. Even better, she's the grandmother of two swell kids.

BEVERLY DONOFRIO's memoir *Riding in Cars with Boys* was translated into fifteen languages and made into a movie. Her second memoir, *Looking for Mary*, originated as a commentary on NPR. Her work is collected in several anthologies, and her essays have appeared in the *New York Times*, the *Los Angeles Times*, the *Washington Post*, the *Village Voice*, O, The

Oprah Magazine, Elle, and *Marie Claire,* among other publications. She has written for network television and PBS, and is a commentator for NPR's *All Things Considered.* Donofrio's first children's books were published in 2007: *Mary and the Mouse, the Mouse and Mary,* a picture book illustrated by Barbara McClintock; and *Thank You, Lucky Stars,* a young adult novel. Donofrio lives at Nada Carmelite Hermitage in the mountains of Colorado.

MARCIE FITZGERALD is the pseudonym of a writer who lives in the Midwest.

ELLEN GILCHRIST, winner of the National Book Award for her collection *Victory Over Japan,* is the author of more than twenty books, including novels, short stories, poetry, and a memoir. Her most recent book is *A Dangerous Age,* a novel. She lives in Fayetteville, Arkansas.

MOLLY GILES is the author of the novel *Iron Shoes,* and two short-story collections: *Creek Walk and Other Stories,* which won the Small Press Award for Short Fiction; and *Rough Translations,* which won the Flannery O'Connor Award for Short Fiction. She has received a National Endowment for the Arts Fellowship, two Pushcart Prizes, and the National Book Critics Circle Award for book reviewing. Her short story "Two Words" was included in the 2003 O. *Henry Prize Stories* collection. Other stories have recently been featured on NPR's *Selected Shorts.* Giles teaches creative writing at the University of Arkansas in Fayetteville.

MARITA GOLDEN is the author of the memoirs *Migrations of the Heart, Saving Our Sons,* and *Don't Play in the Sun: One Woman's Journey Through the Color Complex,* as well as the novels *Long Distance Life, The Edge of Heaven,* and most recently *After*, which won both the NAACP Image Award and the Black Caucus Award of the American Library Association. She cofounded the African American Writers Guild and the Hurston/Wright Foundation, and is currently writer in residence at the University of the District of Columbia. Her awards include the 2002 Distinguished Service Award from the Authors Guild and the 2001 Barnes and Noble Writers for Writers Award. Golden lives in Maryland with her husband.

BARBARA GRAHAM is an essayist, author, playwright, and editor. Her essays and articles have appeared in many magazines— including O, *The Oprah Magazine*, where she has been a contributing writer; *Glamour; National Geographic Traveler; Redbook; Tricycle; Time; Vogue*; and *Utne Reader*—and have been collected in many anthologies. Graham is the author of *Women Who Run With the Poodles*, a satirical take on the dark side of the self-help movement. Her plays have been produced Off-Broadway in New York and at theaters around the country. She lives in Washington, D.C.

SUSAN GRIFFIN is an award-winning poet, writer, essayist, playwright, and filmmaker. Her books include *A Chorus of Stones*—a finalist for the Pulitzer Prize and the National Book Award—as well as *The Book of Courtesans, What Her Body Thought, Woman and Nature*, and her latest book, *Wrestling with the Angel of Democracy*. She is the recipient of an Emmy Award, a MacArthur Grant for Peace and International Cooperation, and a grant from the National Endowment for the Arts. Griffin's essays and articles have appeared in the *Los Angeles Times*, the *New York Times*, and *Ms.*, among many other publications.

JUDITH GUEST is the author of five novels. Her first, *Ordinary People*, won the Janet Heidegger Kafka Prize for best first novel in 1976. It was made into a movie that won six Academy Awards, including one for Best Picture. Guest's novel *Second Heaven* was selected as one of *School Library Journal's* Best Books for Young Adults. She has written several screenplays and is currently at work on a suspense novel, *White in the Moon*. Guest divides her time between Minnesota and Michigan.

VIRGINIA IRONSIDE started her career as a rock journalist but has spent the last thirty years writing an advice column for *The Independent* and other publications. She is the author of fifteen books, including the recent *No! I Don't Want to Join a Book Club*, the fictional diary of a sixty-year-old woman besotted with her grandson. She lives in London.

LYNN LAUBER's essays and short stories have appeared in the *New York Times* and have been collected in several anthologies. Her books include *White Girls, 21 Sugar Street*, and *Listen to Me: Writing Life into Meaning*. She lives in Nyack, New York.

KATE LEHRER's novels include *Confessions of a Bigamist, Best Intentions*, and *Out of Eden*, winner of the Western Heritage Award. In addition to her novels, she writes essays, short stories, and book reviews, and she is a frequent guest on the *Diane Rehm Show* on NPR. She lives in Washington, D.C.

BEVERLY LOWRY is the author of six novels and three nonfiction books, including *Crossed Over: A Murder, A Memoir; Her Dream of Dreams: The Rise and Triumph of Madam C. J. Walker;* and *Harriet Tubman: Imagining a Life*. She has written essays and feature articles for *The New Yorker, Granta, Vanity Fair, Redbook,* the *New York Times,* and many other periodicals. In 2007, she received the Richard Wright Literary Achievement Award from the Natchez Literary and Film

Organization. She teaches at George Mason University and lives in Austin, Texas.

RONA MAYNARD is an award-winning journalist and the former editor-in-chief of *Chatelaine*, Canada's leading women's magazine. She is the author of a recently published memoir, *My Mother's Daughter*, and hosts an online community for women. Maynard lives in Toronto.

BHARATI MUKHERJEE, an American citizen born and raised in Kolkata, India, is the author of seven novels and two short-story collections, including *The Middleman and Other Stories*, which won the National Book Award. She has also cowritten two books of nonfiction with her husband, Clark Blaise. Mukherjee is a professor of English at the University of California, Berkeley.

JILL NELSON is a journalist and author of the memoir *Volunteer Slavery: My Authentic Negro Experience*; *Sexual Healing*, a novel; and *Finding Martha's Vineyard: African Americans at Home on an Island*. An avid gardener and budding sailor, she divides her time between New York City and Martha's Vineyard, Massachusetts.

Psychologist MARY PIPHER is the author of eight books, including three *New York Times* best sellers: *Reviving Ophelia*, which has been translated into twenty-five languages; *The Shelter of Each Other*; and *Another Country*—a field guide to understanding the emotional landscape of aging parents and grandparents. Her latest book is *Seeking Peace: Chronicles of the Worst Buddhist in the World*. Pipher's writing is influenced by her rural background, her training in both psychology and anthropology, and her years as a therapist. Her special interest is the way American culture influences mental health.

She lives in Lincoln, Nebraska, with her husband, Jim; her children and grandchildren live nearby.

LETTY COTTIN POGREBIN is a founding editor of *Ms.* magazine, a past president of the Authors Guild, and the author of nine books, most recently *Three Daughters*, a novel. She edited the anthology *Stories for Free Children* and was the editorial consultant on Marlo Thomas's anthology *Free to Be . . . You and Me*; for her work on the television special based on the latter book, she won an Emmy Award. She is a columnist for *Moment* magazine and her work has appeared in the *New York Times*, the *Washington Post*, the *Boston Globe*, *The Nation*, and numerous other publications. She lives in New York City.

CLAIRE ROBERTS is the pseudonym of an author and essayist who lives in the Midwest.

ROXANA ROBINSON is the author of eight books: four novels, most recently *Cost*; three story collections; and a biography of Georgia O'Keeffe. Four of these were named Notable Books of the Year by the *New York Times*. Her work has appeared in *The New Yorker*, *The Atlantic*, *Harper's*, the *New York Times*, *Vogue*, *Best American Short Stories*, and elsewhere. She has received fellowships from the National Endowment for the Arts and the Guggenheim Foundation.

ANNE ROIPHE is a journalist and the author of fourteen books of fiction and nonfiction, including the novels *Up the Sandbox* and *Lovingkindness*; and *1185: A Memoir*. She was a National Book Award finalist for her book *Fruitful: A Real Mother in a Modern World*, and has recently published a memoir: *Epilogue*. She has written essays and reviews for many publications and is currently a contributing editor of the *Jerusalem Report*.

About the Contributors

LYNNE SHARON SCHWARTZ has published novels, short-story collections, essays, poetry, and translations from Italian. Among her novels are *The Writing on the Wall*; *In the Family Way: An Urban Comedy*; *Disturbances in the Field*; *Leaving Brooklyn* (nominated for a PEN/Faulkner Award); and *Rough Strife* (nominated for a National Book Award). She is also the author of the poetry collection *In Solitary* and the memoir *Ruined by Reading*. She recently edited *The Emergence of Memory: Conversations with W. G. Sebald*, a collection of essays and interviews. Her work has been reprinted in *The Best American Short Stories*, *The O. Henry Prize Stories*, *The Best American Essays*, and other anthologies, and her reviews have appeared in leading magazines and newspapers. She teaches at the Bennington Writing Seminars. Her latest book is *Not Now, Voyager*.

SUSAN SHREVE is the author of thirteen novels, most recently *A Student of Living Things*; a memoir, *Warm Springs: Traces of a Childhood at FDR's Polio Haven*; and thirty books for children. She has edited five anthologies, including *Dream Me Home Safely*, and *Outside the Law* and *Tales Out of School*, with Porter Shreve. She is a professor of English and founder of the master of fine arts degree program at George Mason University, and a former president and cochairman of the PEN/Faulkner Foundation. Shreve has received a Guggenheim Fellowship and a National Endowment Award for Fiction.

ABIGAIL THOMAS is the author of one novel, two short-story collections, and two memoirs: *Safekeeping* and *A Three Dog Life*. Her most recent book is *Thinking About Memoir*. She teaches private writing workshops and lives in Woodstock, New York.

SALLIE TISDALE is the author of several books, including *The Best Thing I Ever Tasted*, *Talk Dirty to Me*, and *Women of the*

Way. She is a consulting editor at *Tricycle*. Her work has appeared in numerous publications, including *Harper's*, *The New Yorker, New Republic, Vogue, Tin House, Antioch Review*, and *Creative Nonfiction*. Tisdale is a teacher at Dharma Rain Zen Center in Portland, Oregon. An earlier version of her contribution to this volume appeared on Salon.com.

JUDITH VIORST is the author of many books for children and adults, including the recent *Alexander and the Wonderful, Marvelous, Excellent, Terrific Ninety Days: An Almost Completely Honest Account of What Happened to Our Family When Our Youngest Son, His Wife, Their Baby, Their Toddler, and Their Five-Year-Old Came to Live with Us for Three Months*. (For adults, especially grandmothers and, just in case, their adult children.)

Acknowledgments

Deep bow to Mary Pipher, who opened her heart to this project early on and has since become a dear friend. Profound gratitude to all the contributors for bringing their courage, wisdom, and prodigious gifts—not the least of which is humor—to bear on this always complex, sometimes thorny subject. They have become my friends, too.

I am indebted to my literary agent, Andrew Blauner, for his thoughtful guidance, his sly humor, and his good judgment in matching me up with the fabulous Gail Winston and the wonderful team at Harper, including Jonathan Burnham, Rachel Elinsky, Tina Andreadis, Kyle Hansen, Bobby Brinson, Meredith Rusu, and Jason Sack. Thanks, too, to Elizabeth Shreve and Kate Pinnick Pruss for getting the word out.

My gratitude to the gonzo gang at Grandparents.com who keep the conversation going, especially David Brinker, Jeff Beil, Gary Drevitch, and Lynn Munroe.

Deepest thanks to my posse, who sustained me while I worked on this book: Mark Matousek, Florence Falk, Audrey Ferber, Steven Winn, Julie Bondanza, Mary Willis, Susan

Roberts, Pythia Peay, Eileen Harrington and the rest of the dharma bums—Kevin Berrill, Susan Green, Carolyn Klamp, Betsy Otto, and Jeff Rosenberg; Melina Bellows, Carole Bolsey, Tara Brach, Anna Christensen, Amy Gross, Miriam Karmel, Joyce Kornblatt, Katharine Kravetz, Cathy Madison, Ellie McGrath, Martha Nelson, Grace Ogden, Carolyn Shanoff, Jane Winfrey, Betty Wood, and Patricia Crown for her lovely nest in Paris.

I am grateful to the friends and friends of friends who have supported this project, including Barbara Ascher, Keith Bellows, Steve Bennett and the team at Authorbytes, Dalton Delan, Alan Fallow, Gaby Goddard, Andrew Goldberg, Susan Ito, Carol Jenkins, Lanny Jones, Martha Lear, Marcia Lippman, Joyce Maynard, Marilyn Milloy, Laura Nurse, Pat Towers, Paulette Warren, Victoria Zackheim, and Ande Zellman.

To my mother, Irene Graham, thank you for putting up with me while I've been consumed by this book. My gratitude to the other members of my family who have been so generous, especially Leslie Clayton, John and Judy Delehanty, Ruth and Jerry Foster, Debbie and Michael Freiser, Ken and Cathy Glick, Mike Gottlieb and Ari Shapiro, Brett Graham, Jed Graham and Deborah Solomon, Sheila Kopelman, and Laura Steele.

To the other grandparents who share Isabelle Eva and Azalia Luce with Hugh and me—Gale Gottlieb, Brian McLachlan, and Amanda Smith—deep bows. Ken Gottlieb, you are loved and sorely missed.

To my husband, Hugh Delehanty (aka G-Daddy), who got me from the start, I owe practically everything.

Deepest bows to Clay McLachlan—the white-hot center in the eye of my heart—and the wonderful Tamar McLachlan for bringing Isabelle Eva and Azalia Luce into our lives.